This v
an un
long
choic
resear
focuse
tions
indus
mana
study
gener
ualisn
postn
that
prosp

Th
intere

John
Econ
Dock

ROUTLEDGE STUDIES IN EMPLOYMENT RELATIONS

Series editors: Dr Rick Delbridge and
Professor Edmund Heery
Cardiff Business School

Aspects of the employment relationship are central to numerous courses at both undergraduate and postgraduate level.

Drawing on insights from industrial relations, human resource management and industrial sociology, this series provides an alternative source of research-based materials and texts reviewing key developments in employment research.

Books published in the LSE/Routledge series are works of high academic merit, drawn from a wide range of academic studies in the social sciences for which the LSE has an international reputation.

RETHINKING INDUSTRIAL RELATIONS

Mobilization, collectivism and long waves

John Kelly

London and New York

First published 1998
by Routledge
11 New Fetter Lane, London EC4P 4EE

Simultaneously published in the USA and Canada
by Routledge
29 West 35th Street, New York, NY 10001

Reprinted 1999, 2000

Routledge is an imprint of the Taylor & Francis Group

Typeset in Galliard by Routledge
Printed and bound in Great Britain by MPG Books Ltd, Bodmin

British Library Cataloguing in Publication Data
A catalogue record for this book is available from the British Library

Library of Congress Cataloging in Publication Data
Kelly, John E., 1952–
Rethinking industrial relations : mobilization, collectivism and long waves
/ John Kelly
p. cm.
Includes bibliographic references and index.
1. Industrial relations. 2. Trade-Unions. 3. Long waves (Economics) I.
Title.
HD6971.K423 1998
331–dc21   97-45076
                                                        CIP

ISBN 0–415–18672–2 (hbk)
ISBN 0–415–18673–0 (pbk)

TO CAROLINE, JOANNA, ALEX AND SARAH

CONTENTS

ILLUSTRATIONS

Tables

Figures

ACKNOWLEDGEMENTS

I would like to acknowledge the numerous helpful comments received from many people over the past few years as I presented the ideas in this book at conferences and seminars and tried to make sense of the various reactions they evoked. In particular I would like to thank the following: Stephen Dunn, Christine Edwards, Ed Heery, Pat Fosh, Steve Jefferys, Nicholas Kinnie, Miguel Martinez Lucio, Dave Lyddon, David Metcalf, Peter Nolan, Riccardo Peccei, Ray Richardson, John Salmon, Paul Smith, Paul Stewart, Brian Towers, Peter Turnbull and Stephen Wood. Chapter 7 'Long waves in industrial relations' originally appeared in *Historical Studies in Industrial Relations* 4: 3–35 1997.

ABBREVIATIONS

ACAS   Advisory, Conciliation and Arbitration Service
AEU   Amalgamated Engineering Union (now AEEU)
AEEU   Amalgamated Engineering and Electrical Union
APEX   Association of Professional Executive Clerical and Computer Staff (now GMB)
ASLEF   Associated Society of Locomotive Engineers and Firemen
ASTMS   Association of Scientific Technical and Managerial Staff (now MSF)
AUEW   Amalgamated Union of Engineering Workers (now AEEU)
AUT   Association of University Teachers
BECTU   Broadcasting Entertainment Cinematograph and Theatre Union
BIFU   Banking Insurance and Finance Union
CIR   Commission on Industrial Relations
CMA   Communication Managers Association
CP   Communist Party
CPSA   Civil and Public Services Association
CWU   Communication Workers Union
EETPU   Electrical Electronic Telecommunications and Plumbing Union (now AEEU)
FBU   Fire Brigades Union
FTAT   Furniture Timber and Allied Trades Union (now GMB)
GMB   General Municipal and Boilermakers Union
GPMU   Graphical Paper and Media Union
IRSF   Inland Revenue Staff Federation (now PTC)
MSF   Manufacturing Science Finance
NALGO   National and Local Government Officers Association (now UNISON)
NAPO   National Association of Probation Officers
NATFHE   National Association of Teachers in Further and Higher Education
NCU   National Communications Union (now CWU)

NUCPS	National Union of Civil and Public Servants (now PTC)
NUJ	National Union of Journalists
NUKFAT	National Union of Knitwear Footwear and Apparel Trades
NUM	National Union of Mineworkers
NUMAST	National Union of Marine Aviation and Shipping Transport Officers
NUT	National Union of Teachers
PTC	Public Services Tax and Commerce Union
RCN	Royal College of Nursing
RMT	National Union of Rail Maritime and Transport Workers
SOGAT	Society of Graphical and Allied Trades (now GPMU)
TASS	Technical Administrative and Supervisory Section (of the AUEW)
TGWU	Transport and General Workers Union
UCATT	Union of Construction Allied Trades and Technicians
UDM	Union of Democratic Mineworkers

1

INTRODUCTION

In 1954 Britain's 700,000 coal miners accounted for approximately three-quarters of all recorded strikes. In 1974 a national strike by the Coal Board's 300,000 miners helped to bring down a government. By 1994 the coal mining industry had been reduced to a rump of sixteen pits and about 10,000 miners. According to some commentators, the late twentieth-century workforce is in the throes of a dramatic transformation, from the traditional, class-conscious collectivism of the industrial manual worker to the self-interested individualism of the skilled, mobile and career-centred white-collar worker (Bassett and Cave 1993; Brown 1990). Consequently they argue that trade unions must abandon traditional collectivist principles and practices if they are to have any future. Others take the view that unions and collective bargaining can survive only if these institutions adapt themselves to product market pressures and contribute to the competitive success of firms (e.g. Kochan and Osterman 1994). The adversarial collective bargaining of the past must give way to a more cooperative, 'social partnership' between labour and capital. In the fashionable jargon of management, unions must justify their existence by showing they can 'add value' to the corporation. Common to both these viewpoints is the idea that late twentieth-century industrial relations are passing through an historic transition in which new values, practices and institutions will steadily and surely displace the old (Brown 1990; Lash and Urry 1987).

The principal aim of this book is to show that these fashionable and beguiling notions are seriously flawed and deeply misleading. I do this first of all by setting out a theoretical framework – mobilization theory – that allows us to analyse the processes by which workers acquire a collective definition of their interests in response to employer-generated injustice. It is then possible to show that worker collectivism is an effective and situationally specific response to injustice, not an irrelevant anachronism. By drawing on long wave theory it can be shown that the fluctuating fortunes of national labour movements follow predictable patterns that are closely synchronized with the rhythms of the capitalist economy. Contrary to postmodernist claims that the classical labour movement is in terminal decline, long wave theory suggests that it is more likely to be on the threshold of resurgence.

The structure of the book is as follows. In Chapter 2 I examine the evolution of the field of industrial relations up to the present in order to establish its strengths and weaknesses and to construct a detailed definition of central research problems based around interests, power and conflict. I try to show that a number of attributes of the field, and in particular its theoretical underdevelopment, continue to hamper our capacity to think usefully about these problems. In Chapter 3 I explore micro-level industrial relations and use the work of Charles Tilly (1978) and Doug McAdam (1988) to develop a more satisfactory account of 'collectivism'. Tilly's mobilization theory divides the concept into five components – interest definition, organization, mobilization, opportunity, and action – thereby permitting a far more sophisticated and precise analysis of what has happened to the different facets of collectivism over time. McAdam has developed mobilization theory into a framework that explores the origins of collectivism in perceptions of injustice and then maps out the conditions under which members of subordinate groups will respond individually or collectively, if at all. The theory is then used in Chapter 4 to shed fresh light on a range of major and contemporary industrial relations issues: the growth of non-union workplaces; the alleged decline of worker collectivism; the nature of power in industrial relations; the growth of state and employer authoritarianism and repression; and the prospects and desirability of a new labour–management social partnership. The core argument of this section is that the decline of some traditional forms of collective institution should lead us to develop a more rigorous theory of collectivism instead of embracing the fashionable chimeras of individualism or of non-union forms of worker representation. After demonstrating some of the virtues of mobilization theory I then consider one of the most widely-cited theoretical alternatives, Mancur Olson's *The Logic of Collective Action* (1971) (Chapter 5). I argue that Olson's individualist premises cannot account satisfactorily for the emergence (or decline) of collective organization and I show that his analysis of the role of coercion in the growth and functioning of trade unionism is inadequate and misleading.

The focus then shifts from micro- to macro- and in particular to issues of historical change where I address the argument that we are living through an epochal shift in industrial relations marked by a decline in worker collectivism, organization and militancy. In Chapter 6 I draw on long wave theory to construct an historical account of alternating periods of worker mobilization and state and employer counter-mobilization linked to Kondratieff long waves (upswings and downswings) in the economy. The transition periods between upswing and downswing are marked by unusually intense and wide-ranging class struggles resulting in 'ruptures' to the established patterns of class relations. Long downswings are characterized by the restructuring of productive forces, class relations and the composition of the working class so that viewed in proper historical perspective apparent declines in worker 'collectivism' are a familiar and explicable feature of advanced capitalist economies. Chapter 7 turns to the literature on postmodernism which is probably the most comprehensive expression of

2

the theme of epochal change, embracing as it does trends in politics, culture and the economy (including the arguments about 'lean production' and post-Fordism). I critically review the major arguments from the standpoint of long wave theory and find many of them wanting. The final chapter (Chapter 8) summarizes the themes of the book and draws out their implications for the evolution of the field of industrial relations.

2

THE FIELD OF INDUSTRIAL RELATIONS

In the present chapter I indicate what seem to be the central intellectual problems in contemporary industrial relations. The specification has a threefold purpose. First, and by contrast with some of the HRM literature, it allows us to construct a set of research priorities that do not align the field of industrial relations with the economic and political priorities of employers and the state. Second, it constitutes a benchmark against which we can review the progress of the field of industrial relations in recent decades. Any review of a field of inquiry can deploy purely 'internal' criteria, e.g. are its concepts well-defined? Is there a significant body of theory? Is there a well-established stock of empirical knowledge? But it is equally legitimate to construct a set of intellectual problems or puzzles and use progress towards their solution as an evaluative criterion. Finally, the same problems that are used as benchmarks in the evaluation of existing approaches can also be used in the construction and evaluation of alternative approaches.

According to Blyton and Turnbull (1994) the subject matter of industrial relations is 'the creation of an economic surplus, the co-existence of conflict and cooperation, the indeterminate nature of the exchange relationship, and the asymmetry of power' (1994: 31).

A focus on interests and power, conflict and cooperation in the employment relationship allows us to identify four central and enduring problems in the field. *First, how do workers come to define their interests in collective or individual terms?* This is a central problem for several reasons. There is such a wide and diverse range of employee interests that can be pursued through the employment relationship, e.g. job security, higher wages, training, equal opportunities and career progression, that we need to find some way of categorizing and conceptualizing these interests if we are to explain their variation. Whereas employers are necessarily and primarily concerned with profitability, because of market competition, there is no corresponding mechanism amongst workers that can assign equivalent priority to any one of their many interests (Offe and Wiesenthal 1985: 179). Since workers occupy a subordinate position in the employment relationship, their collective definitions of interest are subject to repeated challenges by employers as they try to redefine and realign worker interests with corporate goals. In the context of the post-1979 period, these attempts have given rise to the frequently

4

heard claim that worker collectivism is in decline. How should we conceptualize worker collectivism in order to think usefully about this issue? Are we now witnessing a unique sea-change in collectivism or does the last two decades of the twentieth century represent a familiar period of cyclical, labour movement decline that will soon give way to union resurgence?

The second central problem concerns power: *what are the most useful ways of conceptualizing the power and power resources of workers, employers and states?* Power is perhaps one of the most widely used concepts in the field of industrial relations but at the same time, as we shall see, one of the least well understood. There is an extensive literature on power *outside* industrial relations but remarkably little of it has penetrated the field even in debates on the post-1979 decline of trade unions. A number of academics have argued that we are witnessing a 'transformation' of existing systems of industrial relations on the untheorized assumption that we are unlikely to see a significant recovery of union power in the future (Kochan *et al.* 1986). But why should this be the case? If union power in the postwar period was underpinned by state commitment to full employment, why should there not be such a policy in the future? Just as there is lack of theoretical clarity about worker interests, so too (at least in the field of industrial relations) there is a surprising lack of work on *the interests pursued by capitalist states*. It is surprising in view of the prominent role of state intervention in capitalist economies throughout the postwar period. Finally, *how should we conceptualize the relationship between worker and employer interests?* This question has become especially important in the recent period of economic recession as growing numbers of employers have sought to recast relations with their workforces in more 'cooperative' and less adversarial ways. This search for a 'mutual gains enterprise' has even been presented by some authors as a new paradigm that can save the field of industrial relations from threatened oblivion in the face of union decline (Kaufman 1993; Kochan and Osterman 1994). The issue of worker–employer relations has also assumed a new importance because of the argument that advanced capitalist economies may be in transition to a 'new industrial relations' following the demise of 'adversarial collective bargaining' (e.g. Bassett 1986; Kaufman 1993; Kochan *et al.* 1986). Too often such arguments have been couched in ahistorical terms without sufficient attempt to locate contemporary changes in historical perspective.

The present chapter begins with these central problems and seeks to establish the gaps and weaknesses in our understanding of them. In the second half of the chapter I will review the field from a different angle in order to try and illuminate some of the reasons that lie behind our inadequate understanding. Both sections of the chapter will then lead into a discussion of an alternative approach in Chapter 3.

Workers' interests

In 1968 Flanders wrote a famous attack on Perry Anderson's influential essay about the limits and possibilities of trade union action. Anderson (1967) had *inter alia* restated the classical Leninist view that through trade union organization and action workers would develop only a 'trade union consciousness', the conviction that it was necessary to organize collectively and fight the capitalists. Since their real interests lay in a revolutionary assault on the capitalist system the role of the Leninist party was to import such consciousness to workers from the outside. Flanders took great exception to these propositions, claiming that workers knew perfectly well what trade unions were for and did not need to be told by outsiders, a view derived from his long-standing and deep-rooted anti-communism (Flanders 1968a; Kelly forthcoming). What is interesting about Flanders' work is that whilst he wrote at great length and often with some rigour about the nature of collective bargaining, his views of workers' interests were very ill-defined. In common with fellow members of the Oxford school such as Hugh Clegg, what passed for analysis of workers' interests and their compatibility (or otherwise) with those of the employers, was a mixture of casual empiricism and woolly platitudes. Unions, he said, aimed to protect workers' 'security, status and self-respect; in short their dignity as human beings' (Flanders 1968a: 42) and to provide them with 'stability of earnings . . . a continually rising standard of living . . . a greater influence on managerial decisions' (Flanders 1965: 112).

Clegg (1979) did not analyse the employment relationship as such but began his famous textbook by declaring that industrial relations was the study of job regulation (1979: 1). Presumably therefore the 'interests' of workers were reflected in the contents of the collective agreements that formed the output of collective bargaining, such as pay, overtime rates, holidays etc. (ibid.: 1–2). So long as industrial relations could be defined (in effect) as the study of collective bargaining then it was obviously convenient, if intellectually lazy, to accept 'workers' interests' as more or less coterminous with their bargaining demands. But reductions in bargaining coverage and scope and employer attempts to commit workers to corporate goals of profitability and competitiveness have fatally undermined this pragmatic solution to what is, in fact, an acute theoretical problem. Contemporary industrial relations textbooks are not much better because despite the exposition of unitary, pluralist, radical (and sometimes human resource management) approaches to the subject, careful reading of the relevant chapters reveals once again the casual empiricism that comes into play when workers' interests in the employment relationship are the topic of discussion. There are scattered references to wages, terms and conditions, occasionally to status or influence, but rigorous analytical treatment of this crucial topic is quite simply non-existent.[1]

There are however several valuable sources of literature about workers' interests, the first being the sociologically-inspired workplace case studies which flourished for about ten years in Britain from the early 1970s and many of which quickly became established as classics. They comprise Lane and Roberts (1971) on the Pilkington's strike, Beynon's (1973, second edn 1984) study of Ford Halewood, Hill (1976) on the dockers, Nichols and Armstrong (1976) and Nichols and Beynon (1977) on the quiescent workforce at ICI, Batstone et al. (1977, 1978) on steward organization in Massey Ferguson, Armstrong et al. (1981) on legitimacy in manufacturing plants, Pollert (1981) on women workers and finally Edwards and Scullion's (1982) account of conflict and control in seven workplaces.[2] The studies were rich in narrative accounts of events and actions and of the arguments that took place amongst stewards and members about the company, their jobs, the union and strikes. They graphically conveyed a tangible sense of shopfloor industrial relations in a variety of settings: militant vehicle assembly plants in Liverpool and Coventry, a quiescent chemicals plant in the North East, and a previously quiet manufacturing plant in St Helens exploding into an unexpected six-week strike. Non-participant observation was the preferred research method and direct quotes from stewards and other workers the favoured mode of data presentation.

The value of these studies lay in their descriptions of the social processes necessary for understanding some of the central problems of industrial relations. They contained data on the social interactions amongst stewards and members in which the former attempted to define or redefine the interests of workers in particular claims or issues, e.g. the wage parity claim in Beynon (1984) or the annual wage claim in Batstone et al. (1978). Other studies tried to account for the absence of collectivist sentiments amongst manual workers or the problems in translating collective definitions of interests into collective organization and action, e.g. Nichols and Beynon (1977) and Pollert (1981). Finally a number of studies examined some of the factors that could impinge on workers' own power resources at the workplace, such as the systems of management control of the labour process (Edwards and Scullion 1982) or the degree of legitimacy enjoyed by managerial rule (Armstrong et al. 1981; and see Brown and Wright 1994 for similar points about power).

The social processes involved in interest definition or mobilization cannot be simply 'described', in a purely empirical way (Hyman 1994a: 170) since any description necessarily entails some concepts and categories however inchoate and rudimentary. Not surprisingly even the most sophisticated cases made explicit use of both: Batstone et al. utilized Lukes' (1974) three-dimensional concept of power and the concept of a 'system of argument', as well as the categories of 'leader' and 'populist' shop steward to distinguish different approaches to worker mobilization. Armstrong et al. (1981) focused on the legitimacy of the employer's authority and distinguished types of argument that eroded or sustained that legitimacy. Edwards and Scullion (1982) examined different modes of control of the labour process and their implications for worker behaviour and mobilization.

These studies represented the intellectual high-water mark of a brief period of fertile and highly insightful accounts of social processes at the workplace.[3]

Perhaps their main thrust was to emphasize the extent to which workers' expressed interests are 'socially constructed'. 'Through their own internal processes of communication, discussion and debate . . . unions can help shape workers' own definitions of their individual and collective interests' (Hyman 1994b: 122; and see also Hyman 1989b: 246). Consequently unions have pursued a wide and varied range of interests (as well as methods for their pursuit), from narrow workplace issues affecting a very specific group of workers to political issues affecting a national (sometimes even international) working-class constituency (Hyman 1994b: 120–122, 133–136).

If we turn to more recent studies, there are two that stand out for their theoretical contribution. Offe and Wiesenthal (1985) examined what they called the 'logics of collective action' confronting labour and capital respectively and argued that workers faced particular difficulty in identifying their 'real interests', by comparison with capitalists for whom profitability provided an agreed and clearcut measure. Since there is no equivalent to profit on the workers' side they are obliged to construct definitions of interest through debate inside their own organizations. Creating and maintaining such organizations is harder for workers than for employers since the effectiveness of the former depends not only on the members' willingness to pay union dues but on their 'willingness to act' collectively. By contrast, organizations of capitalists can function quite adequately so long as their members are 'willing to pay'. In addition workers' organizations are subject to bureaucratization as well as to external pressures which seriously distort the process of interest identification. Offe and Wiesenthal's argument is important in emphasizing the structural factors that permeate workplace industrial relations and create real difficulties for workers in establishing their interests. On the other hand they have very little to say about the micro-level processes of interest identification within the workplace or union.

Paul Edwards has argued that the most appropriate way to establish how workers define their 'interests'[4] is through analysis of what they do rather than what they say, and through a focus on groups rather than individuals. Workers' behaviour is complex because they 'resist' exploitation as well as cooperate with the employer to ensure the viability of their particular firm (cf Cressey and MacInnes 1980). As a consequence relations between workers and employers necessarily involve conflict *and* cooperation. Within concrete labour processes these relations take a variety of forms depending *inter alia* on whether workers' 'orientations' to the employer are militant or acquiescent and individualist or collectivist and on whether such orientations have been translated into collective organization (Edwards 1986: 226–229). Edwards' work is particularly valuable for its anchoring of the concept of interests in a theory of capitalist exploitation, for its insistence on multiple levels of analysis and for its recognition of the complexity of workers' interests under capitalism. The distinction between collective orientations and collective organization is analytically very important and will be picked up in the next chapter.

If we accept that workers' interests are (in part) contingent products of social construction then the processes by which interests are defined and redefined and the range of interests and strategies that are constituted, both become central issues for industrial relations (cf Balbus 1971). What factors shape the definitions of workers' interests proffered by shop stewards? How do they convey these definitions to union members and how are they reworked in the course of interactions at the workplace and beyond? What factors influence the susceptibility of workers to individualistic and collectivist definitions of interests and strategies for their achievement? What factors condition the success (or failure) of employers' efforts to undermine elements of collectivism (e.g. in pay determination) and substitute elements of individualism? These are the questions raised, but not yet adequately resolved.

Power and collective bargaining

Most industrial relations academics would probably accept the following claims: workers join unions in order to overcome their weakness as individuals in the employment relationship. A group of workers organized in a trade union meets the employer on a more equal footing than the individual, and confronts the employer with collective power. When union and employer engage in collective bargaining their relationship involves the threat or deployment of power and the outcomes of bargaining reflect the balance of power. Workers' power however is fragile and is particularly susceptible to the corrosive effects of high unemployment.

Yet the truly remarkable thing about 'power' is that for a concept which lies at the heart of industrial relations it has received very little discussion by mainstream industrial relations researchers (Martin 1992 is a notable and recent exception). Of the ten textbooks of industrial relations that are currently available, six of their authors either consider power to be so unimportant or its meaning so obvious that the term does not even appear in the index (Beaumont 1990; Edwards 1995a; Farnham and Pimlott 1995; Jackson 1991; Kessler and Bayliss 1995; and Rollinson 1993), whilst only three of them have any sustained discussion of the concept and its different definitions and usages (Gospel and Palmer 1993; Hyman 1975 but not 1989c; and Salamon 1992). Since this may be thought a rather casual and superficial exercise, we can turn to recent reviews that have reached similar judgements.

> The notion of power is commonly used, almost unconsciously and in a 'taken-for-granted' fashion, by lay observers . . . in employment relations. . . . This 'taken-for-granted' utilization of power as an explanatory variable is mirrored in the theoretical literature of employment relations.
>
> (Kirkbride 1992: 67; and see also Kirkbride 1985: 44)

9

> Orthodox industrial relations scholars have recognized the central importance of power, but not subjected it to conceptual analysis, or used it extensively in empirical research.
>
> (Martin 1992: 2; and see also Martin 1981: 105)

Where power has been discussed at all, it is in one of four ways: by the use of proxy variables, by reference to structural determinants or correlates, by examining the outcomes of bargaining and by reference to subjective variables (cf Lukes 1974).[5]

As unemployment rises, union density falls; as union density falls, union power falls. Conversely if unemployment is low or falling union power is high and/or rising. Reasoning such as this leads to the use of proxy measures of union power such as union density, bargaining coverage and strike frequency, the last on the grounds that striking constitutes the most visible expression of union power (cf Armstrong *et al.* 1977; Levinson 1969; Martin 1981, 1992). Empirical evidence for the period 1951–1968 showed no relationship between changes in strike frequency on the one hand and changes in union density or hourly earnings on the other, a curious and unexpected result if the first two variables are proxies for power, and earnings are influenced by the exercise of power (Armstrong *et al.* 1977; and see also Levinson 1969; Martin 1981). Armstrong *et al.* (1977) pointed out some of the obvious difficulties in the use of proxy measures such as strikes: unions may strike when they are weak; strong unions may not need to strike at all; workers can use sanctions other than strikes (on which there is no reliable time-series data: Milner 1993); and strikes emerge from the interaction between the parties and will therefore reflect the power of the employer as well as that of the union.[6] In other words, two of the most widely used proxies for trade union power – strike frequency and union density – are unreliable and possibly invalid. This was no doubt why Armstrong *et al.* concluded their investigation of proxy measures by saying that, 'In order to resolve these ambiguities the development of a more detailed theoretical analysis of the sources, weapons and objectives of union power is required' (Armstrong *et al.* 1977: 98).

Almost ten years later Mike Terry (1986) was equally unsuccessful in the search for useful indices of changes in the balance of power. Organizational measures, such as the degree of sophistication of shop steward organization, showed little overall change between 1980 and 1984, and consequently if growing sophistication was indicative of rising steward power in the 1970s then its stability to 1984 suggested there had been no decline in steward power in the early 1980s, a conclusion Terry was wisely unwilling to accept. Whilst some case study research pointed to declining union power (e.g. Chadwick 1983), the evidence was impressionistic and the mechanisms – rising unemployment and fear of redundancy – inadequately theorized. As Terry concluded, if union power had declined, 'we remain ignorant about the precise mechanisms of such changes and how best to investigate and estimate them' (1986: 176).

Several writers have listed sets of structural factors that are likely to influence union power: product markets, labour markets, strategic position of workgroups in the production process, degree of labour substitutability, type of payment system, management control systems, employer strategies, structure and sophistication of union organization and scope and depth of collective bargaining (e.g. Batstone 1988b; Brown 1973: 144–145; Martin 1992: 14–16). However the impact of such variables on the balance of power is far from obvious. On the one hand, union power is likely to be weakened in recession by product market competition and by mass unemployment. On the other hand, increasingly competitive product markets may also weaken employers since they will be anxious to avoid interruptions to production (unless high stock levels provide the ability to resist any industrial action): 'as long as the employer wants production, the workers have some degree of power' (Batstone and Gourlay 1986: 18).

The low levels of strike activity in the 1980s may therefore reflect common weakness rather than a simple shift in the balance of power from workers to employers (Batstone 1988a, b; Batstone and Gourlay 1986: 1–10; Batstone *et al.* 1987). Evidence of successful strikes such as the 1989–1991 engineering campaign for a shorter working week would bear out the Batstone *et al.* argument but still leave us uncertain about the overall parameters of union power decline (Richardson and Rubin 1993).[7]

It is clear from a number of studies that whilst structural factors may facilitate the exercise of power, they do not necessarily generate any awareness of the 'possession' of power or provide the motivation to use it (Edwards and Heery 1989: 177). Goodman *et al.*'s (1977) study of the footwear industry described a classic example of a setting where production line interdependencies, product market competition, payment-by-results and high union density and union centralization seemed to place workers in a very powerful position, whilst insecurity of earnings and employment provided the necessary motivation to exercise that power through militant bargaining and industrial action (1977: 188–201). Yet such action was conspicuous by its absence. Part of Goodman *et al.*'s explanation was that the exercise of power requires a number of subjective pre-conditions, such as group cohesion, that were absent from the footwear plants (cf also Lukes 1974). An individualistic workplace culture with little group formation or consciousness, and low cohesion amongst groups that did form, was inimical not only to the exercise of power via collective action but to the awareness that workers had any power.

One way round some of these problems has been to focus on the outcomes of decisions by asking the parties which of them can get their own way across a range of issues in collective bargaining (Edwards 1978, 1983). Typically such work reveals that unions are 'powerful' on a relatively narrow range of issues and that most decisions are controlled by management. This type of research certainly throws light on the results of exercising power, but it does not tell us much about the processes by which groups acquire and mobilize power resources in the first place (Kirkbride 1992: 70). Once we admit subjective variables such as group consciousness, that may be implicated in the awareness and acquisition of power,

11

the issues of conceptualization and measurement become immensely more difficult. One attempt to theorize the role of subjective factors was by Phelps Brown whose *Origins of Trade Union Power* argued that the decisive change in the postwar period was 'the readiness of the employee to use the power of the strike' (Brown 1986: 158), a readiness underpinned, he said, by full employment, union strike funds and past strike victories. It was reinforced by the disappearance from union leaderships of the generation socialized in the 1930s Depression and their replacement by the new generation of union activists who had only ever known full employment (1986: 164–165). What Brown called the 'readiness' to strike is very similar to Offe and Wiesenthal's (1985) concept of the 'willingness to act' as the essential component of union power (and see Booth 1995: 56, 72 for a similar emphasis on strike action from a labour economist). Brown's analysis is potentially valuable, and unusual, in highlighting historical shifts in the balance of power between workers and employers. In particular it raises the possibility of a recovery of union power in the future, given the appropriate economic, political and psychological conditions.

But conceptions of power which emphasize the subjective willingness to strike as its core also have their problems, for as Kirkbride noted,

> In the majority of instances in employment relations, however, no action is taken by the parties and indeed, rhetoric, or the 'tactical action' dimension of power . . . is employed. Rhetoric . . . represents both the articulation of 'legitimizing principles' or 'vocabularies of motive' and the signalling of the possession and threatened use of resources.
> (1992: 77; and cf also Hyman 1994b: 128–129)

Legitimizing principles are important because employers not only 'want production', they may also want to rule the workplace with the consent of the workforce (cf Burawoy 1979, 1985; Thompson 1989: Chapter 6). As the authors of one of the best workplace case studies put it,

> The workplace is seen, therefore, as a stage on which the cross-currents of interests, supported by varying degrees of power, are mediated by appeals to value systems and moral perspectives and expressed in the debate between workers, their representatives and management.
> (Armstrong *et al.* 1981: 15; and see also Hyman 1975: 23–27 and
> Gospel and Palmer 1993: 192–194 for similar and equally useful
> discussions)

Many of these points about subjectivity are useful, as we shall see, but they need to be incorporated into a more rigorous theoretical framework and not left standing as isolated observations.

We have now come a long way from the commonplace notion that union power is an inverse function of unemployment, but we have not reached any precise conclusion. There is in other words no consensus on how the concept of power should be defined or measured; there is no agreed theoretical framework for studying its determinants; and consequently there is no consensus about precisely what has happened to union power since 1979 beyond the obvious general fact that it has declined.

Capitalist states

The role of the state in modern capitalist economies can hardly be ignored. Whether through legislation, macro-economic policy or its role as an employer, the presence of the state is pervasive. But what can be ignored is the relationship of the capitalist state to class interests and to the process of capital accumulation. Once again the available textbooks of industrial relations are highly revealing. Of the ten that are currently available only one – Hyman's (1975) Marxist introduction – has any extended treatment of the class nature of the capitalist state. There is a modest amount of discussion in Hyman (1989c) and in Gospel and Palmer (1993) and just a few lines in Beaumont (1990), Farnham and Pimlott (1995) and Salamon (1992). Remarkably there is absolutely no discussion of this topic in five textbooks: Clegg (1979), Edwards (1995a, the successor to Bain 1983), Jackson (1991), Kessler and Bayliss (1995) and Rollinson (1993). Miliband's classic study *The State in Capitalist Society* (1969) is referenced in only three textbooks (Blyton and Turnbull, Gospel and Palmer and Hyman) whilst Jessop's equally important book *The Capitalist State* (1982) is not mentioned in any of them. There is an extensive literature on 'corporatist industrial relations' which examined *inter alia* the role of governments in a process of political exchange with organized labour and representatives of capital (e.g. Crouch 1992, 1993; Panitch 1981). With the disintegration of Britain's 'bargained corporatism' from 1979 the topic gradually disappeared from the intellectual agenda of most British researchers. One of the few exceptions is Edwards, whose *Conflict at Work* (1986) contains a lengthy analysis, drawing on contemporary Marxist state theory, of the role of the capitalist state in regulating the workplace (and see also Edwards 1994). His analysis accepts that capitalist states enjoy a degree of relative autonomy from social classes in part because state managers are able to exploit intra-class divisions. The broad but contradictory objectives of these states are to maintain the accumulation of capital whilst legitimating the capitalist system of production. Once particular policies are enacted, however, they acquire a logic of their own, constraining future policy options.

This is a valuable account of the basic functioning of capitalist states to which I shall return in a later chapter. For the moment there are two important observations to be made about the legitimation of capitalist rule. It is one thing to observe that capitalist states will strive to achieve this objective but there can be no presumption that they will succeed. Consequently there is now a large body of attitudinal survey research that has found substantial minorities, sometimes majorities, of British respondents appear not to endorse some of the central features of a capitalist society, such as pronounced income inequality (e.g. Marshall *et al.* 1988: 152–162). The incompleteness of legitimation directs our attention to a more familiar method of rule, namely the use of repression. It became fashionable for a time to stress the degree to which capitalist rule was reproduced through 'ideological hegemony' and to downplay the relevance of force, but after the displays of state force used against groups such as the miners in the strike of 1984–1985 and the printers in 1986 it is surely time to reappraise the significance of repression, and I shall return to the issue in Chapter 4.

Worker–employer relations[8]

As the post-1979 decline of trade unionism gathered pace and showed few signs of letting up, academic and other commentators increasingly turned their minds from the analysis of decline to the prognosis for growth. The old 'adversarial' industrial relations was castigated as destructive and irrelevant in the current era of intensified world competition. Implicit in much of this writing is the idea that a militant response by workers to the current demands of employers would be self-defeating and that any return to a more 'adversarial' pattern of industrial relations is either highly improbable or, if it is thought possible, would be undesirable for all those involved (Kochan *et al.* 1986). Taken to extremes, unions were exhorted to abandon the strike weapon, icon of the 'trench warfare' of the 'old industrial relations' (to use the terminology of Dunn 1990), or (in the American case) to reconcile themselves to the near-total disappearance of collective bargaining (Edwards 1993: 97; Heckscher 1996). A significant number of writers (both in Europe and the USA) came to the conclusion that union survival and recovery turned on the willingness of unions and their members to behave 'moderately' and to offer concessions to the employer as part of a new social partnership between labour and capital (Bacon and Storey 1996; Bassett 1986; Beaumont 1995; Blanchflower and Freeman 1992; Cave 1994; Crouch 1986; Kelley and Harrison 1992; Kern and Sabel 1992; Kochan *et al.* 1986; Kochan and Osterman 1994; Storey and Sisson 1993: 217–221, 233–34; Taylor 1994; Turner 1991). Consequently much of the 'social partnership' literature consists of (rather uncritical) explorations of particular examples of this relationship, such as the Saturn, NUMMI, Xerox and Polaroid companies in America (e.g. Kochan and Osterman 1994; Rubinstein *et al.* 1993; Turner 1991; Verma and Cutcher-Gershenfeld 1993). There is a striking parallel between the social partnership and human resource management literatures, evident most clearly in the way that employers' priorities have come to dominate the intellectual agenda of researchers, but equally apparent in the reluctance of these writers to address what I call the malign face of employer power: actions such as derecognition of unions and victimization of union activists. What is also apparent in much of the social partnership literature is an absence of any historical analysis of patterns of labour–management relations. Union cooperation with employers has been promoted repeatedly throughout the history of capitalism, and defended on the now-familiar grounds that union militancy is anachronistic and destructive (see Chapter 6). Yet the persistence of industrial conflict and the regular outbreak of strike waves over the past century ought to have cast at least some doubt on the validity of these latter claims.

Explaining the gaps

How are we to account for the gaps in our understanding of issues such as power, interests and collectivism? The general problem of shortcomings in industrial relations research is hardly novel since it was addressed over twenty years ago in the influential review by Bain and Clegg (1974), then Deputy Director and Director respectively of the recently formed Industrial Relations Research Unit at Warwick. It is worth recapitulating their main criticisms so that we might then consider whether they are still valid, and if so, whether they help us make sense of the gaps in contemporary research. They argued that British industrial relations research and analysis displayed a series of major weaknesses, the first being that it was largely *descriptive*. Material was organized in the 'categories which were to hand' and there was very little hypothesis testing (Bain and Clegg 1974: 99). Second, there was a strong bias towards the description (sometimes the analysis) of the *institutions* of trade unions and collective bargaining arrangements at the expense of social processes such as influence and mobilization (ibid.: 93–95).[9] Third, researchers rarely used *theory*, either to organize data, to generate and test hypotheses or to develop analysis and argument. Fourth, the few attempts at theory that had been made were marked by significant *conceptual underdevelopment and ambiguity* and finally the industrial relations research agenda was *policy-driven* in that the issues for investigation had increasingly come to reflect the priorities of policy-makers concerned with industrial relations order and reform (for similar criticisms see also Allen 1971; Blain and Gennard 1970; Cappelli 1985; and Goldthorpe 1977; and for more detailed reviews see Poole 1984). Of these five weaknesses, it was the lack of theory that was thought to be most significant:

> the chief current need in industrial relations research is to develop verifiable theory which is interdisciplinary in nature. . . . There is less scope than in the past for fact-finding and case studies merely for the purpose of description . . . [and] for the most part, research should be undertaken not simply because it will increase the stock of knowledge about a given phenomenon but because it is relevant to the development and testing of theory.
>
> (Bain and Clegg 1974: 108)

The limitations of description, the narrowness of institutionalism and the bias towards policy-driven research derived from the theoretical and conceptual underdevelopment of the field. To what extent have these problems been over-come in the ensuing twenty years?

Description

I have already commented on the intellectual value of the workplace case studies of the 1970s in helping our understanding of the ways in which workers come to define their interests. The 1980s witnessed the temporary eclipse of such studies because although examples of the genre continued to be published their quality often compared unfavourably with their predecessors (e.g. Cavendish 1982; Spencer 1989; Thompson and Bannon 1985; Westwood 1984) and the impact of even the better quality cases was slight (e.g. Woolfson and Foster 1988). The historical case studies of engineering plants in Terry and Edwards (1988) were the exception to this trend, whilst the studies by Darlington (1993, 1994, 1995) and Scott (1994) represent a welcome revival of the 1970s tradition. From the late 1980s there was an upsurge of case study investigations of the impact of manage-ment techniques and practices but despite its critical focus this research often lacked the earlier concern with social processes of interest definition and mobi-lization (or its absence) (e.g. Blyton and Turnbull 1992a; Marchington and Parker 1990; Storey 1992; Tailby and Whitston 1989).[10]

Descriptive research took a different form in the 1980s and 1990s, that of the large-scale quantitative survey of establishments and companies with sophisti-cated sampling procedures and instrument design and the use of statistical analysis. Industrial relations surveys themselves were not new: the Donovan Commission had directly and indirectly given rise to three (McCarthy and Parker 1968; Parker 1974, 1975), but the Warwick Survey of 1977/78, published three years later (Brown 1981), inaugurated a veritable flood of sequels and offshoots.[11] Prodigious quantities of useful data, some of it spanning a whole decade, are now available on the major institutional features of British industrial relations and on the structural and institutional differences between union and non-union establishments, a topic of growing interest and concern amongst academics and policy-makers. The authors of most of these surveys have typically professed both descriptive and theoretical ambitions and the Introduction to *Changing Contours* was typical. 'Its principal objective was to . . . allow an assess-ment of the extent of change . . . to construct an institutional "map" [and] to cast light on a wide range of theories and controversies' (Brown 1981: 1; see also Daniel and Millward 1983: 1–2; Millward and Stevens 1986: 1; Millward *et al.* 1992: xi–xii).

Yet with few exceptions the survey reports have largely confined themselves to presenting raw frequencies on the incidence of various practices and proce-dures and cross-tabulations with familiar 'categories to hand' such as manual/non-manual, public/private, industry/services, establishment size and union/non-union (cf also McCarthy 1992, 1994). Most of the textual discus-sions have focused on the scale of various practices (or rates of change in the later surveys) and on their association with structural variables such as those just listed. Where 'hypotheses' have been used to frame discussions, these are not so much theoretically-derived propositions as ad hoc suggestions about issues such as the incidence of new management practices or the scale of industrial action. In addition the surveys contain far more information about institutions and structures than about social processes and to that extent have reinforced the institutionalism of which Bain and Clegg so eloquently and rightly complained (cf again McCarthy 1994). Attempts to use survey data to explore process issues such as industrial relations climate have proved less than satisfactory because of the unavoidable crudeness of survey measures (cf Fernie *et al.* 1994, the criticisms in McCarthy 1994 and the responses by Fernie and Woodland 1995 and Millward and Hawes 1995).[12] Whilst conceding these limitations, Marginson (1998) rightly pointed out that many of them could be overcome by the use of multiple methods (so that surveys are used in tandem with cases) and in particular by the development of better theory.

Institutionalism

The continuing institutionalist bias in the field can be illustrated clearly from our unbalanced knowledge of collective bargaining. We know a great deal about the *structure and scope* of bargaining across different industries and about changes over time. We also know a lot about the correlates of bargaining structure, such as strike activity, wage settlements and productivity levels and trends at many different levels of aggregation – industry, whole economy and internationally (Brown and Walsh 1991; Millward *et al.* 1992; Paloheimo 1990; Purcell 1991). By contrast our knowledge of the bargaining *process* is astonishingly slight. Purcell's (1979, 1981) work is the obvious exception to this stricture but fifteen years after his 1979 study of bargaining reform it is still the case that the bargaining process has been the subject of hardly any systematic research (the obvious contemporary exception being Purcell's former research student Bruce Ahlstrand (1990), as well as the work of Kelly and Heery (1994) on full-time union officers). Equally indicative of this lacuna in research is the fate of Walton and McKersie's *Behavioral Theory of Labor Negotiations* (1965), reissued in 1991 as a classic text. If frequency of citation is the hallmark of a classic then Walton and McKersie's status is beyond doubt, but as Beaumont rightly observed the *Behavioral Theory* has been subjected to hardly any empirical testing in field settings (1990: 132–133).

Policy and research

Although a policy-driven research agenda does not necessarily preclude theoretical development and testing, it has a tendency to do so because of the pressure to focus quickly on the question of *whether* a given policy has or has not worked. Nowhere is this clearer than in the dramatic reorientation of industrial relations research towards the study of management and more recently 'human resource management'. It has been argued that this research is not entirely policy-driven since the best of it is highly critical and has sought to explore 'the contradictions of management and the conflict and processes of negotiation which arise from this fact' (Edwards 1995b: 55). Whilst critical research is clearly preferable to uncritical, we still need to ask how far the research in question advances our understanding of some of the central problems in industrial relations such as interest definition, the formation of collectivism and the acquisition of power resources. For the most part, the recent literature on human resource management has not addressed these questions and I would argue that this is partly because of its orientation towards the empirical evaluation of management policy and practice without the aid of well-developed theoretical frameworks. The new interest in employers and employer policies has been added to a continuing interest in state policies. On the legal side much of the research is again descriptive evaluation, i.e. to what extent have the government's various legal measures achieved their desired effects? Consequently we have thorough empirical evaluations of the laws on balloting (Undy et al. 1996), the closed shop (Dunn and Wright 1993) and industrial action (Elgar and Simpson 1993) to name just three areas.[13] Looking back over the past twenty years it is striking to see how the research agenda of industrial relations has shifted in line with the changing priorities of employers and the state, a trend that was already clear in 1987 (Hyman 1989b: 12–15).

Theory in industrial relations

The field of industrial relations is not quite so devoid of theory as is sometimes imagined, though as we shall see this is a case of first appearances being deceptive. Apart from an older tradition represented by Dunlop's Systems Theory and its offshoots, we have Kochan et al.'s Strategic Choice Theory, a tradition of Marxist analysis and numerous middle-range theories of strike activity and union membership.[14] Dunlop's ideas have been carefully reviewed elsewhere (Poole 1984), so there is no need to repeat what others have written. It is worth stressing however that Dunlop's concept of an industrial relations system (actors, rules and rule making, contexts and ideology) had a dual purpose. It was intended both to establish the analytical focus for an emerging discipline and to function as testable theory (Dunlop 1993: 46).[15] But an assessment of *Industrial Relations Systems* several years ago confirmed what everybody knows: 'it is widely embraced around the world as a device for organizing industrial relations courses and text books. . . . Its major failure, however, has been its inability to stimulate hypothesis-testing research' (Adams 1991: 2; see also Kaufman 1993: 101–102).

And another analyst went on to observe that,

18

> Even if we focus on the research that has been done . . . few if any of the applications conducted statistical tests of hypotheses which were generated by the model. Instead the model has served as a general framework to organize a *description* of the interaction between the actors, the environmental contexts and the ideologies.
>
> (Meltz 1991: 14, my emphasis)[16]

Much the same could be said of Clegg's *Trade Unionism Under Collective Bargaining* (1976), probably the high-water mark of Institutionalist theory in the Dunlop-Flanders tradition. Taking the structure of collective bargaining as his key independent variable, Clegg hypothesized that variations in eight dimensions of bargaining could account for international variations in seven major facets of industrial relations such as union membership, workplace organization and strikes.

For Kochan *et al.* (1986) this tradition of theorizing overestimated some key features of existing industrial relations systems: the stability of the institutions, the ideological consensus between the parties, in particular, management's commitment to trade unionism, and the determining role of the environment. In reality the actors made *strategic choices* in the light of their own values as well as environmental pressures within the three tiers of an industrial relations system: long-term strategy and policy-making at the top level, collective bargaining and personnel policy, and finally workplace activity. In the case of the United States, growing competitive pressures since the 1970s in conjunction with anti-union values amongst management had generated increasing hostility towards collective bargaining and trade unions and stimulated more and more employers to search for an alternative, non-union system of industrial relations.[17]

The strategic choice approach is valuable in highlighting variation amongst employers and across national systems of industrial relations (Clark *et al.* 1988; McLoughlin and Clark 1988; Marchington and Parker 1990; Poole 1986a). Yet it remains unclear whether it is management values that have changed in the past twenty years or the opportunity for their expression because of shifts in the balance of power (Bigoness 1990). In fact Kochan *et al.* have remarkably little to say about power in industrial relations and the degree to which it is not only the 'strategic choices' of the actors that are crucial but the balance of power which enables some actors to impose their choices on others. Their support for union adaptation to employers' demands suggests that they envisage an enduring imbalance of power in favour of employers and that in order to prosper unions must therefore become more 'reasonable' and conciliatory, a fashionable view among pro-labour US academics (cf many of the contributions in Kaufman and Kleiner 1993). But this view of the balance of power is not made explicit; the nature of power in industrial relations is not explored; and there is little discussion of the ways in which actors can accumulate power resources for themselves as well as denying them to their opponents (for instance through utilizing the state: Edwards 1995c: 21).

19

No such charges can be levelled at Richard Hyman whose exposition of Marxism (particularly in the 1970s) pursued three principal objectives: exposing the conservative ideological assumptions of the pluralist academic orthodoxy in industrial relations; demonstrating the necessity to analyse industrial relations as antagonistic class relations between labour and capital; and defending the rationality and legitimacy of workers' struggles (Hinton and Hyman 1975; Hyman 1971, 1972, 1974, 1975, 1978; Hyman and Brough 1975). Much of this work took the form of critiques of other writers and their approaches and thereby helped to demarcate and preserve a distinctively Marxist section of the industrial relations community, with an intellectual agenda centred around the relations between class struggle, union organization and class consciousness (see for instance the reader edited by Clarke and Clements 1977). These topics increasingly preoccupied industrial sociologists in the 1970s, giving rise to the extremely valuable workplace case studies discussed earlier. In the 1980s and 1990s Marxist research on the employment relationship was increasingly conducted within the orbit of 'labour process theory'. Since that body of work has been extensively reviewed elsewhere there is no need to cover the same ground except to make one observation (see Brown 1992: Chapter 5; Littler 1990; Thompson 1989, 1990). It can be argued that the growing interest in human resource management and its associated managerialist agenda poses a challenge to the traditional emphasis in the industrial relations field on worker organization and action. A similar trend can be discerned in the labour process literature where recent interest in management strategy and practices has far outstripped any interest in worker organization and mobilization (Thompson and Ackroyd 1995).

Middle-range theory has arguably fared rather better in recent years, especially on the two subjects where we have a large volume of time-series data, viz. trade union membership and strikes. But it seems unlikely that the presence of data in and of itself has been responsible for the production of theory, since there are many other topics on which there are substantial quantities of data but very little theory (e.g. the range of issues covered by collective agreements for instance). What is perhaps more significant about the research on union membership and strikes is its multidisciplinary character. The strikes literature for instance, has been developed by researchers from sociology, political economy, economics, political science and psychology who have all 'imported' into industrial relations well-developed concepts and theories from their parent disciplines (see Edwards 1992). The result has been to enrich our understanding of many of the different facets of strike activity as well as the broader patterns of conflict of which strikes comprise a key part (for an excellent example see Franzosi 1995). In addition the reliance of many researchers on reasonably coherent, if differing theories, has facilitated an accumulation of knowledge in the form of generalized propositions rather than a simple agglomeration of facts. One basic lesson from this literature, to be taken up in Chapter 3, is the importance of theory in helping to frame problems in ways that yield fresh insights.

However, it is still the case that the bulk of industrial relations research neither derives from nor contributes to either general or middle-range theory. In the burgeoning field of comparative industrial relations, for instance, a recent text noted that

> a good deal of the existing work . . . although often rich and insightful, has not so far been explicitly theoretical in either its purpose or method. . . . Many studies present empirically derived information arising from cross-national investigations, often relating to institutions and practices, which is then analysed and interpreted with little direct orientation towards theoretical considerations.
>
> (Bean 1994: 9)

For the most part the specification of research problems and the discussion of findings has relied less on theory and more on ad hoc hypotheses. These can conveniently be labelled as the trend, policy outcome, correlational and multi-factor hypotheses respectively.

Research hypotheses

Trend hypotheses are propositions which simply assert that over a certain period there has been a greater or lesser incidence of a particular phenomenon, whether it be human resource management, decentralized bargaining or membership of the closed shop. Time-series survey data has facilitated discussion of trends, but so too has the traditional penchant in industrial relations for descriptive studies. Perhaps the clearest expression of trend hypotheses was to be found in the 1980s debates about 'continuity vs change' in British industrial relations where large piles of evidence were pored over to defend one position or another (e.g. Bassett 1986; Batstone 1984, 1988b; MacInnes 1987; Millward and Stevens 1986). What is remarkable in hindsight is how little theoretical or conceptual discussion occurred in order to establish what were the most salient criteria for determining the existence of a 'new industrial relations': changes in institutions, in behaviour or attitudes? And in each case how much change was required, and for how long, before one could confidently proclaim fundamental change? (cf Block 1990; Morris and Wood 1991).

Policy outcome hypotheses normally consist of little more than statements about the possible outcomes of various types of state and employer policies. For critics of such policies 'hypotheses' will be cast in the form of propositions that such and such a measure is unlikely to work, that its effects have been exaggerated or that unsubstantiated claims have been made on its behalf. Such criticism is often coupled with complaints about the poor quality of previous work and statements of the need for new and more rigorous studies to test the policy's effectiveness. Research on schemes of 'employee involvement' and on the post-1979 anti-union laws has largely conformed to this model (see for instance Baddon *et al.* 1989 and Poole and Jenkins 1990 on share schemes; Collard and

21

Dale 1989 on quality circles; Dunn and Metcalf 1996 and Elgar and Simpson 1993 on labour laws). What this research can tell us is that under the particular conditions investigated, quality circles for instance 'worked', but under others they did not, and researchers may then hazard a guess as to the differences between these conditions, but in a purely inductive and ad hoc way. Valuable though it is to know *whether* a particular policy has 'worked' (assuming agreement on criteria), it would be even more valuable to know *why* it has worked (or not, as the case may be). To answer this latter question would require the use of theory to identify the mechanisms (or processes) by which a particular policy might produce its intended effects and the boundary conditions within which such mechanisms would operate. But the overwhelming majority of the policy outcome research has been atheoretical, that is neither derived from nor contributing to theory.

Correlational hypotheses propose that one variable is associated with another and data is then collected to see whether this is the case. Examples include product diversification and decentralized bargaining, or human resource management practices and the presence of trade unionism. In the latter case there has been debate over the WIRS111 finding that three types of human resource management practice (direct communications between management and employees, single status terms and conditions, and checks on start and finishing times) were more common in the unionized than the non-unionized sector (Guest and Hoque 1996; Millward 1994: Chapter 5). According to one view the correlation between union presence and human resource management shows that the two can co-exist (Sisson 1993; TUC 1994). Yet it is possible to conclude precisely the opposite: if human resource management is in some sense inherently anti-union it *would* be most common in the unionized sector because that is where employers have most need of its anti-union effects. By contrast, since most non-union employers face no immediate prospect of unionization then there is little sign of human resource management in that sector. As with policy outcome research, it is hard to progress much further in understanding the evidence without some theory to specify the mechanisms connecting human resource management practices and trade unionism.

The multifactor hypothesis is perhaps the most common of all. Sometimes described as a model or framework, occasionally even a theory, it consists of the proposition that a given phenomenon or event is a complex function of many different factors whose relative importance is unknown. For instance, the prospects for local bargaining in public services were said by Bach and Winchester (1994) to depend on political, organizational and occupational characteristics of the parties and their industrial relations. Yet as Beadle (1995) pointed out this multifactor explanation was entirely ad hoc and the authors provided no guidance as to how this set of factors could be used theoretically to yield explanations of other, similar phenomena. On a broader canvas, Poole has produced a number of multifactor 'models' which identify an enormous range of variables without clearly specifying their relative importance or indicating any ways in which their

22

importance could be determined. For instance, the characteristics of different national industrial relations systems were analysed as a function of environmental conditions (values, ideologies and policies; social, economic, political, technological, legal and demographic structures), intervening conditions (organizational structures and processes and industrial relations institutions), proximal conditions (industrial relations processes, in particular the marshalling of power resources), and the strategic choices of the actors (Poole 1986b: 11–37). It is difficult to think of anything that is *not* included in these 'frameworks' and consequently they entail the proposition that everything is important. Any piece of evidence could therefore be 'fitted' into such analytical frameworks and 'accounted for' but it is not at all clear what we would learn. Multifactor frameworks or models of this kind may be useful as checklists for researchers but once they include everything but the kitchen sink they lose all meaning.

Conclusions

In his 1983 review of industrial relations Winchester echoed the earlier views of Bain and Clegg, noting that the 'discipline' was still marked by a predominance of fact-finding and institutional description (even though such tendencies had abated since the 1950s and 1960s), the underdevelopment of theory and concepts and the continued influence of government and state policy on research agendas. Fifteen years later there is no reason to depart radically from these conclusions, despite the undoubted advances in middle-range theories. Consequently we have made limited progress in tackling what I regard as the central problems in industrial relations. We don't know whether workers are less collectivist and more individualist in orientation and we don't know how to conceptualize their interests in order to answer this question. Power has rarely been conceptualized by industrial relations writers and the concept tends to be used in a purely commonsensical way without definition or explication. Because we have no clear and agreed definition of power in industrial relations, we lack a reliable way of measuring it and we do not have a convincing theory of its acquisition and deployment. As a result we don't know precisely why and how union power declined or by how much in the 1980s, and to what extent its decline could have been attenuated or avoided given different policies by one or more of the chief industrial relations actors, including the state. Finally, we don't know whether the British system of industrial relations is undergoing major or minor changes and whether these are short-term or long-term, cyclical or secular. Not only are we lacking answers to many fundamental questions, but we often lack the conceptual and theoretical tools that would enable us to think about these questions in a fruitful way. It is therefore to the elaboration of those tools that we turn in the next chapter.

3

MOBILIZATION THEORY

Introduction

Over the past twenty years political scientists, sociologists and social psychologists have developed a large body of work on social movements and collective action. One of the main attractions of this literature is that its research agenda maps very closely onto the central problems of industrial relations: first, how do individuals acquire a sense of collective, as opposed to individual grievance? Second, how, and under what conditions, do individuals organize collectively to pursue their grievances (or interests, more broadly defined)? Third, how, and under what conditions, will such individuals take collective action, that is 'cooperative action taken by a number of individuals acting in concert and with common goals' (Scott 1992: 128; and Tilly 1978: 7 for a similar definition).

These questions entail analysis of the ways in which groups perceive and acquire power resources and deploy them in the construction of different types of conflictual and collaborative relationships. A clearer understanding of the conditions under which workers formulate their interests in collective terms should enable us to transcend the woolliness and imprecision that has marred debates about the alleged decline of worker collectivism (see Chapter 2). There is no single theory of mobilization and I have therefore drawn on the work of several writers, in particular Tilly (1978), McAdam (1988) and Gamson (1992, 1995). The chapter begins with definitions of terms and basic assumptions, and then sets out the main social and cognitive processes thought to be involved in the transformation of individuals into collective actors (and vice versa), under the headings of interests and mobilization. In the next chapter I then explore the implications of the theory for the central problems in the field.

Basic assumptions and definitions

Tilly's (1978) mobilization 'theory'[1] begins from a set of Marxist premises. Society is composed of a ruling class and a subordinate (or working) class who have conflicting interests. The ruling class comprises senior state officials, such as judges and top civil servants as well as employers, and seeks to secure and maintain its domination over the subordinate class both in society and in the economy. Employers hire workers and seek to exploit their capacity to work in order to produce both value (sufficient to cover the worker's wage or salary) and surplus value (to cover the employer's profit as well as interest, rent and dividends to shareholders). It is this inevitable exploitation and domination of labour by capital that creates the conflict of interest between the social classes. The process of exploitation requires considerable organization, however, for two reasons: first because the production of surplus value is primarily of interest to the employer not the employee, and second because the employment contract is necessarily incomplete and does not specify the quantity or quality of work to be performed. Employers must therefore translate the capacity to work (which is what they hire) into actual performance (or labour power into labour to use Marx's terms). The conflict of interest that lies at the heart of the capitalist employment relationship does not necessarily give rise to conflict behaviour. Since workers depend on employers to hire their capacity to work, then they too have an interest in the viability of their particular employing organization. Moreover, the subordinate class often exists in a state of disorganization, lacking an agreed view of its interests and without the organizational resources with which to pursue them. From time to time, however, subordinate groups do display some degree of organization (as in trade unions for example) and we observe both long-run fluctuations and cross-sectional variations in the incidence of collective organization and action. It is these fluctuations and variations in 'individualism' and 'collectivism' that form the central theoretical objects of Tilly's work (cf also Brown 1988 and Edwards 1986: 58–77 for similar assumptions about the employment relationship).

Tilly proposed that a useful theory of collective action (and its absence) must have five components, dealing respectively with interests, organization, mobilization, opportunity and the different forms of action (see Figure 3.1).[2] The fulcrum of the model is *interests* and the ways in which people (particularly members of subordinate groups) come to define them. To what extent do they believe their interests to be similar to, different from, or opposed to, those of the ruling group? Do they define their interests in individual, semi-collective or collective terms (or some combination),[3] and if the latter, then to what group or groups does the term refer: an informal group, a department, a social class etc.? The concept of *organization* refers to the structure of a group, and in particular those aspects which affect its capacity for collective action. Examples include centralization of power and scope of representation (sometimes referred to as inclusiveness). *Mobilization* refers to 'the process by which a group acquires collective control over the resources needed for action' (Tilly 1978: 7), or the ways in which individuals are transformed into a collective actor (ibid.: 69). The concept of *opportunity* is itself divided into three components: the balance of power between the parties, the costs of repression by the ruling group and the opportunities available for subordinate groups to pursue their claims (ibid.: 55). Ruling groups may be said to engage in *counter-mobilization* in order to change subordinate

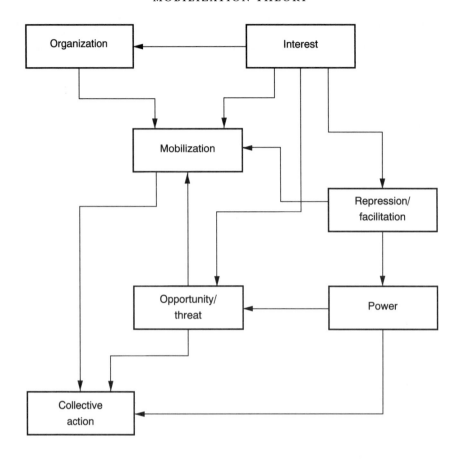

Figure 3.1 Tilly's mobilization model
Source: Tilly (1978: 56)

definitions of interests, to thwart the creation of effective collective organization and to repress attempts at mobilization and collective action (see Franzosi 1995: Chapter 8). Finally *collective action* can take different forms according to the balance between interests, organization, mobilization and opportunity.

Tilly's theory has three significant advantages in the light of the central problems of industrial relations described earlier. First, it helps us to transcend the very general debates about 'the decline of collectivism' and to think much more precisely about different facets of collectivism and individualism. Second, it enables us to recognize that there may be disjunctures between the different facets of collectivism so that, for example, the absence of collective organization in a particular workplace in and of itself tells us nothing about the degree of collective interest definition amongst the workforce. Third, it helps to resolve a number of puzzles or anomalies in the literature of collective action. One example, explicitly addressed by Tilly, is the Kerr and Siegel (1954) hypothesis that a homogeneous mass of workers living in isolated communities (coal miners, for instance) would show unusually high levels of strike activity. The empirical evidence has thrown up numerous variations between countries and regions, and across time, which do not fit the hypothesis (Edwards 1977). Tilly was able to show that many of these discrepant findings begin to make sense when you take into account variations in the mobilization potential of different groups and fluctuations in the opportunity structures for collective action (1978: 65–69).[4]

Industrial relations research has actually covered a lot of useful ground in the areas of organization and opportunity although significant gaps remain, particularly in our understanding of power. We have good time-series data from the British Workplace Industrial Relations Surveys on the structures of trade unionism at the workplace, and the structures of collective bargaining, and there is additional material from the Union Balloting project on union organization throughout the 1980s and early 1990s (Undy *et al.* 1996). Union membership has been reasonably well covered, both descriptively and analytically (Disney 1990; Millward *et al.* 1992: 58–77). Research is also beginning to appear on the different forms of collective action (e.g. Milner 1993). It is in the areas of interest definition and mobilization that we are weak (as we saw in Chapter 2) although there were useful workplace studies of both topics in the 1970s.

Worker definitions of interests

Social movement theorists have broken down the issue of interest definition into two major questions: first, how and why do people acquire a sense of *injustice or grievance*, and second, how do they develop a sense of their grievance being *collective*?[5]

From dissatisfaction to injustice

According to McAdam (1988) grievances arise when people are 'cognitively liberated' from a belief in the legitimacy of the status quo and his model of how this comes about is shown in Figure 3.2. Dissatisfaction may be necessary to motivate collective action but it is not sufficient. For example, an employee may be unhappy with a company pay freeze, but if he or she feels the measure was either fair (everybody suffered the same outcome) or unavoidable (the firm was facing bankruptcy), then behavioural consequences are unlikely. The *sine qua non* for collective action is a sense of injustice, the conviction that an event, action or situation is 'wrong' or 'illegitimate' (see also Gamson 1995: 90–94; Klandermans 1992: 85–86; Snow *et al.* 1986: 466; Taylor and Moghaddam 1987: 79, for similar ideas). Ruling groups seek to legitimate their actions in three ways: by claiming they conform to established rules such as national laws, European Directives or collective agreements; by reference to beliefs shared with their subordinates such as ideas of fairness; and by arguing that employee

27

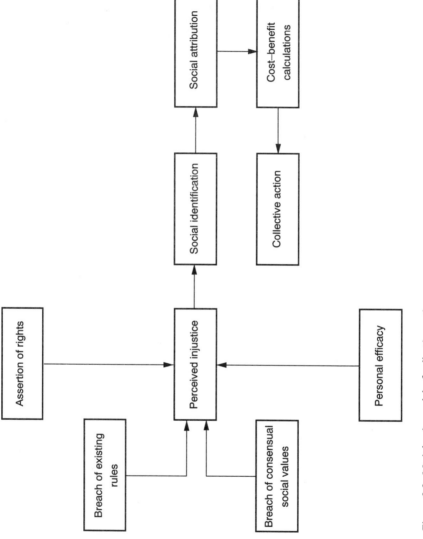

Figure 3.2 McAdam's model of collective action
Source: Adapted from McAdam (1988)

consent can be inferred from their actions, such as signing a contract or undertaking new duties (Beetham 1991: 15–20). Injustice can therefore arise when management violates established rules, e.g. instructing people to do work that is not part of their job (Batstone *et al.* 1978: 47–48). It can also arise when employer actions conflict with shared beliefs. Gouldner's (1954) classic study of a wildcat strike described a gypsum plant in which the employer had traditionally tolerated *inter alia* petty theft of materials and 'clocking off' early. New management attempts to crack down on this 'indulgency pattern' led to a number of strikes. Finally, injustice may appear when employees withhold their consent through actions, e.g. declining to participate in quality circles or purchase company shares (Kelly and Kelly 1991: 36). Workplace case studies have provided numerous other day-to-day examples of contests over the legitimacy of managerial decisions (Armstrong *et al.* 1981: Chapter 8; Beynon 1984: Chapter 6; Edwards and Scullion 1982: Chapter 5; Nichols and Beynon 1977: Chapter 8).

McAdam (1988) identified two other components of 'cognitive liberation', the assertion by employees of their rights and the perception of personal efficacy. It is not enough for employees to feel aggrieved: they must also feel entitled to their demands and feel that there is some chance that their situation can be changed by 'collective agency' (Gamson 1992: 7; Klandermans 1997: 41–43; Melucci 1988). Both points raise crucial questions about the sources of social beliefs and take us into a discussion of ideology. In the context of the employment relationship, ideologies play at least three significant roles: they help identify the most salient features of the relationship, such as the wage–effort exchange; they supply a set of emotionally loaded categories for thinking about this exchange in terms of group interests, e.g. exploitation, social partnership; and they provide a set of categories and ideas that label the interests of one's own group as rights. In Snow and Benford's (1992) terms ideologies 'frame' an issue, event or situation. Injustice (or illegitimacy) frames are critical for collective organization and action because they begin the process of detaching subordinate group members from loyalty to ruling groups (or in Marx's 1847 terms converting a class-in-itself into a class-for-itself). The abstract ideologies that circulate within the labour movement – varieties of Marxism, Christian socialism, social partnership, etc. – are consequently of fundamental importance in understanding the concrete, day-to-day behaviours of workers.

From injustice to collective interest

How does a set of individuals with a sense of injustice or illegitimacy coalesce into a social group with a collective interest? According to social movement theorists there are three critical processes in effecting this transition: attribution, social identification and leadership. It is vital that aggrieved individuals blame an agency for their problems, rather than attributing them to uncontrollable forces or events. That agency can then become the target for collective organization and action. Social identification entails the process whereby people develop a sense of themselves as a distinct group, 'we', defined in opposition to an outgroup, 'them', which has different interests and values. Both attributions and social identities are socially constructed by activists or leaders (Fantasia 1988; Gamson 1995; Klandermans 1997: 38–44).

Attribution

An attribution is an explanation for an event or action in terms of reasons, causes, or both. The action can be one's own or other people's; it can involve individuals or groups; and there is no presumption as to whether attributions are 'true' or 'false'. It is now conventional to classify attributions along three dimensions of causality: personal (or internal) vs external (or situational), stable vs unstable and controllable vs uncontrollable (Hewstone 1989: Chapter 3). For example, if a union negotiating team signs an unsatisfactory agreement with the employer some team members may blame themselves for using poor negotiating arguments whilst others may prefer external attributions, such as the company's poor market position or the lack of militancy of the union's members. Each attribution has very different consequences for future behaviour, and could lead, respectively, to better preparation, fatalism and mobilization of the members. Attributions can also refer to stable or unstable factors and in the example just used some negotiators would regard the level of workforce militancy as unstable, i.e. capable of being changed with more campaigning, whereas others will regard it as stable, treating it as a fixed constraint within which they must operate. Closely related is the dimension of controllability. Workforce militancy, for instance, may be seen as influenced by factors such as unemployment rates that lie beyond the control of local union negotiators.[6]

Social identification

According to social identity theory each individual has a personal identity, which is that unique set of personal traits and attributes sometimes described as personality or character, and a social identity, which comprises the social categories to which we belong and the positive or negative evaluations of those categories.

> Categorization thus brings the world into sharper focus and creates a perceptual environment in which things are more black and white, less fuzzy and ambiguous. It imposes structure on the world and our experiences . . . [and] satisfies a basic human need for cognitive parsimony.
>
> (Hogg and Abrams 1988: 72)

Evaluations of these categories derive from social comparisons with members of other groups (outgroups) along dimensions normally favouring one's own group, e.g. skilled workers differentiate themselves from semi-skilled workers by reference to their qualifications (Brown 1978). A person's social identity might consist of categories such as university lecturer, socialist, or trade unionist, for instance.[7]

Two of the consequences of categorization are stereotyping and social attribution (see Figure 3.3). Stereotypes are defined as perceptions that involve the ascription to every member of a group of those features (positive, negative or neutral) that are thought to typify the group as a whole. For example, left-wing union activists might hold a negative stereotype of managers which states they are untrustworthy. Stereotypical perception will heavily influence the attribution process and predispose people to explain the behaviour of their own group and outgroups in characteristic ways. Positive in-group behaviour and negative out-group behaviour are the expected results from a stereotypical viewpoint: the trade union's wage claim reflects social justice and equity, the management's offer reflects their contempt for the workforce (Kelly and Heery 1994: 151–154, 165–166). These social attributions are also self-serving insofar as one of their functions is to protect group identity. Departures from stereotypical behaviour can thus be 'explained away' by resorting to external attributions (Hewstone 1989: 173). The union's acceptance of a poor pay offer was forced on it by an intransigent employer in a competitive market; the employer's generous redundancy terms reflected last year's unusually high profits. Attributions of this type explain away deviant behaviour that is apparently at odds with negative group stereotypes and thereby help to preserve them (cf Waddington's 1987 study of the Ansells' Brewery dispute for an application of some of these ideas).

One important implication of the personal identity/social identity distinction is that it suggests each person can think and act individually *and* collectively depending on which facet of their identity is currently dominant or 'salient'. Once we conceptualize individualism and collectivism as situationally specific responses to social cues then it becomes almost meaningless to ask whether a particular person is one or the other. Under the right conditions, social identity theory (as well as social movement theorists such as McAdam) would suggest that anyone can think and act collectively. For example, the social identity of 'trade union activist' could be rendered salient ('switched on') by a television news item about a strike, by an argument with a supervisor or by the sight of a picket line.

Even when social identities have been created and switched on, it is rarely the case that there is only one way of categorizing the world. Workers faced with redundancy could represent their problem in terms of governments and government policy, foreign imports, subsidized or cheap foreign labour, the remote decisions of corporate headquarters or the greed of corporate shareholders anxious to cut costs. The social categories have different implications for the interpretation of redundancies and responses to it, but the social identity literature has little to offer in telling us how and why people deploy one social category rather than another (cf Hogg and Abrams 1988: Chapter 4; Hogg and McGarty 1990; Turner *et al.* 1987: Chapter 3). On that topic we must return to the social movement literature and the subject of leadership.

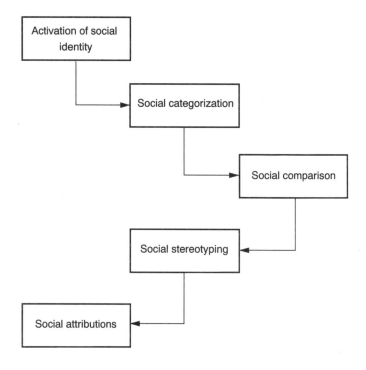

Figure 3.3 Social identity and its consequences

Leadership

The role of leadership in social movements is best illustrated in Fantasia's (1988: Chapter 3) observations of unofficial strikes in an American metals plant. He documented the ways in which informal group leaders persistently talked to their colleagues about the sacking of a worker for sleeping on the job, and in a second case, repeatedly complained about the lack of heating in a changing room despite a series of complaints to management about low temperatures. One of the achievements of the leaders in both cases was to frame issues so as to promote a sense of injustice about what had happened. When workers' leaders pressed the first of their demands (reinstatement of the dismissed co-worker) with the foreman, he became hostile and threatened further dismissals, but the leaders stood their ground, thereby encouraging other workers to do the same. As the arguments continued, management threats engendered a growing degree of cohesion amongst the workers, a process that soon culminated in a walk-out. It was the hostile interaction between determined leaders and intransigent foremen that engendered work-group cohesion, a result that went hand in hand with a strong sense of work-group identity. This cycle of inter-group conflict, hostility and in-group cohesion leading to further conflict is a classical pattern of inter-group relations graphically described and analysed in Sherif's summer-camp studies in the early 1950s (see Brown 1988 for details of the research and theory, now known as realistic conflict theory).

Other examples of similar social processes can be found in Batstone *et al.*'s (1977, 1978) studies of a motor vehicle plant where both formal and informal shopfloor leaders were frequently engaged in discussions with fellow workers, designed to erode managerial legitimacy and emphasize the need for a collective response to management proposals. Likewise, shop stewards in Brown's (1973: 148–151) engineering plants and Beynon's (1984: 213–245) car plants often tried to transform vague feelings of discontent into a firmer sense of injustice. One example was the campaign by Ford stewards around the issue of inter-plant wage parity and the implication of Beynon's account is that the activists' campaign was essential in shaping workers' interest in the issue (cf also Johnston (1994) for other examples, and Marwell and Oliver (1993) for theoretical discussion of the importance of a 'critical mass' of activists in generating collective action).

One final issue worth emphasizing is the role of language in shaping people's definitions of their interests. An informal work-group norm about minimum staffing levels can be described with the neutral label of 'job control' or with the more familiar term 'restrictive practice', which carries an obvious connotation of illegitimacy. The action of a manager can be described in particularistic terms as an expression of individual personality or in social categorical terms as behaviour that is typical of management as a social group. In the context of class struggles, differences in terminology can become critical as Foster and Woolfson (1986) showed in their analysis of the 1971 UCS work-in. The communist leadership of the workforce persistently talked about the shipyards as a whole, and not about individual yards; they talked about the interests of workers, not just shipyard workers, in job security; and they emphasized the degree to which the proposed redundancies were the result of decisions made by English capitalists, thus incorporating a national dimension into the class struggle. It is clear from Foster and Woolfson's (1986) account that the communist leadership of the work-in had thought these issues through very carefully and was deliberately using language as a power resource to 'frame' a particular definition of interests amongst the workforce and to construct a broad alliance of class forces against the employer.

Mobilization

Tilly assumes that once individuals belong to groups then mobilization depends on definitions of interests, the degree of organization and the costs and benefits of taking action. McAdam's model of collective action (Figure 3.2 above) also identified cost–benefit calculations as the key intervening variable between perceived injustice and collective action. In this section I first discuss the most sophisticated theory of individual calculations about collective action, Klandermans' value–expectancy theory, before turning to the social processes of leadership and interaction that are implicated in mobilization.

Calculating the costs and benefits of collective action

Klandermans (1984 a, b) argued that individuals committed to a particular goal or demand will decide whether to engage in collective action by calculating the personal costs and benefits under three headings: goal, social and reward motives. Goal motives comprise beliefs about the number of people expected to participate, the idea that high turnout is necessary for success and that the proposed collective action will make a difference. Social motives refer to the perceived reactions of significant others (family, friends, fellow workers) and the value placed on those reactions. Reward motives refer to the personal consequences of participation, such as loss of pay, and the value placed on those consequences. The individual's willingness to participate in action is said to be a weighted sum of these three motives and evidence from studies of three Dutch union campaigns appeared to lend strong support to the theory. Questionnaire measures of the three motives accounted for between 40 and 60 per cent of the variance in people's willingness to participate.

It is clear from studies of mobilization for strike action that workers *do* talk about the cost and outcomes of collective action and it seems likely that these deliberations play some part in their decisions (cf for instance Woolfson and Foster 1988). However, Klandermans' early work tried to explain the emergence of a collective phenomenon out of individual decisions without specifying the social context in which the decisions are made or the ways in which union leaders attempted to mobilize people (Kelly and Kelly 1992). As McAdam (1988) pointed out the individual's decision to participate assumes there is already the prospect of collective action, but we then need to know how this prospect was organized and came into being. In any case it is not obvious that people are mobilized solely on the basis of instrumental calculations of individual self-interest, a point now acknowledged by Klandermans (1989a). Individuals with a strong sense of social identity, 'switched on' during a mobilization campaign, may think in terms of *group* interests and *group* gains and losses (Fireman and Gamson 1979; Gamson 1992: 57; Turner *et al.* 1987: 65). Others may be mobilized on the basis of compliance with social norms or involvement through networks of friends (Klandermans 1989a). Fantasia's study of a 'wildcat strike' confirmed the existence of these multiple bases of mobilization: the minority of union activists needed little encouragement to propose strike action; a second group of workers was initially uncertain, but on perceiving the action was likely to be effective, soon joined in, whilst a third group was always reluctant but complied with social pressure (1988: 83–85).

Leadership and social interaction

Though often mentioned in the literature, the nature and effects of leadership on mobilization have rarely been theorized (cf McAdam 1988; but see Klandermans 1989b and Marwell and Oliver 1993 for rare exceptions). Fantasia's (1988) study, cited earlier, is again very suggestive. It appears from his case studies that leaders play at least three critical roles in mobilizing workers for collective action once they have imbued them with a sense of injustice: first, they promote group cohesion and identity which encourages workers to think about their collective interests. It also discourages any tendency towards free-riding and is likely to facilitate negative stereotyping of management. Second, leaders will urge workers to take collective action, a process of persuasion that is assumed to be essential because of the costs of such action and the inexperience of many people with its different forms and consequences. Finally, leaders will have to defend collective action in the face of counter-mobilizing arguments that it is illegitimate. The last of these points is especially important in contexts where such action is either illegal (as in one of Fantasia's cases) or regarded by workers as being of dubious legitimacy because procedures for resolving disputes may not have been fully utilized. A similar point was made by Batstone et al. (1978) who reported that workers' support for strike action often turned on the belief that management had broken agreements or was being unfair, whilst worker opposition to strike action reflected the view that there were procedural alternatives which had not been fully exhausted (1978: 46–57).

The role of leadership has also been documented in historical and contemporary studies of workplace union organization by Fishman (1995) and Darlington (1994) respectively. Both reported the key role of left-wing union militants in building and sustaining union organization and adversarial industrial relations. Conversely the absence of mobilizing leadership has been cited as one factor explaining the absence of collective identification and action in particular organizations (Armstrong et al. 1981: 82–83; Edwards and Scullion 1982: 173, 175; Nichols and Armstrong 1976: 98–110).

If we turn to the theoretical and empirical literature on leadership there are some helpful insights into the leadership process. Classically, leaders were seen as high-status role occupants who supplied their subordinates with the facilities and resources to get a job done. In return subordinates received various rewards, including pay bonuses and promotion. In this 'transactional' view the leader–member relationship is largely instrumental, but an alternative, 'transformational' approach has recently become the subject of intense debate. It originated in the observation that certain 'charismatic' business and political leaders seemed to evoke subordinate behaviour by securing their commitment to corporate or other goals rather than exploiting their self-interested commitment to personal goals (Bryman 1992; Guest 1996).[8] Another way of describing these activities is to say that transformational leaders activate particular social identities and that 'subordinates' then behave in terms of their group identity. But precisely how do 'transformational' leaders achieve this outcome? Rule (1989) suggested one possibility in a discussion of the relationship between emotion and rationality. Emotional appeals, he argued, could be understood as, efforts to increase the *salience* of particular interests, values, identifications or concerns. . . . Such appeals are most likely to succeed in conjunction with dramatic public events that seem to cry out for an expressive response – . . . the role of *leaders* in mobilization is to engender in followers just such dramatic perceptions.

(Rule 1989: 154)

It may be that transformational leaders are more likely than transactional counterparts to behave in this way and achieve such results. Rule went on to make the equally important point that the arousal of particular values or identifications does not prevent people from calculating the costs and benefits of collective action: what it means is that they are more likely to think about *group* costs and benefits.

It is a truism that interaction is vital for mobilization (cf McAdam 1988; Melucci 1988) (and hence the legislation by the British Conservative government in 1984 to individualize strike decision-making and to shift it from the workplace to people's homes). For McAdam perceptions of injustice, attribution and costs and benefits occur through discussions and arguments amongst people in what he calls the 'micro-mobilization context': 'that small group setting in which processes of collective attribution are combined with rudimentary forms of organization to produce mobilization for collective action' (1988: 134–135).

Yet the *precise* functions of social interaction are less well documented. One is simply to allow the assessment by individuals of how many others share their grievance, dispelling what Merton (cited in Rule 1989) called 'pluralistic ignorance', a situation where people wrongly feel their grievances are not shared by others. A second function is to allow people to assess the level of support for collective action. In Fantasia's case studies this was particularly important because of the illegality of strike action during the term of a contract and because of the lack of experience of the workers with any form of collective action (1988: 83–85, 96–97, 129–130, 137–138). If these functions can be satisfied by *intra*-group interaction, then *inter*-group interaction serves a different set of purposes. According to realistic conflict theory it is likely to solidify group boundaries, increase group cohesion and promote out-group stereotyping (Brown 1988: Chapters 7 and 8).

Organization, opportunity and the forms of collective action

These three remaining components of Tilly's theory have been covered to some degree in the industrial relations literature, and therefore require much briefer discussion than interests and mobilization.

Organization

The industrial relations literature has covered union organization quite well though in a purely narrow, structural sense. The total size of the union movement (membership and density) has been the subject of considerable research, much of it by labour economists because of the presence of good time-series and cross-sectional data. There is also a large amount of evidence on structural properties of workplace organization, such as steward numbers and steward–member ratios and on those union decision-making procedures now regulated by law (Undy *et al.* 1996). For mobilization theorists such as Tilly these are important variables in helping us understand collective organization and action but he argues that we need to look more deeply and try to gauge the extent to which members identify with the organization and the degree of interaction, or density of social networks, amongst members. For Tilly (and for others) it is variations on these two dimensions that largely shape the 'real' degree of group organization. After all, union density *per se* tells you very little about the willingness of organized workers to act collectively.

Opportunity

The fourth component of Tilly's framework is opportunity, and in particular the policies and actions of employers and the state, and the balance of power between rulers and subordinates. On the face of it this looks like the one area where 'traditional' industrial relations research might be expected to have performed well. There is an extensive literature on labour legislation, and employer policies have come to occupy a prominent place in contemporary industrial relations research. There are, however, two lacunae: the first relates to the specific question of employer repression (discussed more fully in the next chapter). There is an extensive literature on HRM and other employer attempts to inculcate worker commitment to corporate goals, but very much less on the authoritarianism of the 1980s and 1990s: unfair dismissals, derecognition of unions, imposition of new work practices and pay systems, unilateral changes in bargaining and consultative arrangements, to name only a few manifestations.[9] The second omission has already been extensively discussed in the previous chapter and that is the concept of power, and its corollary, balance of power.

Forms of collective action

Most industrial relations literature on collective action is about strikes, although there are a few studies that have examined other forms of action such as overtime bans, go-slows and works-to-rule (e.g. Edwards and Scullion 1982; Kelly and Nicholson 1980; Milner 1993). But petitions, lobbies, collective appeals and the many other forms of non-cooperation and threats to employer legitimacy remain largely unexplored (for examples of these in the white-collar sector see Foley

(1992), and for good discussions of the issues, Edwards and Scullion (1982) and Edwards (1986)). A focus on strikes is defensible on several grounds: we have time-series data back to 1888, as well as comparative data (though there are very difficult problems of comparability); the strike is usually the most powerful sanction available to workers and often the most costly for the employer; and strikes are sufficiently frequent and widespread to allow us insights into the industrial relations system as a whole. During a downturn in class struggle (or a period of counter-mobilization) as in the 1980s and 1990s, these reasons seem less compelling. But even for the high points of strike activity – in the 1890s, 1910–1920, the 1940s, 1968–1974 – we still know remarkably little about the forms of collective action (or their absence) in the thousands of unremarkable plants that did not hit the headlines or participate in the great strike waves of those times.

Conclusions

Mobilization theory constitutes a significant shift in the focus of industrial relations research. At its heart is the fundamental question of how individuals are transformed into collective actors willing and able to create and sustain collective organization and engage in collective action against their employers. (By the same token, of course, the theory should prove equally illuminating on the absence of collectivism.) It redirects our attention away from bargaining structures and institutions and towards the social processes of industrial relations. Second, the theory provides both a general and a specific framework for thinking about these processes. The former comprises five concepts: interests, mobilization, organization, opportunity, and the forms of collective action. The more specific framework highlights the roles of injustice, agency, identity, and attribution in shaping the ways people define their interests. These attributions and categories will often be derived from general ideologies and will be reinforced, reworked or abandoned in the course of workplace social interaction. It is these discussions that provide the opportunities for leaders to frame issues in particular ways, intensifying or moderating employees' sense of injustice. Third, the process of mobilization entails calculations by employees of the costs and benefits of collective action, and these will also be influenced by the behaviours and arguments of union activists (and managers) in what McAdam calls the 'micro-mobilization context'. Mobilization theory therefore provides a set of interconnected concepts that focuses our attention on particular social processes and helps us think analytically about them.

4

MOBILIZATION AND
INDUSTRIAL RELATIONS

In this chapter I want to explore the implications of mobilization theory for the central problems identified in Chapter 2: the alleged decline in worker 'collectivism' and the rise of non-unionism, the concept of power, the nature of the capitalist state and relations between workers and employers. In each of these areas I aim to show how mobilization theory directs our attention to novel issues or helps us conceptualize familiar ones in a more fruitful way.

Worker interests: the alleged decline of worker collectivism and the rise of non-unionism

Worker collectivism

The decline of trade union membership and collective action in Britain and other advanced capitalist countries during the 1980s was initially addressed in the literature through familiar ideas such as the business cycle and changing class composition. But a growing number of commentators began to argue that what underlay the sharp and dramatic decline of the labour movement was a pervasive and secular transformation in popular attitudes, a decline in the collectivist values intimately associated with post-1945 patterns of industrial relations (Bassett and Cave 1993; Brown 1990; Cave 1994; Valkenburg and Zoll 1995; and for critiques see Hyman 1992 and Rentoul 1989).[1] The most sophisticated, and most frequently cited, exposition of the argument is in Phelps Brown's (1990) essay 'The Counter-Revolution of our Time', and the authority of its author alone is sufficient reason to examine the article in detail. The argument is an historical one, presented discursively and through broad generalizations, but without the aid of detailed evidence or any articulated theoretical framework.[2] Brown's case has to some extent to be reconstructed and it seems to go as follows. In the nineteenth century the working class was strongly collectivist in outlook because of the deprivations of working life, particularly poverty, job insecurity, unemployment and employer power. This common set of conditions created a widespread sense of mutual interdependence and solidarity, features of the working class that were reinforced by employment concentration in large factories and by housing concentration in the poor areas of large towns and cities. Trade unionism thus took on the character of a broad social movement aspiring to the defence and promotion of class interests through a radical reconstruction of society. It was this deep-rooted collectivism that expressed itself in the solidarity of the 1926 General Strike in support of the miners, and in the trade union attachment to national as against local (and therefore sectional) collective bargaining.

But in the latter half of the twentieth century this collectivism has been dramatically eroded. Workers have become more affluent and are now more concerned than previous generations with the acquisition of consumer goods and services. Owner occupation, the spread of conurbations and the growth of private transport have broken up old occupational communities and allowed geographical dispersal and mobility of workers. More and more employees work in small units or work for themselves, and see education and training as the main devices for self-improvement rather than collective organization and adversarial industrial relations. When the miners called for solidarity action during the 1984–1985 strike the silence was deafening: contemporary trade unionism, according to Phelps Brown, represents the interests of discrete individuals in local bargaining units, not the class interests of a militant proletariat.

Some of Brown's description of patterns and trends is accurate (particularly in the field of consumption), and there is a lot of survey evidence that some (though by no means all) of the reasons people give for joining (or not joining) unions are instrumental (Gallie 1996; Kelly and Waddington 1995; Marshall *et al.* 1988; Millward 1990). But one of the main problems with Brown's argument is that there is no attempt to distinguish analytically or empirically between different facets of collectivism (and the same weakness is to be found in Bassett and Cave 1993). He therefore appeared to assume that changes in collective interests, organization, mobilization and collective action necessarily went hand in hand, even though mobilization theory suggests, for instance, that workers may have a collective definition of interests but lack the organizational means for their pursuit.

Second, Brown presented a rather romanticized view of the 'Golden Age' of worker collectivism from which sectionalism, political divisions and the sheer effort required to organize workers have been excised (Hyman 1992: 160; 1994b: 117–118). Third, his argument that worker collectivism is rooted in poverty and deprivation and reinforced by employment concentration and residential segregation, makes it difficult to account for the upsurge of collective organization and action during the world strike wave of 1968–1974. These strikes frequently involved relatively well-paid workers, non-manual as well as manual, in disputes over wages (an average of 57 per cent of strikes each year in Britain from 1968–1974). Brown might argue that this was merely the collective action of instrumental individuals, but the proportion of wage strikes was even higher in the period 1910–1920 (an annual average of 66 per cent) described by Brown himself as the heyday of collectivism (Kelly 1988: 102, 105). In any case the 1968–1974 strike wave was particularly notable in Britain for the unusually high level of solidarity strikes and for the return of the class-wide political strike (Kelly 1988: 136–144).

Even more curious in the light of Brown's argument are the varied fortunes of British unions in the 1980s. Although the union movement as a whole has lost members, some individual unions actually increased their membership over the period 1979–1996 (see Table 4.1). One striking feature of this list is the preponderance of unions organizing relatively well-paid, skilled manual and white-collar professional workers. Yet according to Phelps Brown these are precisely the types of worker who should be most prone to individualism and least susceptible to union organization. It is true that most of the unions shown in the table organize in public sector services where employers have generally continued to recognize unions for collective bargaining and where demand for labour has been high or rising. But these structural factors tell only part of the story. The growth of public service unionism has also been associated with relatively high levels of worker discontent, themselves expressed in major strikes every year since 1980 (Bailey 1996: 145). Although the incidence of strike action has fallen significantly since 1979, the decline in the public sector has been very much less than in the private sector (see Table 4.2).

All of this evidence suggests that the collectivism of poverty is just one form, not the form, of collectivism and that labour movements in Britain and elsewhere have been able to construct collective identities and movements amongst a wide range of workers at many different levels of affluence. For mobilization theorists it

Table 4.1 British TUC unions with 1996 membership totals above their 1979 levels

---

Association of First Division Civil Servants

Association of University Teachers

British Actors Equity Association

British Airline Pilots Association

Chartered Society of Physiotherapy

Educational Institute of Scotland

Fire Brigades Union

National Association of Probation Officers

National Association of School Masters Union of Women Teachers

National Association of Teachers in Further and Higher Education

Prison Officers Association

Scottish Prison Officers Association

Society of Radiographers

Writers Guild of Great Britain

Sources: TUC General Council Report 1980; TUC Directory 1997

Note: The table excludes recent affiliates to the TUC

Table 4.2 Strike incidence in the British public and private sectors 1974–1990

	Private sector		Public sector		Private: public ratio (%)
	Strikes	Strikes per million union members	Strikes	Strikes per million union members	
1974	2,379	368.2	543	104.2	19%
1979	1,517	215.4	563	90.3	27%
1985	465	90.7	438	79.1	49%
1990	265	47.4	365	74.0	58%

Source: Dickerson and Stewart (1993: Table 6)

is not the absolute level of 'affluence' or earnings that is critical for collective organization and activity, but the sense of injustice. For all these reasons, then,
Brown's argument for the decline of worker collectivism is seriously flawed.

The growth of non-unionism

Even if one were to reject the broad historical sweep of Brown's argument, it
would still be possible to contend that the recent growth of non-unionism represented a significant new trend in contemporary industrial relations that called into
question previous assumptions about the union form of worker representation. It
is therefore only in the last few years that the study of non-unionism has really
started to take off, and Blyton and Turnbull's (1994) textbook, for instance, is the
first (and to date the only) one to feature a whole chapter on the topic. I shall first
review the literature on non-unionism and then indicate how and where mobilization theory can make a fresh and important contribution.

Four approaches to the topic can be distinguished in the literature, each of
which actually picks up on one of the themes explored by Phelps Brown: structural correlates of density and recognition (or its absence), case studies of
managerial practices in non-union firms, surveys of union recruitment activity
and surveys of employee attitudes. These are analytically distinct approaches but
empirically they may co-exist (as in McLoughlin and Gourlay 1994). The first
approach often uses Workplace Industrial Relations Survey data to discover the
structural correlates of non-unionism, such as enterprise and establishment size
and age of firm (e.g. McLoughlin and Beardwell 1989; Millward 1994: 21–30;
Millward *et al.* 1992: 70–77; Milner and Richards 1991). This type of research is
useful in mapping the terrain of non-unionism and in charting changes over time,
and may in addition indicate hypotheses for further research. For instance, the
extent of union recognition in establishments opened after 1980 was only half
that of pre-1980 plants (Millward 1994: 27–31; Millward *et al.* 1992: 73), a
difference that could alert us to a significant change in employer policy coinciding
with the early 1980s recession and the arrival in power of a right-wing administra-

tion. However, the mainly structural and cross-sectional character of the Workplace Industrial Relations Survey data means it is difficult to shed much light on the *processes* by which recognition is obtained and to draw causal inferences.

The second approach consists of studies of managerial practices in non-union firms, and is premised on the idea that such practices play a critical role in keeping unions out. Hence, there are case studies of prominent non-union firms such as IBM (Dickson *et al.* 1988) and Marks and Spencer (Blyton and Turnbull 1994: 228–233), and surveys of management in non-union companies (e.g. Bassett 1988; Beaumont 1987: Chapter 5; Blyton and Turnbull 1994: Chapter 9; Flood and Toner 1997; Foulkes 1980; Guest and Hoque 1994, 1996; Guest and Rosenthal 1993; McLoughlin and Gourlay 1994: 40–65; Rainnie 1989).[3] These studies have proved useful in identifying some of the employer policies and practices – in reward systems, work organization and employee representation – that *may* inhibit either worker desires for trade unionism or the opportunity to translate such desires into action. The research has also generated typologies based on multiple dimensions of managerial behaviour. Guest and Hoque's (1994) study of British greenfield sites classified firms along two dimensions: degree of strategic integration of human resource policies and the extent of human resource policies, to produce a 2×2 matrix comprising four types of non-union firm (cf also McLoughlin and Gourlay 1994). However, it is rare in these largely descriptive studies to find any evidence, systematic or otherwise, on the responses of employees to managerial policies and on their effectiveness in deterring trade unionism (McLoughlin and Gourlay 1994 and Scott 1994 are the exceptions: see below).

Third, we have survey evidence on union recruitment, either taken from Workplace Industrial Relations Survey data (Millward *et al.* 1992: 68–70), from union head offices (Beaumont and Harris 1990; Mason and Bain 1991) or from union officers themselves (Kelly and Heery 1989; 1994: 101–111). This research is useful in documenting just how few resources unions devote to recruitment and recognition, a fact which perhaps explains some of the failure to penetrate the growing ranks of non-unionism. On the other hand we have no reliable, contemporary evidence on organizing drives *per se*, on the way they come about, the issues involved and the responses of the workforce and of management (at least not for this country: there is very interesting American evidence in Fantasia 1988: 121–179 and Johnston 1994). Consequently we know virtually nothing about the differences between successful and unsuccessful union campaigns.

The fourth approach to non-unionism is based on employee attitude surveys, making use of the growing number of national data sets, such as British Social Attitudes, the Labour Force Survey and the Employment in Britain Survey, as well as customized, one-off surveys of both national samples and particular groups such as young workers (e.g. Cregan and Johnston 1990; Gallie 1996; Gallie and White 1993; McLoughlin and Gourlay 1994: 93–116; Marshall *et al.* 1988; Millward 1990). Researchers have principally explored workers' general attitudes towards unions, their beliefs about union power and effectiveness, and their reasons for not joining unions. In line with the more rigorous (if sometimes narrow) research in America, these findings have confirmed it is the availability and perceived effectiveness of unions which encourages people to join (see Barling *et al.* 1992 and Hartley 1992 for reviews). Evidence on the effects of employer hostility to unions is mixed, with some studies showing that it deters employees from joining (e.g. Gallie 1996) though others disagree (e.g. Gallie and White 1993: 42). What still remains unclear from all four approaches is how unionism ever gets started up in a workplace.

Mobilization theory argues that collective organization and activity ultimately stem from employer actions that generate amongst employees a sense of injustice or illegitimacy. Employees must also acquire a sense of common identity which differentiates them from the employer; they must attribute the perceived injustice to the employer; and they must be willing to engage in some form of collective organization and activity. This whole process of collectivization is heavily dependent on the actions of small numbers of leaders or activists.

Much of the available evidence on these processes can be found in *British Social Attitudes*, an annual opinion survey of a representative sample of approximately 3,000 members of the British adult population. The surveys began in 1983 and the most recent was conducted in 1995, so on some items we have a time series spanning thirteen years (see Jowell *et al.* 1984–1996). There are two other data sets that we can also draw upon, the first of which is the national *Employment in Britain* attitudinal survey, carried out in 1992 and comprising a sample of 3,458 employees (Gallie and White 1993). The second is the data assembled by the Citizens' Advice Bureaux from callers to their offices throughout Britain (NACAB 1990, 1993, 1997).

Injustice at work

One possible explanation for the rise of non-unionism is that fewer and fewer employees experience work-related injustices that are sufficiently serious to encourage unionization. If we look first of all at the broad incidence of employee grievances over the past ten years we actually find a very different picture (see Table 4.3).

Whilst the category of 'complaints' does not necessarily equate with that of injustice, it is apparent from the content of the complaints that there is probably a lot of overlap. To cite just two examples:

> A CAB in Lancashire reports that they referred a case to the Factory Inspectorate. The clients in question were employed in an unheated warehouse. Some days later the employer asked the staff who had contacted the Factory Inspectorate. When the clients admitted it they were immediately dismissed and escorted from the premises.
>
> (NACAB 1990: 8)

Table 4.3 Numbers of work-related complaints reported to Citizens' Advice Bureaux 1983–1997

1983	469,000
1987	625,735
1990	709,570
1993	882,257
1997	610,000

Source: Hobby (1994); NACAB (1997: 9)

> A CAB in Avon reports a 19-year-old client who was employed at a gardening centre. He worked from 8am to 5pm six days a week, at an hourly rate of £2.00. He had no written contract. His hours were gradually increased to 70 per week, with no overtime pay. When he protested, he was sacked.
>
> (NACAB 1993: 11)

The evidence suggests that, far from declining, the level of worker grievances about employment almost doubled between 1983 and 1993.[4] Most of the grievances logged by the Citizens' Advice Bureaux emanated from the non-union sector and in view of its expansion since 1983, some rise in grievances might have been anticipated (NACAB 1990: 5). But this can only be part of the story because the number of non-union employees rose by approximately 31 per cent from 1983 to 1993, whereas the number of grievances rose by a staggering 88 per cent. If we turn to *British Social Attitudes* data we have evidence on attitudes to pay and decision-making at the workplace, shown in Table 4.4.

Asked about the gap between high and low incomes at their own workplace, a growing proportion of employees, up from 38 per cent in 1984 to 50 per cent in 1995, believes that pay differentials are too large. How far this perception translates into a sense of grievance is not clear because when asked if their own pay is reasonable, a stable 55–60 per cent of employees have said 'yes' over the past ten years. If we turn to employee views about participation in workplace decision-making, then the evidence seems fairly unequivocal. A declining percentage believe they would have a say in decisions affecting their work and there is a corresponding fall in the level of satisfaction with participation.[5] Overall this evidence suggests that in recent years more employees, not fewer, have become discontented with some aspect of their work and so the rise in non-unionism over this period cannot be accounted for by a fall in the volume of employee grievances.

Identity and attribution

As mobilization theorists argue, grievances are necessary but not sufficient for employees to become collectivized. What is also essential is that workers blame the employer or the management for their problems. After all, if aggrieved employees believed they could resolve their problems through discussion with

45

Table 4.4 British attitudes to pay and participation 1984–1995

	1984	1985	1986	1987	1989	1990	1991	1993	1994	1995
% of employees:										
who agree that the gap between high and low incomes is too large at their own place of work										
	38	39	39	41	45	47	44	46	52	50
who perceive their own pay as reasonable										
	55	56	55	54	56	59	63	60	56	58
who have a say in decisions affecting their work										
	–	62	–	51	50	–	54	52	–	–
who are satisfied with their say in decisions affecting their work										
	–	63	–	53	54	–	54	47	–	–

Sources: Hedges (1994); Spencer (1996)

Note: – indicates data not collected that year

management, then their incentive to unionize would be diminished correspondingly, as the US literature on union joining has shown (Barling *et al.* 1992; Premack and Hunter 1988). On this topic the *British Social Attitudes* data is far from perfect since it comprises items measuring general attitudes towards management and trust in management, rather than attribution for workplace problems. Nevertheless it is worth recording because *ceteris paribus*, employees who are critical of management are less likely to identify with them and will be more receptive to the argument that management is to blame for their problems (see Table 4.5).

Asked whether management would 'try to get the better of employees if it gets the chance', the evidence shows that levels of mistrust in management amongst the general population have risen significantly, if not spectacularly since 1985, rising sharply in 1986–1987 and steadily thereafter. Likewise there has been a recent steady growth in the numbers of people who believe business benefits owners at the expense of workers. Even more revealing are the questions that have been put to employees, where the two management items from *British Social Attitudes* have charted a significant deterioration in workers' assessment of the quality of management–employee relations and the quality of management itself. A small but steadily rising percentage of employees believes that relations at their workplace are not very good whilst there has been a steep decline in the percentage who think their workplace is very well managed, from 30 per cent to 23 per cent. The differences in some of these numbers over a twelve-year span may not seem especially dramatic but by the normal standards of attitudinal change these are in fact significant shifts.

Table 4.5 British attitudes to management 1983–1995

	1983	1984	1985	1986	1987	1989	1990	1991	1993	1994	1995
'Management will always try to get the better of employees if it gets the chance'											
% Agree	–	–	51.5	51.6	60.9	–	61.3	57.9	62.7	63.4	64.0
% Disagree	–	–	24.6	27.3	19.8	–	19.0	19.2	15.4	15.0	14.2
'Big business benefits owners at the expense of workers'											
% Agree	–	–	–	53.9	51.1	52.8	52.4	49.5	54.8	60.1	61.7
% Disagree	–	–	–	19.0	22.1	21.5	22.6	18.5	17.0	13.6	15.3
% employees:											
who would describe relations between management and other employees at your workplace as											
Very good	37	36	38	34	34	32	38	34	31	29	30
Quite good	47	47	45	47	48	49	44	45	47	47	45
Not very good/ not at all good	15	16	16	19	18	18	17	21	20	24	24
who in general would say their workplace was											
Very well managed	30	28	28	27	26	26	26	25	26	22	23
Quite well managed	50	51	53	52	54	54	55	55	52	54	54
Not well managed	20	19	18	20	20	18	19	20	21	23	23

Source: Jowell, R. *et al.* (1984–1996)

Taken as a whole this evidence suggests that we cannot account for declining unionization in Britain by reference to improvements in worker attitudes to, and trust in, management. The growing mistrust of management is potentially good news for trade unions because it implies that recruitment literature focused on managerial deficiencies is likely to fall on receptive ears. Yet even if this point were to be accepted it does not necessarily follow that employees will join unions.

The willingness to act collectively

Writers such as Phelps Brown (1990) and Bassett and Cave (1993) claim to have identified a generalized decline in the willingness of employees to resolve workplace problems by collective means. *British Social Attitudes* cannot tell us much about the willingness of employees to organize and act collectively at the workplace, but it does contain very interesting time-series data for the general population. People were asked to imagine there was an unjust Bill going through the House of Commons and to say which of several forms of action (if any) they would take in response. The options ran from mild forms of activity such as signing a petition to one of the classic forms of collective action, the protest or demonstration (see Table 4.6).

The evidence shows that far from being less willing to engage in such action, people have actually become more willing to do so over the years. As a check on the reliability of the data, people were also asked to report if they had in fact ever demonstrated and the numbers are sufficiently small to suggest that on the whole respondents are probably being honest.

If we take this data at face value it does raise the interesting question as to why British trade union membership continued to decline despite falling unemployment between 1986 and 1989 and again from 1994. One hypothesis which can be derived from mobilization theory is that employees are deterred from joining because they believe unions are simply too weak to be able to resolve workplace injustices. Evidence from *British Social Attitudes* shows that a growing number of people have indeed come to believe unions have too little power, a perception which would certainly not encourage them to join (Table 4.7).

By focusing on the separate components of collectivization, mobilization theory allows us to analyse the different factors which may (or may not) be responsible for the rise of non-unionism in Britain and elsewhere. Although the future of trade unionism depends partly on structural factors, such as the level of unemployment, even a favourable environment will leave unions with the task of 'collectivizing employees'. The evidence reviewed here suggests that union decline in the 1980s and 1990s cannot be accounted for by reference to a decline in employee grievances; it cannot be explained by growing trust in management, consequent on better management of the workplace; and it does not derive from a generalized decline in people's willingness to act collectively. All of this evidence actually augurs well for the future of trade unionism since many of the essential attitudinal prerequisites for recovery are in place. The central problem now faced

Table 4.6 Percentages of the British population who would protest/demonstrate against an unjust Bill

1983	1984	1986	1989	1991	1994
8	9	10.5	14.0	13.6	16.4
(2)	N/A	(5.7)	(8.4)	(9.1)	(8.9)*

Source: Jowell, R. *et al.* (1984–1995)

Note:* Figure in brackets is those who say they have ever been on a protest or demonstration

Table 4.7 'Trade unions in Britain have too little power' (% agreeing)

1983	1986	1989	1994
5.0	11.1	18.5	28.4

Source: Jowell, R. *et al.* (1984–1995)

by unions is the perception that they may be too weak to 'make a difference'. We know this belief has been overcome in the past, but what we do not know is the precise mechanisms through which this attitudinal change comes about. Greater legal rights for unions ought to make a difference and so too should an increase in strike frequency, especially if the latter is associated with a rising union win rate, since both developments ought to erode the perception of union weakness.

Leadership

It was suggested in Chapter 3 that leaders play four major roles in the overall process of mobilization: they imbue workers with a sense of grievance, create a sense of social identity, urge collective action and legitimate such action in the face of hostile criticism. Evidence collected by the Commission on Industrial Relations (CIR 1969–1974) in the course of union recognition disputes demonstrates that campaigns for recognition are frequently initiated and led by very small numbers of pro-union activists (CIR Reports 26, 28, 43, 44, 53, 57, 71, 72 and 81). Consequently unionizing drives are highly vulnerable to employer dismissal of such activists and in some cases may have actually collapsed as a result (CIR Reports 44, 72, 81). The CIR data provides some justification for the stress on leadership, both positively (their presence makes a difference) and negatively (their dismissal often terminates the process of collectivization), though there is insufficient detail to distinguish the four roles mapped out by the theory and to analyse the bases of leader support (cf Fantasia's 1988 study, Chapter 3, by contrast).

Support for the role of leadership in building union organization *after* union recognition comes from the historical case studies of the British postwar engineering industry edited by Terry and Edwards (1988). In their concluding chapter they argued:

> the ending of the war led to fresh problems for steward organizations. Paramount among these was the need to build and strengthen member- ship as the protection provided by wartime controls was lost. Key to this process in many factories were a handful of activists and, for the TGWU at least, a full-time official, Jack Jones. . . . The case studies support an 'activist' approach to union organization.
>
> (Edwards and Terry 1988: 220–221)

The theoretical emphasis on leadership implies that non-unionism is thriving partly because of an absence of activists willing to challenge the employer. Up until the 1970s many union militants belonged to the Communist Party (CP), whose membership averaged 32,500 between 1945 and 1979 (Thompson 1992: 218). It was CP members who played a key role in building union organization in major industries such as motor vehicles and engineering from the 1930s onwards (Fishman 1995: Chapter 8; Hinton 1983: 153–154; Jefferys 1988). Its declining membership and influence from the early 1970s until its demise in 1991, notwith- standing the limited growth of several Trotskyist groups in the same period, could well be part of the explanation for the persistence of non-unionism.[6] However, mobilization theory certainly does not require union activists to be members of left-wing political parties (even of the Labour Party, whose membership also declined between the early 1970s and the late 1980s: Kavanagh 1990: 170). Repression of potential or actual union activists can also be critical in demobi- lizing workers and despite a law prohibiting discipline and dismissal of employees on grounds of union activity, there is some anecdotal evidence that in industries such as hotels and catering union activists have been illegally dismissed (see various issues of the TGWU *Record*). There is even firmer evidence from America and Italy that employers have eliminated unionism or held it at bay through the selective dismissal of activists (Franzosi 1995: 213–220; Freeman 1985).

What is also important in understanding non-unionism is the different forms of collective action. Conventionally we think of the main forms as strikes, over- time bans and go-slows but despite their differences they all have in common the fact that they tend overwhelmingly to be organized by unionized workers. Mobilization theory places no such restriction on the forms of action and thereby acknowledges that there may be forms of collective action in non-union firms which might not normally be thought of as belonging to that category. We now have a number of recent and valuable case studies which have used observation and interview to illuminate worker responses to injustice in non-union settings (Ram 1994; Scott 1994). In one instance the management of a chocolate plant wanted to change the system of differential shift payments and introduce a single premium for all shifts. But when 'job involvement' meetings were held to announce and explain the decision there were very strong protests from workers, and as a result management scrapped the proposal (Scott 1994: 121). In Ram's clothing factories, negotiations took place over piece rates despite the absence of a union or any formal system of worker representation.

> it would be unduly simplistic to characterize the effort bargaining process as management autocracy. . . . In negotiations around the actual piece-rate, management and [individual – JK] workers struck informal bargains.
>
> (Ram 1994: 122)[7]

In these two instances we see the classic alternative to unionism, other than quitting: collective (non-union) voice, and individual voice. It may be that employees perceived these mechanisms (respectively) to be sufficiently effective to inhibit any desire for unionism, but this would be a very strong, and probably unjustified, inference. CIR data, referred to earlier, showed repeatedly that even in the midst of recognition struggles where unionism was becoming increasingly legitimate, the number of employees prepared to join was often small and was far below the numbers who said they supported trade unionism (CIR Reports 57, 58, 63, 67, 68, 70, 71, 74, 75, 81 and 82). As always we must be careful not to infer attitudes from behaviour, particularly where behaviours (such as union joining) can prove very costly for the individuals in question.

Mobilization theory directs our attention to the social relations of the workplace and the processes by which employees perceive and respond to injustice and assert their rights. Out of these interactions emerges the desire for unionism, a particular form of collective representation. Yet the current research bias towards structural correlates of recognition and questionnaire surveys of management practices and employee attitudes is unlikely to shed very much light on these processes.

The concept of power

In Chapter 2 I examined the ways in which power had been conceptualized within British industrial relations literature and showed that much of what had been written was rather commonsensical. For example, as unemployment falls, union power rises, or as product market competition increases, union power falls. The problem with such arguments is not that they are wrong *tout court* but that there are interesting exceptions, such as Britain and Italy in the late 1960s and early 1970s (when strike rates and unemployment both rose), which show that the link between labour markets and union power is more complex. It was this realization which led Eric Batstone (1988b) to analyse a multiplicity of determinants of power resources and the interactions between them. Since purely structural accounts of power omitted the attitudes and strategies of the actors, Batstone formally incorporated these into his framework but was unable to take his ideas much further before his death. Kirkbride (1992) argued forcefully that the actors' perceptions of power resources were critical in understanding power struggles, and also pointed out that such struggles involved not only an exchange of sanctions (strikes, etc.) but an exchange of arguments, designed to bolster the legitimacy of one side whilst undermining that of their opponents.

What does mobilization theory add to these accounts? First, it directs our attention to the role of ideologies in framing issues around which people can be mobilized for action. Since the workers' 'willingness to act' is one of the key power resources for unions, then the ways in which employees think about workplace and employment issues is a vital component of the mobilization process. Second, the theory alerts us to the role of repression in raising the costs of collective organization and action, a topic I shall examine in the next section, on the capitalist state.

Trade unions are often viewed primarily, if not exclusively, as bargaining agents whose principal function is to secure improvements in their members' terms and conditions of employment through collective bargaining. Political action may also be used, but as an adjunct to extend the scope or coverage of bargaining or to protect the right to organize and bargain. Union action has thus been seen as primarily instrumental in character, designed to secure particular ends (cf Crouch 1982: Chapter 6). The traditional emphasis on collective bargaining is evident for example in the attention devoted to bargaining structure as an object of research (in WIRS and other surveys for instance) and in its use as an explanatory variable. By contrast the volume of writing and research on union links with the Labour Party for instance, is minimal and confined mainly to political scientists: David Coates (1975, 1980), Ben Pimlott (Pimlott and Cook 1991), Andrew Taylor (1987) and above all, Lewis Minkin (1991), as well as one or two writers from outside the academic mainstream (the MEP Ken Coates – see Coates and Topham 1986 – and the journalist Robert Taylor – see his 1993).[8] Textbooks of industrial relations typically cover union–party links in just one or two pages (e.g. Blyton and Turnbull 1994: 117–120; Edwards 1995a: 40–41).

Unions can also be seen, however, as components of a social movement, whose aims and methods include, but are not coterminous with, collective bargaining and some of whose actions are expressive of the movement's core values and instrumental in reinforcing and winning support for those values. The instrumental/expressive distinction is an analytical one and will not necessarily correspond to distinct empirical types of union action. Indeed we can readily think of actions such as solidarity strikes which are both instrumental and expressive. Nonetheless the value of the distinction is that it focuses our attention on different facets of trade unionism and opens up different types of research question for investigation, such as the political differences between unions.

As a first approximation these can be captured by the categories of 'left' and 'right', but clearly more refined categories are necessary. Hyman (1996: 70) distinguished what he called five union identities according to the focus and the key function of union activity, viz. guild, friendly society, company union, social partner and social movement. In practice however any given union is likely to display many, if not all of these faces, so it remains to be seen how far this framework can be developed (Kelly 1997). Operationally we can begin to obtain some idea of how unions differ politically by looking at their political affiliations, both to the Labour Party, but more particularly to other social movements, such as Anti-Apartheid, the Campaign for Nuclear Disarmament (CND) and the Cuba Solidarity Campaign. It is certainly true that the most obvious index of political character – affiliation to the Labour Party – is largely the preserve of manual unions (with notable exceptions such as COHSE, now UNISON), and that the increasingly significant white-collar and/or public sector unions have often shunned party affiliation. Yet this is a misleading index, since many of these same, non-Labour unions, *do* have left-wing political affiliations of a non-party character (Table 4.8).

It could be objected that the payment of £100 per annum to join CND tells us very little about the politics of an organization with tens of thousands of members and an annual turnover of millions of pounds. But the *differences* between unions *do* signify something: the fact that the Fire Brigades Union affiliated to CND with little debate, whilst APEX (now part of GMB) refused to affiliate despite a lengthy debate is highly informative about the balance of political opinion amongst the activists who attended the conferences and sat on the national executive committees of those respective bodies. The fact that the white-collar and technical union MSF debated solidarity with the former Sandinista government of Nicaragua whilst the white-collar and technical union, the EMA, did not, is equally revealing about the political views of their activists.

Table 4.8 Political affiliations of some non-Labour trade unions

	Organizations				
Unions	AAM	AI	CND	Liberty	CSC
BECTU	x			x	x
BIFU		x			
CMA		x			
Equity			x		x
IRSF*			x		
NALGO**	x	x	x	x	x
NAPO			x		
NATFHE	x	x	x	x	x
NUCPS*		x			
NUMAST	x	x			

Sources: Maksymiw *et al.* (1990); *Cuba Si* (CSC magazine); Barnes (1995)

Notes:
AAM = Anti-Apartheid Movement
AI = Amnesty International
CND = Campaign for Nuclear Disarmament
Liberty = Formerly NCCL, National Council for Civil Liberties
CSC = Cuba Solidarity Campaign
* Now PTC
** Now UNISON

Mobilization theory also directs our attention to the internal politics of trade unions, and in particular the factional struggles waged between various shades of social democrats and Marxists for supremacy in the unions' policy-making bodies. In the terms of mobilization theory, many of these struggles involve debates over the most appropriate ways of 'framing' issues that face the union or the union movement. For example, is an employer demand for greater flexibility a negotiable claim arising out of competitive pressures or an illegitimate desire to intensify labour that reflects corporate greed? Is involvement in international solidarity work (as with Cuba) a legitimate expression of the 'social movement face' of trade unionism or a politically inspired distortion of union aims? Apart from Undy *et al.*'s (1981) study of factions in the major unions, particularly the AUEW, the TGWU and NALGO, there is practically no literature at all on the structure, size, finances, politics and influence of factions based on the Communist Party, Socialist Workers' Party and the Militant Tendency, now Militant Labour (the exceptions are Carter 1997 on MSF; Seifert 1984 on the NUT; and Undy *et al.* 1996: 182–187). Yet trade union policy has long been the subject of fierce debate in many unions between organized political factions, anxious (at least on the left) to promote the solidarity and collectivism that some critics (e.g. Phelps Brown 1990) claim they can no longer detect. The Communist Party had a significant, organized presence amongst officers, on the National Executive Committee and amongst shop stewards in a large number of key unions until the late 1970s: the AEU, ASTMS, NUM, NUT, SOGAT, TASS, TGWU and UCATT, as well as significant representation in some smaller unions, such as ASLEF, AUT, FBU and FTAT. There were also important Trotskyist factions in some (mainly) public service unions such as ASTMS, CPSA, Equity, NALGO, NATFHE, NCU, NUT and the TGWU (Callinicos 1982; Crick 1984: 203; Fishman 1995; McIlroy and Campbell 1997; Shipley 1976: 37, 53, 86, 138–139; Undy *et al.* 1981: 105, 107, 118, 124–125).[9] At the height of the Cold War, communist activity in the unions was simply anathematized by many industrial relations academics (cf Flanders' revealing discussion of 'Communist *penetration*' (my italics) of unions: 1952: 145). During the 1960s it was largely ignored, disguised in the famous and misleading formula that 'stewards were lubricants not irritants'. (Edwards and Terry (1988: 220–221) are amongst the few to have argued for the importance of activist leadership in unions.) The central point to make here is that unions are the site of often intense ideological struggles between different groups of activists about the definitions of member interests and the most appropriate means for their pursuit, yet our knowledge of these activities is astonishingly slight.

Such ideological struggles not only take place within unions, but they are also to be found within the collective bargaining arena. It has long been accepted that the process of collective bargaining is both economic and political in character, in other words it fixes both substantive terms and conditions of employment as well as some of the rules governing the employment relationship (cf the Flanders–Fox debate on this subject in which Fox was right as against Flanders: Flanders 1968b;

Fox 1975). Yet bargaining is political in a deeper sense in that different systems of union argument, to management but especially to members and shop stewards, can reinforce or undermine the legitimacy of managerial rule (some arguments may be neutral, but this seems unlikely). Armstrong *et al.* (1981) (and see Chapter 2 above) classified negotiating arguments under three headings: managerial, worker and consensual, and were thus able to explore the ways in which their differential use varied between workplaces and between issues, and contributed to the maintenance or erosion of managerial authority. In similar vein Batstone *et al.* (1978: 48) classified the 'vocabularies of motive' used by shopfloor workers in a single factory, to justify twenty-four separate incidents of industrial action. The most frequently cited reason was managerial breach of agreements (27 per cent of 112 arguments). Kelly and Heery showed significant differences amongst full-time union officers in their use of 'managerial' arguments in negotiations, and found that the type of officers most likely to use such arguments were older, right-wing officers who were more hostile to strikes and to shop steward power (1994: 158, 169).

Employers are increasingly aware of the role played by language in framing the way employees think about issues. As a result there has been a proliferation of new terminology designed either to neutralize the emotive impact of 'negative' situations or to encourage a 'positive' view of situations and events. Sisson (1994: 15) gave several examples of the former in his essay on contemporary personnel management some of which are by now very familiar. Organizations no longer 'sack' or 'fire' workers, they 'downsize'; 'total quality management' actually means 'doing more with less'; employers no longer 'control' employees, they 'empower' them; telephone or computer 'surveillance' of staff is relabelled as staff 'feedback and development'. Despite the cynical transparency of some of these linguistic devices, with their echoes of Orwellian Newspeak, they reflect applications of the well-established psychological principle that the words available in language provide the categories we use to think about the world.

These few examples show how we can begin to recast the topic of collective bargaining and think analytically about its nature. Even if collective bargaining proved at certain periods and on particular issues to have little impact on economic outcomes for union members (cf Chadwick 1983), this purely economic focus overlooks the political dimension of the bargaining process, in which the parties exchange arguments, contesting and consolidating managerial authority. It is that exchange which should occupy more of our attention in studies of bargaining, not least because of its astonishing neglect over the past thirty years (cf Walton and McKersie 1991: xii; Beaumont 1990: 132).

The role of the capitalist state

Contemporary textbooks describe the 'modern state' as having a variety of roles or functions: as legislator, employer, agency of conflict resolution, economic manager and regulator of industrial relations. These roles are then typically illustrated by reference to the considerable literatures on the content and impact of labour law and on the institutions of public sector industrial relations. Yet what is striking about this material is the omission of any theoretical perspective on the *capitalist* character of the state and its consequent role in maintaining the economic and political conditions necessary for capital accumulation (cf the classic works by Jessop 1982 and Miliband 1969). In Chapter 2 I showed that only three industrial relations textbooks contained any reference to these classic texts, viz. Blyton and Turnbull (1994), Gospel and Palmer (1993) and Hyman (1989c).

A few industrial relations studies have made use of the Marxist argument that capitalist states are caught in a contradiction between the logic of accumulation, which periodically requires cutbacks in workers' terms and conditions of employment, and the logic of legitimation, which requires that the victims of capitalist accumulation are protected from its costs if the system is to survive with their support (cf Coates 1989; Ferner 1988). One difficulty with this argument became apparent as the costs of legitimation, through welfare expenditure for instance, became too high in relation to existing levels of corporate profitability (as in Britain, America and other capitalist countries in the 1970s). If subordinate group loyalty could no longer be secured through the provision of benefits then subordinate resistance to the logic of capital accumulation would increasingly have to be met with repression, a topic discussed by many writers on mobilization theory but one that is conspicuous by its absence from mainstream industrial relations textbooks. General works on the subject such as Jeffery and Hennessy *States of Emergency* (1983), Peak *Troops in Strikes* (1984), Geary *Policing Industrial Disputes* (1985) and Hain *Political Strikes* (1986) are simply not referred to and neither is the substantial literature on repression in the 1984–1985 miners' strike, such as Beynon (1985) and Fine and Millar (1985).[10]

Mobilization theory is particularly valuable in highlighting the role played by ruling groups in repressing contenders, i.e. raising the costs of collective action (Tilly 1978: 55). Clearly this is not the only strategy adopted by ruling groups and there are many employers who continue to recognize unions and to negotiate with them. But it would be equally untenable to claim or imply that repression is of little or no consequence in industrial relations. Repression can be targeted either at individuals, for instance by victimization, or at groups such as trade unions by legal prohibitions on certain types of action, e.g. unballoted official strikes, political strikes or strikes during the period of a contract. Second, repression can be organized by several different agents apart from the state. During the past thirty years, American employers have become increasingly willing to break the law by dismissing trade union organizers in order to thwart union recognition drives (Freeman 1985: 52–54). Trade unions can also raise the costs of action by sections of their own memberships. A number of British unions in the late 1940s, including the TGWU, banned communists from holding office, thereby removing some militants from positions of influence.

In relation to strikes the emphasis of state repression has shifted historically from attacking strikers towards the protection of strike breakers, with prime responsibility for this role switching from troops to police early in the twentieth century (Geary 1985). The 1984–1985 miners' strike, however, witnessed radical changes in both the nature and scale of police tactics as the forces of the state engaged with an unusually large number of determined strikers. Police road-blocks were established up to 150 miles away from areas of unrest and pickets travelling to those areas were either turned back or arrested for refusing to do so. Regional police forces achieved an unprecedented degree of coordination and centralization in decision-making. Riot police, first pioneered in the 1970s as a response to the strike wave of that period, were frequently deployed and anti-strike tactics became markedly aggressive. Charges by mounted police followed through by riot police on foot became the principal method used to disperse large groups of pickets (Fine and Millar 1985; Green 1990: Chapter 3; McIlroy 1985). Troops continued to be used in the late twentieth century but primarily as a strike-breaking labour force in industries such as docks, transport, utilities and the emergency services (Peak 1984). Other branches of the state also played a part in the counter-mobilization against the miners. In the midst of the strike, the courts began to attach novel conditions to bail awards which prevented striking miners travelling within a specified radius of any coal mine other than their own until their case came up in court (Green 1990: 95–97). A few years earlier (in 1980), the welfare benefits system had been altered so that social security benefits were reduced by £16 per week (the amount of union strike pay miners were deemed to receive, whether they did or not) and urgent needs payments to strikers and their families were abolished (Jones and Novak 1985). Finally the intelligence services were allegedly involved in a variety of ways: surveillance, telephone tapping, deployment of agents provocateurs and maintenance of at least one secret agent in the upper reaches of the miners' union (Milne 1994). Some of these activities have also been carried out on a more routine and longer-term basis. The head-quarters of the Communist Party was apparently bugged until 1975 when a small transmitter was found in the building, and from time to time named individuals have been revealed as having worked secretly for the intelligence services whilst being active trade unionists (Bunyan 1977: 182–183). Files were kept in the 1960s and 1970s (and probably since) on senior trade union leaders and regularly passed to the government ministers who met them (Hollingsworth and Norton-Taylor 1988: 122–126).

Employers too have taken measures in order to contain the possibility of collective challenge to their power and the use of secret (or now, not so secret) blacklists was one of the most widely discussed mechanisms. Until its demise in the 1990s, an organization called the Economic League (founded in 1919) had maintained files on thousands of trade union activists, and companies obtained access to this information by subscribing to the League. In this way they could either avoid hiring such people in the first place or, if they were already employees, find ways of getting rid of them (Hollingsworth and Norton-Taylor 1988: Chapters 7, 8 and 9). The list of companies that subscribed to the League until the late 1980s (though whether they used its blacklist is unknown) included many of Britain's largest firms: BT, Grand Metropolitan, BET, Royal Dutch Shell, ICI, Barclays Bank, GEC and Hanson Trust amongst others (Hollingsworth and Tremayne 1989: 91–102). Precise data on the numbers of employees refused work, disciplined or dismissed on the grounds of trade union activity does not exist, although there are a few well-known cases described in the literature, such as the Ford Motor Company's dismissal of seventeen leading shop stewards in 1962 (Beynon 1984: 65–69). Similar activities have been described in Italy where the Roman Catholic Church and the anti-communist union federation CISL were involved in blacklisting communist militants in the 1950s and 1960s (Franzosi 1995: 48–49, 213–221). The Italian case points up the potential significance of trade unionists in facilitating state and/or employer repression. Anti-communist factions still exist in a number of British trade unions, particularly the engineers (AEEU), and they are thought to be connected with the Catholic Church, though whether this takes the form of financial support from the Church is unclear.

One obvious objection to this type of material is that it covers the outer fringes rather than the mainstream of industrial relations activity. Surely day-to-day collective bargaining, grievance handling and consultation in thousands of firms up and down the country is hardly touched by the activities of the Special Branch, MI5, troops or riot police? Doesn't the dramatic character of this evidence only serve to underline its marginal place within contemporary industrial relations? For mobilization theory the significance of repression cannot be measured simply by the numbers of people involved. For example, suppose a terrorist bomb were to kill the entire British cabinet and it was said that 'only' twenty-five people out of a population of 56 million had died. The statement would instantly be recognized as fatuous and the nature of the error involved would be clear. The role and power of government ministers means that their assassination could have far-reaching consequences despite the 'small' number of deaths. Likewise with union activists:

> The 1983 Assolombarda Report on the state of labour relations in Milanese firms showed how a handful of layoffs could rid a plant of troubles for years to come: No one would want the job of union representative on the shop floor.
>
> (Franzosi 1995: 323)

We saw in Chapter 3 that mobilization theory places great stress on the role of leaders in legitimating workers' discontents and channelling them via collective organization into collective action against the employer. It follows that effective repression of actual or potential leaders can seriously impair the capacity of a group to organize and act collectively. In America illegal firings of union activists significantly depress the chances of union victory in certification elections (Freeman 1985: 58).

The second reason for believing repression to be highly significant is that it is often targeted at powerful groups of workers, so its effects may be very far-reaching. We know from the literature on why workers join unions that their perceptions of union effectiveness are a key factor in decision-making (e.g. Millward 1990). Well publicized defeats of militant groups such as British miners (1985), printers (1986) and dockers (1989), Italian car workers (1980) or American air traffic controllers (1981), may radically alter employee perceptions of general union instrumentality and thereby raise the expected costs of collective organization and action across many sectors of the economy far removed from the direct hand of state repression (cf Deshpande and Fiorito 1989 on general and specific union attitudes). Third, state and employer repression can be understood as a delineation of the boundaries beyond which 'normal' industrial relations should not pass. The three British strikes referred to just now all confirmed management's right to implement radical changes in work practices and to dismiss those who opposed them by collective means. Though few in number and unusual for their degree of violence and repression, these strikes could be seen as highly significant for the 'normal' industrial relations to which they are sometimes counterposed. Far from being marginal to 'normal' industrial relations they may have been vital in reinforcing the ideological precept of 'management's right to manage'. By focusing on the role of coercion in industrial relations we may therefore come to have more insight into the day-to-day consent that is often taken to be a feature of more 'mainstream' employment relations. To put the point more abstractly, it is the dialectical interplay of coercion and consent that should be the focus of our inquiry, rather than a one-sided concern with the latter at the expense of the former.

Worker–employer relations: union militancy and 'social partnership'[11]

The rise of 'human resource management', in a context of economic recession, union decline and right-wing government has led some union leaders and academics to rethink union relations with employers. On the one hand, it has been argued that the adverse balance of power appears to rule out the feasibility of unions recovering membership and influence by threatening uncooperative employers with sanctions. On the other hand, the rhetoric of human resource management emphasizes employee skills and commitment, stresses the importance of quality – of employees, processes and products – and features, however disingenuously, the idea of employee empowerment. Union leaders such as TUC General Secretary, John Monks, have stated that, 'We do not fear the agenda of the human resource development manager. We prefer a people-oriented system' (Monks 1993: 223). Consequently, he went on, 'We are encouraging a new language for activists with new terms – partnership; quality products and quality services; becoming competitive and staying there' (ibid.). The argument goes that if unions offer benefits to employers such as cooperation in flexibility agreements and involvement in training programmes, then they are more likely to extract concessions in return, such as recognition for collective bargaining and influence in decision-making.

The detailed arguments in favour of this type of 'social partnership' have been reviewed at length elsewhere (Kelly 1996) and can therefore be briefly summarized before we consider the contribution of mobilization theory. In no order of importance the arguments are as follows. Strikes are said to be ineffective insofar as they either fail to achieve their objectives or achieve them at such heavy financial cost to the strikers that they constitute purely Pyrrhic victories. A more defensible version of the argument is that wage strikes lasting more than about four days almost certainly generate more costs for the strikers in lost wages than they will recoup through employer concessions in wage bargaining. Militant unionism (a somewhat ill-defined category) is said to be vulnerable to employer counter-attack under conditions of recession in a way that more 'moderate' unionism is not. There are various payoffs to moderate unionism, including union recognition in unorganized plants, especially where unions agree to binding arbitration in the event of dispute, and forego the strike weapon. As a consequence it is claimed that 'moderate unionism', such as that of the former EETPU and the RCN, records faster growth rates than its more militant rivals such as the TGWU or the NUM. Unions such as the EETPU have also claimed that their policies have given them more influence over workplace decision-making than is customary in manufacturing industry, often through channels such as company or works councils outside of the collective bargaining machinery.

Underpinning these concrete arguments is a profound sense of union weakness and decline, arising from years of economic recession, right-wing government and anti-union laws, but reinforced by the increased competitive pressures in world markets and the internationalization of production and corporate organization. Competitive pressures subject employers to seemingly continuous pressures to reduce costs, whilst internationalization puts key corporate decisions increasingly beyond the reach of workplace (and perhaps even national) unionism. Because of this hostile environment, it is argued that unions are in no position to challenge fundamentally the priorities and interests of employers but must adapt as best they can, seeking out those issues on which they can forge common or compatible objectives with employers.

Mobilization theory takes serious issue with this analysis and the associated prognosis by virtue of its roots in Marxism. Let us start however with definitions of terms because this area of debate is littered with ill-defined terminology: militancy and moderation, resistance and collaboration, conflict and cooperation, to name only a few. For the purpose of this discussion I propose to analyse union policy, rather than sets of union–management relations, although the two are empirically connected. The terms 'militancy' and 'moderation' are sensible ones to use provided we decompose them into five dimensions: goals, methods, membership resources, institutional resources, and ideology (see Table 4.9).

Although Table 4.9 depicts two polar types, it is clear from the continuous nature of the goal and method components that militancy and moderation are

Table 4.9 Components of union militancy and moderation

Component	Militancy	Moderation
Goals	Ambitious demands (scale and scope) with few concessions	Moderate demands with some or many concessions
Membership resources	Strong reliance on mobilization of union membership	Strong reliance on employers, third parties or law
Institutional resources	Exclusive reliance on collective bargaining	Willingness to experiment with/support non-bargaining institutions
Methods	Frequent threat or use of industrial action	Infrequent threat or use of industrial action
Ideology	Ideology of conflicting interests	Ideology of partnership

best understood as two ends of a continuum. It is also true that unions are not free agents when it comes to goals, methods or resources. Other parties, particularly employers and the state, can constrain or suppress particular types of demand, e.g. those featured in 'political' strikes; as well as particular methods, e.g. solidarity action; and particular resources, e.g. abolition of bargaining machinery or fair wage laws. Any observed degree of union militancy and moderation therefore results from an interaction between unions and their environments and cannot necessarily be regarded as a true measure of the preferences of the union and its constituent elements (rank and file, shop stewards, officers). The labels of militant and moderate can be applied to unions as a whole but also to super-union bodies (federations) and to intra-union bodies (factions, regions, etc.). The meaning of these terms will vary between countries and over time. Resort to membership mobilization in the midst of recession arguably signifies a greater degree of militancy than a similar scale of mobilization during a long economic upswing.

For mobilization theorists the period since the late 1970s has witnessed a dramatic and far-reaching employer and state offensive against trade unionism, as employers have sought both to increase profitability and to 'reassert their managerial prerogative' against joint regulation with trade unionism. The two objectives are intertwined, insofar as the reassertion of employer power in the production process is designed to assist the improvement of labour and capital productivity and hence of profits. But on the assumption that ruling groups always wish to preserve their own power as an end in itself it would be mistaken to regard employers' concern with their own power as a purely economic reflex. Consequently we have witnessed a rise in employer militancy that expresses itself in four ways: hostility to union recognition, derecognition, antipathy to collective bargaining, and attempts to bypass and marginalize workplace trade unionism.

The incidence of union recognition has declined as non-union employers (and even union employers) have opened up new plants and successfully kept most of them union-free even in the face of worker demands, through secret ballots, for union representation. It has also declined because of a growing tide of partial and total derecognition of unions whose incidence has risen from approximately twenty-five cases per annum between 1987 and 1988 to almost seventy cases per year between 1988 and 1994 (Claydon 1989, 1996; Gall and McKay 1994; Heery 1997). Derecognition is beginning to spread from its original enclaves of publishing and coastal shipping and has even penetrated the highly organized oil industry, where some or all of its manual unions have now been derecognized by all of the major oil companies, BP, Esso, Mobil and Shell (Higgs 1994).

Collective bargaining has also come under attack and for the first time since the late 1930s now covers a minority of the workforce (47 per cent in 1990 according to Brown 1993: see also Milner 1995b). A growing number of union-ized employers have moved towards unilateral imposition of new terms and conditions of employment, sometimes derecognizing unions at the same time and despite employee resistance. Performance related pay has been imposed in local government (Kessler 1994); Saturday opening was imposed by the clearing banks; and more classroom contact hours have been imposed by the new universi-ties and by further education colleges. WIRS3 confirmed that the scope of collective bargaining contracted between 1984 and 1990 although the effect was smaller than in the 1980–1984 period (Millward *et al.* 1992: 253). The main employers' organization, the CBI, has called into question the continued rele-vance of collective bargaining. According to its Director of Employment Affairs, writing about WIRS3: 'Collective bargaining no longer presents itself as the only or even the most obvious method of handling relations at work; and fewer employees – and employers – feel the need of union mediation in their dealings' (Gilbert 1993: 252). The Advisory, Conciliation and Arbitration Service, once obliged to promote collective bargaining, is no longer required to do so, following the passage of the Trade Union Reform and Employment Rights Act (1993).

Finally there is growing evidence of employer attempts to bypass or marginalize trade unions. For instance, between 1984 and 1990 the incidence of direct communications between junior managers (or supervisors) and their subordinates showed a significant increase, especially in unionized settings, a change interpreted by Millward as, 'one designed to supplement or partially replace trade unions as one of the principal channels of communication between management and employees' (Millward 1994: 88).

This type of evidence graphically confirms earlier data from case studies (Marchington and Parker 1990) and could be interpreted as consistent with the anti-union logic of human resource management (Guest 1989). There is indeed evidence that some of the larger companies using HRM in a fairly sophisticated way are trying to reduce the range of issues over which unions exert influence. According to Storey's study of fifteen major British private companies and public corporations, fourteen of them had made some attempts to 'marginalize' shop stewards (1992: 82–83). There was

> a generally more aggressive stance towards the unions but without any apparent agenda (hidden or otherwise) to displace them. . . . Union leaders at both national and workplace level were left on the sidelines of most of the managerial initiatives during the period.
>
> (Storey 1992: 246, 250)

All of this evidence demonstrates a wide-ranging hostility to union presence, activity and organization on the part of employers and suggests that the scale and intensity of such hostility gathered pace in the late 1980s and early 1990s. It also suggests that the TUC is being seriously complacent in assuming that the association between HRM policies and unionization indicates that the former is no threat to the latter (TUC 1994). The significance of this growing tide of employer hostility is that it calls into question the appropriateness and value of union policies of collaboration and partnership. It is, after all, difficult for a union to construct a partnership with an employer who would prefer that the union simply did not exist (cf Yates 1992 on American and Canadian car workers' responses to employer demands for concessions).

If we re-examine the evidence on union recognition we find that whilst unions offering no-strike deals recruited about 20,000 employees between 1988 and 1994, unions that pursued more conventional approaches (without 'no-strike deals') achieved a similar level of membership growth. This evidence is consistent with data on disaggregated union growth rates which shows that the fastest growing unions include both militant organizations such as BIFU (up 30 per cent between 1979 and 1991) and the FBU (up 73 per cent 1979–1992) as well as 'moderate' unions such as the RCN. If we turn to the coal mining industry for a straight comparison between the militant NUM and the avowedly moderate UDM, the evidence shows that between 1986 (when the latter was issued with a certificate of independence) and 1992, the NUM lost 56 per cent of its total membership, the UDM slightly more at 59 per cent! Time-series data on union membership and strike activity suggests that the periods of most substantial union growth have coincided with the periods of large-scale mobilization and militancy: 1889–1892, 1910–1920, 1935–1945 and 1968–1974 (Cronin 1979, and Chapter 6, below). Cohn's (1993) detailed investigation of the outcomes of striking by French coal miners provided one possible explanation for this link:

> The empirical analysis showed that, so long as the labor movement remained undivided, the optimal strategy was to strike frequently. . . . Militancy raised wages by convincing authorities that workers were interested in striking for its own sake. By doing so, the latter induced employers to provide them with extra wages as a peace payment.
>
> (Cohn 1993: 213)

Where unions have visibly demonstrated their effectiveness in pursuing, and winning, employee claims and grievances through strike action, then non-union workers have been encouraged to join in unusually large numbers.

Such effectiveness is unlikely to be demonstrated through policies of moderation, even where unions attempt to pursue issues that are purportedly of equal interest to employers, such as training, equal opportunities, and health and safety. The most recent reviews of union progress in these areas show a continuing reluctance by employers to engage in meaningful discussions, which only serves to underline the degree of employer hostility that now exists towards joint regulation. By emphasizing the conflicts of interest in the employment relationship, mobilization theory encourages a highly critical orientation towards the currently fashionable proposals for union–management cooperation.

Conclusions

This chapter has explored the relevance of mobilization theory for a wide range of issues in industrial relations. Central to the theory is injustice, a starting point derived from Marxist analyses of exploitation and domination within capitalist economies. Perceived injustice is the origin of workers' collective definitions of interests and from those definitions in turn flow collective organization and action. Mobilization theory therefore rejects the fashionable idea that one of the major tasks of industrial relations research is to trace out the logic of competitiveness by exploring employer responses to market pressures, such as human resource management, and then seeking to investigate union and worker responses to those initiatives.

In this chapter I have explored the contribution of the theory to the four central problems of industrial relations described earlier, viz. interest definition, the nature of power, the role of the state, and relations between workers and employers. First, mobilization theory allows us to rethink popular arguments about the decline of worker collectivism in Britain. It is important to distinguish between interests, organization, mobilization and forms of action because changes in these four aspects of collectivism do not necessarily coincide. The observed decline in collective action in the advanced capitalist world after 1979 in and of itself tells us nothing about changes in collective interest definition amongst the workforce. Moreover, since collective interest definition is most likely to emerge as a response to injustice, it is wrong to argue (as does Phelps Brown) that worker collectivism can only be a response to absolute poverty and deprivation. The theory also allows us to go beyond the existing literature on the structural correlates of non-unionism (such as firm size), the management and union recruitment practices (if any) to be found in non-union firms and the general attitudes to unions of non-union employees. Mobilization theory focuses instead on the processes by which employees acquire a sense of injustice (or illegitimacy), identifying the importance of activists who promote a sense of group identity and who argue the benefits of collective organization and action.

Activists' notions of workers' rights are often derived from general ideologies which implicate unions in political campaigns that go beyond the workplace. It follows that the role of the union is not confined to being an agency of collective bargaining (or individual grievance handling) but also embraces political activity as part of a social movement, an aspect of their functioning traditionally neglected in the industrial relations literature. One of the most important institutions in the wider society is the capitalist state, traditionally viewed in pluralist terms as a law-maker, agent of conflict resolution and employer. By identifying the state as an agency of class rule, mobilization theory brings into view its repressive face, a subject on which there has been a dearth of industrial relations research. Finally, the theory opens up a critical perspective on the fashionable idea of social partner-ship because of its focus on collective interest definition, organization and activity by subordinate groups against ruling groups.

Mobilization theory enables us to think analytically about some of the most important issues in contemporary industrial relations and it can therefore help to overcome some of the weaknesses in the field, identified in earlier chapters. It can help us avoid the biases towards description and institutionalism, reduce our reliance on policy initiatives as a source of research topics, and it provides a set of linked concepts that can overcome the well-established theoretical and concep-tual underdevelopment of the field. Mobilization theory however is not the only approach that could achieve these objectives and it is therefore important to show not only the strengths of this theory but the weaknesses of its rivals. In the litera-ture on collective organization and action there is one alternative approach that stands out as having been especially influential and that is Olson's *Logic of Collective Action*. It is therefore to Olsonian theory that we now turn.

5

OLSONIAN THEORY AND COLLECTIVE ACTION

A critique

Introduction

Mancur Olson's *The Logic of Collective Action* (1971)[1] is an extraordinarily influential book whose impact has been felt in a wide range of disciplines including economics, sociology, political science, public administration and psychology. There is even a well-established school of Marxism that has taken over some of his ideas (e.g. Buchanan 1979). Olson's theory belongs to a broader class of theories normally described as rational choice models of behaviour which take as their starting point the individual acting to maximize his or her interests. These interests are normally (though not necessarily) assumed to be personal interests which individuals are thought to rank in order of importance and pursue by appropriate means or resources. In choosing between courses of action people weigh up the costs and benefits (or act as if they do) so as to opt for the one that is least costly and most beneficial.

Olson's ideas deserve attention for several reasons: first, they constitute a radically different approach to the genesis of collective organization and action as compared to mobilization theory. Second, Olson claims to offer a theory of the links between individual interests and group behaviour which might therefore provide some insight into a number of central problems in industrial relations: under what conditions do workers become collectively organized and take collective action? How are we to account for the decline in union membership in many countries since 1979? Third, two of Olson's chapters actually dealt with industrial relations issues (trade unionism and class action). Finally, Olson's work has in fact been used by a number of contemporary writers to explore industrial relations issues, viz. Crouch (1982) in his wide-ranging study of trade unionism, and Golden's (1997) analysis of the rationality of union resistance to job losses. This chapter begins with a brief and critical exposition of the basic assumptions of rational choice theory. I then outline Olson's ideas in some detail before proceeding to a critical appraisal and then looking briefly at some post-Olsonian work.

Rational choice theory: the basic assumptions

There is no single version of rational choice theory and in fact some writers prefer to speak of rational choice models or approaches (Crouch 1982: 40).[2] In what follows I set out the core propositions shared by most rational choice theories in the literature (cf Barry 1978: Chapter 2; Dunleavy 1991: 3–4 for similar accounts). The theory deals with individuals as the proper unit of analysis and most, though by no means all, theorists are committed to the doctrine of methodological individualism according to which, 'all social phenomena – their structure and their change – are in principle explicable in ways that only involve individuals – their properties, their goals, their beliefs and their actions' (Elster 1985: 5).

Second, actors are assumed to be self-interested agents (Abell 1991: xi; Elster 1979: 141–146; Fireman and Gamson 1979; Hardin 1982; Hindess 1988: 29; Taylor 1988: 66) a statement which implies that they are not motivated to act in other people's interests and that they do not pursue the interests of any groups to which they belong, unless those other interests happen to coincide with their own. Third, behaviour is future-oriented rather than determined by the past. Rational agents have goals which they seek to pursue and their behaviour is to be understood as intentional action designed to achieve those goals (Coleman 1986: 1310; Elster 1982: 453; Friedman and Hechter 1988: 202).[3]

Fourth, agents are thought to have sets of preferences ranked transitively in order of value (or utility). Transitivity means that if A is preferred to B and B is preferred to C then A will also be preferred to C (Dunleavy 1991: 3–4; Friedman and Hechter 1988: 202; Goldfield and Gilbert 1995: 276; Heath 1976: Chapter 2; Sen 1977: 322–323). Fifth, agents use 'appropriate' or 'logical' means to pursue their ends (Barry 1978; Elster 1983: 11; Goldfield and Gilbert 1995: 276–277). Taking paracetamol to relieve a headache is rational; writing to your Member of Parliament to demand a cure is not. The presumption here is that not only should the chosen means be appropriate but it should be the *most* appropriate, i.e. the least costly and/or the most effective. Sixth, rational agents act strategically, so that in choosing their own course of action they take into account how other agents are likely to act (Abell 1991: xi; Coleman 1986; Crouch 1982: 42; Elster 1979: 117–123). If those interested in a job vacancy are invited to turn up at nine o'clock the next morning then it makes sense for each one to go early if they assume that many other people will be interested and that the job will go to the first suitable applicant. Finally, the theory is often defended because it generates testable predictions even if some or all of its assumptions are unrealistic (Crouch 1982: 43; Hogarth and Reder 1987: 2–5, but see Friedman and Hechter 1988 and Hindess 1988: Chapter 3 for different views).

Rational choice theory applied: Olson's logic of collective action

One reason for the tremendous impact of Olson's work is that it overturned conventional wisdom about collective action and appeared to demonstrate the far-reaching analytical power of rational choice theory. I shall draw almost entirely on *The Logic of Collective Action* because it is clear from subsequent writings that Olson continues to believe in the validity of its main lines of argument (Olson 1982: 17–35; 1992). Olson's book began by setting out the popular notion that individuals with a common interest would act together so as to achieve that interest. In contrast his own view was that,

> unless the number of individuals in a group is quite small, or unless there is coercion or some other special device to make individuals act in their common interest, *rational, self-interested individuals will not act to achieve their common or group interests.*
>
> (Olson 1971: 2, italics in original)

Olson was particularly concerned with group interests that were public (sometimes called collective) goods. These are goods which have the property of non-excludability so that if they are supplied to one member of a group they must be supplied to all members of the group and none can feasibly be excluded. A union-negotiated wage rise is a public good because all workers in the relevant bargaining unit receive the rise irrespective of whether they belong to the union. According to Olson the rational individual will reason as follows: I will receive the benefits of union action whether I belong to the union or not. Therefore I might as well save the cost of contributing to the union and free-ride on my colleagues. In any case my own contribution won't make a noticeable difference to the outcome of the union's action and furthermore nobody will notice if I don't contribute. But, if everybody reasons like this and aspires to free-ride, then nobody will join the union, there will be no collective organization or action and there will be no ride for anyone, free or otherwise. Hence the predicted absence of collective organization and action. Empirically, however, we observe that trade unions do exist and take action and that often these unions are large organizations where Olsonian logic and thus free-riding should be pervasive. How can these facts be accounted for?

Olson's answer was that collective organization and action is achieved through the provision of selective incentives (or private goods) – rewards for participation or punishments for free-riding – that are only available to group members and which therefore change the calculations and the actions of rational individuals. Craft unions, for instance, may supply private goods, such as access to certain kinds of employment. Alternatively unions can seek to discourage non-membership through the 'coercion' of the closed shop and the picket line. The rational individual will then join the union and take part in strikes because the alternative course of action (free-riding) is more costly. And the same 'logic of collective action' also applies to working-class political action, as discussed in Marxist theory. Since revolution is a public good, the rational worker will elect to avoid the costs but obtain the rewards of revolution by free-riding on his revolutionary colleagues. And once more the result is that if everyone reasons this way there is no revolutionary action, no revolution and no free-ride unless participation can be induced by selective incentives (Buchanan 1979).

To this general argument Olson introduced an important qualification about group size. In small groups it was likely that the individual's own contribution would make a difference and that individuals who tried to free-ride would readily be detected and might suffer sanctions. Collective action was therefore more likely in small than in large groups. Olson also identified what he called 'privileged' groups where a collective good could be achieved by the actions of just one of its members because the benefits for that individual would be sufficiently large to outweigh his/her personal costs (and he also noted the case where personal costs were so negligible that no prediction could be made about free-riding). Finally, Olson identified 'intermediate' groups for which no predictions about collective action could be made. On the one hand no single member had the incentive to provide the collective good, but on the other hand the group was small enough to allow free-riders to be detected. Hence the outcome for collective action was indeterminate.

Writing mainly though not exclusively about America, Olson therefore argued that 'By far the single most important factor enabling large national unions to survive was that membership in those unions, and support of the strikes they called, was to a great degree compulsory' (1971: 68). He noted that unions often began as small groups that were therefore exempt from the free-riding logic of collective action. They grew, he argued, by supplying private goods, such as welfare benefits, to their members but over time the role of these benefits had dwindled.

> In short unions can no longer draw a great deal of strength from small groups, and a union's noncollective benefits cannot usually be sufficient to bring in many members. Smallness and noncollective benefits can probably now explain only the exceptional union. In most cases it is compulsory membership and coercive picket lines that are the source of the union's membership. Compulsory membership is now the rule. In recent years roughly 95 per cent of the unionized workers have been covered by various types of 'union security' (or sometimes dues check-off) that normally make it impossible, or at least exceedingly difficult for a worker to avoid being a member of the union under whose jurisdiction he falls.
>
> (Olson 1971: 75)

Compulsion was also necessary because of the logic of free-riding.

> most of the achievements of a union . . . could offer the rational worker no incentive to join; his individual efforts would not have a noticeable effect on the outcome, and whether he supported the union or not he would still get the benefit of its achievements.
>
> (ibid.: 76)

Historically, therefore, he claimed that the major growth periods of American unionism – 1897–1904 and 1935–1945 – had been marked by compulsion. Hence his conclusion that 'compulsory membership is usually essential for an enduring, stable labor movement' (ibid.: 88).

The core assumptions of Olson's theory

What does it mean to say that an action is rational? According to Olson an action is rational if it is, 'pursued by means that are efficient and effective for achieving these objectives' (Olson 1971: 65). Barry (1978), Elster (1983: 2), Hardin (1982) and Heath (1976: 79) offer similar definitions which describe the means–end relationship as 'logical' or 'consistent'. There are many situations where judgements of rationality on this definition can be made. If I want to buy a car but lack the money to do so then it may be rational to borrow or save the money required. But this and other textbook examples are unusual in the clarity of means–end links. When we turn to industrial relations and particularly collective action, means–end relationships are often opaque. Take for instance the announcement by British Coal in October 1992 that it was to shut thirty-one pits within six months, putting 30,000 miners out of work and jeopardizing the jobs of another 40–70,000 workers in ancillary industries. The speed and scale of the closures outraged the miners themselves (not to mention public opinion) and the principal union, the NUM, voted to ballot its members on strike action if a public campaign of meetings, lobbies and demonstrations was unsuccessful.

Would a strike against job losses have been rational? The strikers would have been using a readily available means (or resource) to bring pressure to bear on the government at a time when it was sensitive to public opinion because of its unpopular management of the economy. Sufficient pressure may have forced a change of policy and saved the pits. But the rationality of such strike action could be challenged on two grounds. First, coal stocks at pits and power stations were sufficient to supply the country's energy needs for almost twelve months, so any strike would be extremely lengthy and therefore costly. Second, strikes would stop production at pits that the government and the employer had already decided to shut down so the strike might serve only to hasten pit closures not halt them (cf Golden 1997: 108–112).

How can we adjudicate between these competing interpretations of the miners' proposed action in order to establish whether a strike would be rational? One answer is to say that it is the agent's own beliefs about means–end links that should count. If agents themselves believe that their chosen means are an efficient

70

and effective way of achieving their ends then they are acting rationally (Abell 1991: xi; Heath 1976; Taylor 1988: 66). For instance if I pick up a glass of clear liquid and proceed to drink it because I am thirsty, my action is rational given I believe the liquid is water even though it is in fact sulphuric acid. But once beliefs are introduced in this way what are we to say of a miner who supports strike action and another who is opposed? Given their different beliefs each may be acting rationally, yet this conclusion leaves rational choice theory unable to predict which course of action will be chosen by a rational individual unless auxiliary propositions are introduced. The collective outcome for a group of miners may therefore be indeterminate.[4]

In setting out the postulate of individual self-interest, Olson made his own assumptions admirably clear, reasoning by analogy with individual firms in a competitive market. Each firm wants the highest price for its product but none of them wishes to cut its own output in order to boost prices, hoping instead that other firms will cut output whilst their own is maintained (1971: 9–16). Firms are self-interested and free-riding is attractive because the contribution of a single firm to the collective good will make only a marginal difference. But is a group of firms a reasonable analogy to a group of individuals interested in a public good? There is one key difference, which is that firms are necessarily engaged in competitive relations, individuals are not. Firms do not simply pursue gains for themselves, they pursue gains at the expense of their rivals. One firm's increase in market share is another's decrease even if both are recording higher profits and sales because of market expansion. On the other hand, individuals contemplating the formation of a union may hope to gain for themselves but there is no theoretical reason for supposing that they need to gain at the expense of fellow workers since they could equally gain at the expense of employers or consumers. Consequently, while cooperation between firms to produce a collective good may well founder on the hard logic of free-riding, it is not obvious that this is an equally powerful obstacle to cooperation between individual workers with a common interest in better terms and conditions of employment. The effect of Olson's argument by analogy is therefore to exaggerate the probability of free-riding.

One further objection to the assumption of individual self-interest is that people may also act on behalf of group interests, reflected in social norms. As Fireman and Gamson wrote

> calculations of what may be gained and lost through collective action are very important to actors' decisions to join in collective action. But contrary to utilitarian logic, we think that actors assess what their group may gain or lose as well as what they may gain or lose as individuals.
>
> (1979: 15; see also Callinicos 1987: 199; Margolis 1981: 236; Miller 1991: 86–87; Shaw 1984: 16–20)

Individuals comply with group norms, 'a scale of values defining the range of acceptable and unacceptable behaviours' (Brown 1988: 42), for a variety of reasons, some of which are compatible with Olsonian theory, e.g. to obtain rewards and/or avoid punishments (Olson 1971: 60–61; and see also Akerlof 1980; Booth 1985; Coleman 1986; Elster 1989a: 15; 1989b: 35; Naylor 1989). But a second basis for norm compliance, strongly emphasized by mobilization theorists, poses a more serious challenge to Olsonian theory. If we make the non-Olsonian assumption that people identify with a particular group, then we can follow social identity theory and argue that some of their behaviour will derive from the internalization of group norms as personal standards of conduct (Chapter 3 above, and Brown 1988; Dunleavy 1991: 55–57; Hogg and Abrams 1988: Chapter 8; Turner *et al.* 1987: 65). This idea was illustrated and explored in a series of laboratory experiments on collective action. Brewer and Schneider (1990) found that the activation of group (social) identity had pronounced effects on the incidence of free-riding. In a Commons dilemma game (all share the costs but only some benefit) the activation of social identity significantly reduced the incidence of free-riding in all sizes of group. By contrast, in a public goods game (all benefit, a few pay) social identity reduced free-riding in small groups but increased its incidence in large groups. In another series of experiments Marwell and his colleagues examined the effects of social norms in settings where norm violation was virtually impossible to detect and punish. They still found substantial numbers of people who refused to free-ride because they said it was unfair and declared they were concerned about fairness (Marwell and Ames 1979, 1981).[5]

The critical point is that people's behaviour is regulated both by their personal interests and by the interests of those groups with whom they identify, whether it be women, trade unionists or lawyers, for example. Once this point is established we have opened up a much bigger set of issues about the formation of interests. How do employees come to define their interests in individual or collective terms? How do collective and individual definitions of interests change over time or as a consequence of employer actions? How do non-union employees come to believe that collective organization and action may be necessary to pursue their interests? Olson's individualist bias prevented him from appreciating and addressing these important issues about the formation of interests and their definition in individualist or collectivist terms. The same bias prevented him from recognizing the distinct dynamics of group and inter-group behaviour analysed by social identity and mobilization theorists (Chapters 3 and 4 above). Rather than assign theoretical privilege to individualism and treat departures from it as theoretically deviant we should treat individual and social actions as different forms of behaviour that emerge under different conditions. Some critics might well concede some or all of these points but defend Olsonian theory on the grounds that it has generated testable predictions that have turned out to be valid. After all, free-riding is widespread, unions do (or at least did) organize closed shops and industrial relations do involve coercion.

Olson's account of trade unionism

Theoretical ambiguities

According to Taylor,

> there is now a great deal of evidence . . . which supports the thin theory
> of collective action . . . where large numbers of people share a common
> interest in a public good, relatively few do anything about it.
> (Taylor 1988: 83–84)[6]

Even if we agree with the view that relatively few are involved in the provision of
collective goods and that many people appear to free-ride, these facts do not
necessarily support Olsonian theory. For Olson's claim was that 'there is a
tendency for large groups to fail to provide themselves with any collective good at
all' (Olson 1971: 28).

If a workplace trade union with 40 per cent density and only weak selective
incentives negotiates a wage rise, does this activity support Olsonian theory
because many workers free-ride, or contradict the theory because a large group
has supplied itself with a collective good in the absence of strong selective incentives? This example highlights a second problem which is to do with the nature of
free-riding. Are workers who join a union but fail to take any part in its internal
organization participants in collective action (because they have joined and pay a
subscription) or are they free-riders because they allow a small minority to carry
out the work from which they all benefit?

Precisely why people free-ride is not at all straightforward and Olson actually
set out four reasons as to why a rational individual would not contribute to collective action (see also Dunleavy 1991: 46–48). First, if the collective good is
provided he will obtain the benefits anyway (because of non-excludability: Olson
1971: 11). Second, in large groups the individual's own contribution (or lack of
it) will make only a marginal difference to the burdens falling on other people
(ibid.: 12, 50). Third, the costs of participation relative to personal gain are likely
to be high, especially in large groups (ibid.: 46). And finally he argued that individual contributions (or their absence) were unlikely to be noticed except in small
groups. This multiplicity of reasons for inaction creates a problem. Suppose the
individual's own contribution will make a difference to the group outcome but at
personal cost. Does he participate to make a difference or free-ride to avoid costs?
Or suppose that contributions are cheap relative to gains but that withholding
contributions would go unnoticed. Does the person contribute because of the
favourable cost–benefit ratio or free-ride because of the lack of surveillance?
Olson admits his theory cannot always generate predictions and that the provision of a public good is sometimes indeterminate, which is reasonable enough
(Olson 1971: 43–44). But there is so much indeterminacy in the arguments

about free-riding that it is quite unclear how predictions could be generated in the examples just given.

A number of more recent accounts have argued that it is the high degree of social interaction in small groups that helps stave off the logic of free-riding but precisely why this should be the case is not so clear (Axelrod and Hamilton 1981; Elster 1979, 1986; Taylor 1988). One suggestion is that repeated interaction between people leads them to develop more affection and concern for one another so that they become more averse to free-riding or develop social norms against it (Elster 1979: 146; 1986: 213; Shaw 1984: 23–24). Another possibility is that interaction leads to exchange of information which in turn leads people to behave in ways that depart from Olsonian predictions. Stroebe and Frey (1982) for instance reported that the incidence of free-riding in laboratory games rapidly declined when subjects were allowed to talk to one another about the game. But research by social psychologists into inter-group contact (e.g. Arabs and Israelis, workers and managers) has shown that repeated social interaction does not necessarily lead to any increase in inter-group cooperation or to friendliness (Hewstone and Brown 1986). This is not to dispute the importance of social interaction in the formation of groups or the instigation of collective action, a topic addressed more fully in the previous chapters. But the claim that social interaction will lead to cooperation is as naive and simplistic as the Olsonian idea that individuals will always pursue their own self-interest rather than group interests.

Problems of evidence

Compulsory membership

Let us turn now to the empirical evidence on trade unionism, starting with the American case discussed at length by Olson, where the widespread existence of 'closed shops' (or union security agreements) might appear to lend some weight to Olson's views. Although four out of five workers covered by collective agreements were also covered by closed shops in the early 1970s (Clegg 1976: 18) many of these agreements were voted into existence by workers in accordance with the 1935 Labor Relations Act and its subsequent amendments. Indeed the Taft-Hartley Act of 1947 was premised on the Olsonian-type argument that since unions survived by compulsion, then the mandatory use of secret ballots on closed shops would allow 'conscripted' workers to vote against compulsion. Olson himself reported the results that undermine his own claims:

> These hopes were frustrated. In the first four months under the Act the unions won all but four of the 664 union-shop elections held, with more than 90 per cent of the employees voting for compulsory union membership. In the first four years . . . 97 per cent of the elections were won by the unions.
>
> (Olson 1971: 85)

Olson simply continued writing about the necessity of compulsion oblivious to the significance of the evidence he himself had just quoted. For if rational workers would elect not to join a union but to free-ride on their colleagues why didn't they express this preference when given the opportunity to do so? The fact is that the overwhelming majority of workers freely voted in these ballots to remain in unions and to have everyone else remain in them as well. The number of workers kept in unions by agreements of which they disapproved was insignificant. Far from compulsion being essential to the labour movement this evidence suggests it is quite insignificant. Indeed, only a few pages later Olson reflected on the very question thrown up by the figures he had just quoted, asking if compulsion freely voted on by a group was the same as compulsion imposed by some external force. Where compulsion was unanimously supported in order to make everyone better off then he said 'there would be no more infringement upon the freedoms of those involved than when two people freely sign a contract' (1971: 93). But this is almost exactly the situation of the American closed shops where more than 90 per cent voted in favour!

Olson then tried to defend his theory of closed shop compulsion by looking at US strike statistics. He reported that shortly before and during the Second World War, 'There were many strikes for union security' (1971: 79). But the accompanying footnote tells a rather different story. Whilst there was an upsurge of union recognition strikes from 19 per cent of the total in 1933 to 57.8 per cent in 1937, he was forced to admit that 'many of the strikes for union membership did not have to do with compulsory membership, *at least directly*' (1971: 80, italics added). Since the evidence did not fit the theory, he offered idle speculation and slippery innuendo instead: 'no doubt many of the "union recognition" strikes that were not openly for the closed shop involved devices to encourage employees to join the union' (1971: 80).

Olson may have had 'no doubt' about the validity of his own claims, but he offered nothing by way of evidence or argument to convince a sceptical reader. His own theory clearly stated that coercion was essential for union membership but the evidence shows that the proportion of reluctant members who were compelled in the strict sense of that word was less than ten per cent in the period 1947–1951.

If we turn to the British case we find a similar picture. The most authoritative study of the closed shop (or union membership agreement, UMA) reported that,

> generally UMAs were concluded at very high levels of union membership. . . . In engineering over two-thirds of all closed shop arrangements emerging between 1965 and 1979 were established when union density was at least 90 per cent. . . . Our estimate of the number of employees compelled to join a union when a closed shop was introduced at their place of work must necessarily be very crude. We put the figure at a quarter of a million during the 1970s. . . . As over the same period

membership of TUC affiliated unions increased by 2.9 million, then reluctant joiners accounted for 8 per cent of the growth.

(Dunn and Gennard 1984: 121–122)

British survey evidence has also thrown useful light on the reasons people themselves give for joining unions. Research by Marshall *et al.* (1988), Gallie (1996), Millward (1990) and Waddington and Whitston (1996) contains data from national samples of workers collected in 1984, 1986, 1989 and 1990–1992 respectively. The proportions citing 'compulsion' ('closed shop' or 'it's a condition of having my job') were 41 per cent, 31 per cent, 38 per cent and less than 9 per cent respectively. In view of the decline of the closed shop in the 1980s, the first three of these figures seem surprisingly high, but Millward's data shed more light on this issue because he permitted respondents to offer more than one reason for joining and to rate the importance of each. Of the eight classes of reason 'compulsion' was rated the least important but one, suggesting that even where there was a closed shop a certain proportion of members would have joined the union in any case. Dunn and Gennard (1984) estimated this figure could be as high as 92 per cent (the typical level of union density at the time a closed shop agreement was introduced). So the survey figures of respondents who mentioned a closed shop as a reason for joining (41 per cent, 31 per cent and 38 per cent) would need to be deflated by a factor of as much as 0.92 in order to arrive at a true estimate of the role of compulsion. Applied to the survey figures this calculation would suggest that pure compulsion accounted for no more than 3–4 per cent of those who join unions, a figure remarkably similar to the estimate for American 1940s data reported above.

We can actually test the accuracy of this estimate of pure compulsion because a series of anti-union laws passed between 1980 and 1990 progressively outlawed all forms of compulsory unionism. The numbers of employees covered by closed shop agreements fell by about 3 million between 1984 and 1990 (Millward *et al.* 1992: 99). Now, if Olson is right, we should have seen an equally dramatic fall in union membership and density as the vital prop of compulsion was gradually removed. The well known aggregate fall in British union membership does not clinch the argument because the Olsonian prediction applies only to those areas of the economy covered by closed shop agreements. What happened there was summed up by Millward *et al.*:

> Workplaces that had a closed shop covering all manual workers in 1984 had an average level of manual union density of 99 per cent. These same establishments in 1990 had an average level of manual density of 93 per cent. This is perhaps the clearest indication that the decline of the closed shop had only a limited part to play in the overall drop in union membership during the latter part of the 1980s.
>
> (Millward *et al.* 1992: 100–101; see also Wright 1996)

Coercive picket lines

Olson is no more successful in showing that 'coercive picket lines' were essential for boosting and maintaining union membership. He attributed the violence associated with many US strikes, particularly before the Second World War, to the necessity to control free-riding by,

> those who continue working, or for outside strikebreakers. . . . Should it be surprising, then, that coercion should be applied to keep individual workers from succumbing to the temptation to work during the strike? And that anti-union employers should also use violence?
>
> (Olson 1971: 71)

Notice first how the violence of the employer was presented as an afterthought, or perhaps as a response to the violence of unions. Yet the most recent study of violence in US labour relations reached a very different conclusion:

> Much violence has been sparked by the penchant of American employers to actively break strikes rather than simply wait for their collapse, as British and many other European employers have tended to do. . . . In the United States, employers were not merely above the law, they were the law. Nowhere else in the available history of Western democracies have employers, with impunity, organized vigilante mobs or used mercenary armies to protect their property interests.
>
> (Sexton 1991: 65–66)

Olson was also unclear as to whether any violence used by strikers was directed at their fellow-workers, who were therefore putative free-riders in the Olsonian sense, or against outside strikebreakers brought in to replace the strikers. In the latter case there can be no question of these workers trying to free-ride on the future success of strike action since their own livelihoods as replacement workers now depend on the failure, not the success, of the strike in question. By lumping these two groups of workers together Olson falsely implied that violence directed against either of them was consistent with his theory of compulsion when in fact it was only violence against the former group that fitted the theory.

Since Olson presented the picket line (or as he liked to say, 'the coercive picket line') as the epitome of union compulsion it is worth looking at the available (UK) evidence on picketing. According to the Workplace Industrial Relations Surveys the proportion of strike-bound establishments in 1980, 1984 and 1990 that experienced picketing by their own employees was no more than one-third and the median number of pickets was between five (in 1990) and ten (in 1980) (Millward *et al.* 1992: 303–304). If compulsion is such an integral feature of trade unionism, it is difficult to explain why the majority of British strikes in 1980, 1984 and 1990 involved no picketing at all and why the number of pickets present (where there were any) was so small.

Group size

Olson's argument about the inverse link between group size and collective action is not easy to evaluate because he failed to provide any conceptual or operational definitions of size (Sandler 1992: 9–10). Nonetheless, evidence on group size (treated as a continuous variable) and collective action seems difficult to square with Olson's theory since it is well-established that trade union density and strike incidence are both positively, not negatively, correlated with establishment size (Millward and Stevens 1986: 58–59, 268; Millward *et al.* 1992: 282). Where did Olson's account of size effects go wrong? First, contrary to Olson's claim, collective action by small groups may be very difficult to organize, particularly where they are engaged in inter-group conflict. A small group of strikers is very vulnerable to employer sanctions such as dismissal, and beliefs about these possibilities may be sufficient to deter collective action by such workers. But as group size increases the costs of such 'repression' are spread over larger numbers of people and are either deflated (for each individual) or rendered more bearable. Indeed, when very large groups are engaged in collective action, the costs of repression (for the employer) may become prohibitive and worker knowledge of, or beliefs about, this logic may act as a further incentive for large groups to display more collective action, not less (Barbalet 1991: 457; Elster 1985: 354; Fireman and Gamson 1979; Hardin 1982: Chapter 3). Second, there may be economies of scale in large groups. Olson assumed that with increased group size organization costs will rise (1971: 48), but as Oliver and Marwell (1988) pointed out, this is untrue if there is 'jointness of supply', i.e. the costs of providing a public good are fixed irrespective of the numbers who wish to use it. Holding a union branch meeting costs the same whether the numbers eligible to attend are five or fifty. Third, large groups may be more effective in securing group objectives because of their greater resources, especially if they organize a large proportion of the relevant constituency.[7]

The formation of unions

Much of this evidence then contradicts Olson's claims about 'rational individuals', the pervasiveness of free-riding and the necessity for coercion, but there is an even more serious problem. Olson's entire argument assumes the existence of unions in the first place, since there must be an agency to administer selective incentives to putative free-riders. Now if the rational individual always seeks to free-ride and employers are equally keen to punish those who try to start up unions, why do any rational individuals ever start unions at all (Barbalet 1991: 463; Hardin 1982: 34; Popkin 1988: 14–15)? In other words, if everyone tries to free-ride there is no ride at all, so how does 'the ride' come into being? Olson tried to answer this crucial question by arguing that unions began as small organizations so that the 'logic of collective action' did not apply. Only later, when they had become large organizations, did the problem of free-riding emerge on a serious scale.

This account confuses unions as national organizations with unions at the workplace. American organizing drives in the 1930s got started primarily in the large, not the small, workplaces (Cochran 1977: 103–126). To say this was because of picket line violence during recognition strikes still begs the vital question of how the unions and the picket lines ever managed to overcome the free-rider problem in the first place. To these questions Olson simply has no answer and for very good reason. People who first begin to organize unions in unorganized plants, particularly in the face of employer opposition (the normal situation in the USA and increasingly in Britain) are likely to bear heavy personal costs, including dismissal, blacklisting and violence (cf Fishman's 1995 account of the costs borne by communist union organizers in Britain in the 1930s). Any 'rational' individual, or at least rational in Olson's narrow terms, would be unwilling to bear these costs. Unions must therefore get started by people who defy Olsonian logic.[8]

According to mobilization theory, collective organization and action is often brought about by small numbers of activists or leaders who play a crucial role in promoting a sense of grievance, generating group cohesion and urging and legitimating collective activity against a relevant target (Chapters 3 and 4 above). The same point was made by two of Olson's critics when they argued that one of the key resources for voluntary groups such as unions is a 'critical mass' of activists willing to take on the costs of initiating and organizing collective action.

> Empirical accounts of actual social movements and movement organizations show over and over that most of the action originates from a relatively small number of extremely active participants. The 'free-rider dilemma', correctly analyzed, is the problem of not being able to make a big enough difference in the outcome to compensate for the costs one bears. Thus understood, the theory of collective action does not predict that collective action will never occur, but rather that it will not take the form of small, isolated contributions. Instead the theory of collective action explains why most action comes from a relatively small number of participants who make such big contributions that they know (or think they know) that they can 'make a difference'.
>
> (Oliver and Marwell 1988: 7; see also Frolich and Oppenheimer
> 1970: 119; Marwell and Oliver 1993: 52–57; Oliver 1984;
> Popkin 1988: 16–21)

Crouch on trade unions and the logic of collective action

Crouch's (1982) book was the first (and to date the most comprehensive) attempt to apply rational choice theory to trade unionism and therefore deserves special scrutiny. Crouch actually wrote about a rational choice approach rather than a theory and the difference is significant, as we shall see. For Crouch, actors could be either individuals or collectivities, but even in the former case Crouch's individuals are far more sophisticated than Olson's free-riders. The rational choice approach, says Crouch, involves asking about the chances of success of a collective action, the costs involved, the alternatives available to the actors, the actions and reactions of others and the sanctions or power at the actor's disposal (a framework that is similar to, but broader than, Olson's). After setting out this basic approach the book then focuses on the familiar areas of membership, collective action, union goals, union democracy and political involvement and, as one would expect from the author, it is lucidly and elegantly written.

One obvious test of Crouch's approach is whether it can shed new light on old issues and on this score the book is less than successful. The first substantive chapter, on union membership, concludes that, 'Collective action theory is therefore of limited usefulness in explaining union membership' (Crouch 1982: 67). Crouch therefore abandoned Olson in favour of what he called 'the primary logic of collective action' (1982: 67). This turns out to consist of two variables, the utility and the possibility of joining unions. Utility is a function of the worker's dependency on the employer, which in turn depends on the scope of collective bargaining and the likely impact of unions on wages. The possibility of membership turns out to be the employer's recognition policy. So after a short detour at the end of a long chapter we end up with an explanation of union membership variation that looks remarkably similar to standard institutionalist and business cycle accounts such as those of Clegg (1976) and Bain and Elsheikh (1976), both of whom are cited approvingly. An unfamiliar defence of familiar conclusions can be valuable for reinforcing our confidence in those conclusions but it seems a meagre outcome for a whole new approach in social science. The chapter on collective action consists of a long and inconclusive discussion about strike costs and benefits and the factors that might affect strikers' calculations. However, we are simply not told whether collective action theory or the more broadly defined rational choice approach can tell us anything new about collective action.

Matters get no better when we move on to topics that have rarely been addressed by rational choice theorists, namely union goals and union organization. Crouch argued that, 'workers' actions will usually be incremental, concerned with short-time advantage within known parameters' (1982: 131). As an empirical generalization this is fairly uncontentious but Crouch wanted to show that it follows, or can be derived from, the rational choice approach. He said that workers will often fight much harder for defensive goals than for offensive goals, i.e. to defend what they have as opposed to claiming what they want but do not have (Crouch 1982: 121). Moreover, when they do advance new demands

80

workers are often modest in their ambition, invoking comparisons with other similar groups. Manual workers for instance compare their earnings with other manual workers not with those of their employers. According to Crouch these conclusions follow from relative deprivation theory as expounded by Runciman (1966). This is debatable, and even if it were true it is not clear how it would lend any support to a rational choice approach. Runciman argued that it is frustrated expectations that motivate action not absolute levels of living standard, in other words either the absence of expected improvement or a threat to the status quo. Since these two situations correspond very approximately to Crouch's categories of offensive and defensive goals there is no remit in Runciman for suggesting workers fight harder for the latter than the former. Likewise there is no sound theoretical reason why workers' inter-group pay comparisons should be restricted to similar others and thus reinforce modest incremental goals. Gallie's (1978, 1983) studies of French and British factory workers and Scase's (1977) comparison of Swedish and British manual workers both showed that British manual workers were unusual in their degree of parochialism. Crouch is therefore wrong in attributing this fact to lack of information about other groups of workers. On the other hand he is right to note that workers who have the greatest incentive to pursue radical goals often lack the power to do so, whilst those who have power can often wrest enough concessions from their opponents to take the edge off any radical demands they may have had (cf Arrighi 1990).

The chapter on unions as organizations is a standard analysis of union democracy that owes nothing to rational choice theory, but the final chapter of the book does make use of the Prisoner's Dilemma game to argue that Britain's decentralized bargaining system is highly conducive to small groups of workers free-riding on the contributions of others, e.g. during incomes policies. Overall then one would have to conclude (*pace* Crouch) that the rational choice approach is not especially helpful in studying a number of important aspects of trade unionism.

Conclusions

If most people behaved as Olson suggests then the world of industrial relations would bear no resemblance to the one that actually exists. Olson's account of unions is not just wrong on details: it is radically wrong on fundamentals. His basic concepts of rationality and individual self-interest are ill-defined and of questionable relevance; he has no concept of group identity as a way of understanding the regulation of people's behaviour in group and inter-group contexts; he conceptualizes only individual interests without appreciating the ways in which people can come to think about, and to pursue, group interests; his insistence on the central role of compulsion is contradicted by an overwhelming body of evidence; his theory offers little insight into the contemporary decline of trade unionism; his work is unable to account satisfactorily for the formation of trade unions. In the face of these fundamental problems it simply won't do to say the theory has some validity because there is free-riding. In the world of trade unionism (at least in Britain and America) the clear majority of workers do not free-ride: they either join unions of their own volition or work in non-union establishments where the question of free-riding does not arise. If we want to understand how people come to define their interests in collective terms and embark on the road to collective organization and action, then mobilization theory offers a far richer and more plausible account of the processes involved than is to be found in the strange and impoverished social world depicted in *The Logic of Collective Action*.

6

LONG WAVES IN INDUSTRIAL RELATIONS

Mobilization and counter-mobilization in
historical perspective

Introduction

The last three chapters have concentrated on the analysis of worker mobilization,
as well as state and employer counter-mobilization, over a short time frame. The
focus of mobilization theory as I have expounded and developed it has been on
the short-run, group and inter-group dynamics involved in collective interest
definition, organization, mobilization and action. Yet it is clear from Tilly's
(1978) studies that there are also powerful long-term forces at work shaping the
opportunities and the forms of collective activity. Consequently we must now
examine the processes of mobilization and counter-mobilization in historical
perspective, and one approach that could help do this is long wave theory.

The idea of 'long waves' of economic development is again on the intellectual
agenda, after a long hiatus during the postwar economic boom and the early years
of the late twentieth-century recession. The short business cycle of five to ten
years duration is a familiar and widely used concept, but the notion of long waves
in the economy of approximately fifty years duration is far more contentious and
there is considerable dispute surrounding the underlying mechanisms of any such
phenomenon. They are popularly associated with the Russian economist
Kondratieff, who initiated a major discussion of their existence and significance in
the 1920s.[1] Long waves are now commonly defined as regular patterns of fluctu-
ation in one or more economic indicators (usually prices, output and profit rates)
synchronized across countries, with a total span of approximately fifty years,
consisting of a twenty-five year 'upswing' (of sustained growth), and twenty-five
years of 'downswing' (sporadic growth and recession).

Why should the concept of long waves be of interest to researchers in industrial
relations? First, many of the debates about the 'transformation of industrial relations', the emergence of new systems of labour relations or the alleged decline of
worker collectivism have been conducted in an historical vacuum. Long wave
theorists by contrast insist on the need to situate shifts in labour–capital relations
in an historical perspective. Only then can we begin to delineate what is truly

unique about the present historical period and to appreciate what is familiar from earlier phases of restructuring. Second, it is clear that if you examine aggregate time-series data on British union density and strike activity, there are pronounced discontinuities, with sharp ruptures at those periods identified by long wave writers as the turning points from upswing to downswing and vice versa. Finally, the transition periods from economic upswing to downswing have been characterized by Screpanti (1984) as periods of 'recurring proletarian insurgencies', deeply disruptive of the prevailing social order and for that reason alone of great interest to Marxists and other students of social revolt. The concept of long waves has potentially major implications for analyses of trade union membership, union organization, collective action and collective bargaining (Cronin 1979; Dunlop 1948; Gordon *et al.* 1982; Screpanti 1987; Silver 1992). The first part of this chapter summarizes the major lines of research and thinking on long waves and then considers the implications for industrial relations, looking in turn at strikes, union membership and industrial relations institutions. The next section explores the possible mechanisms behind strike waves and other changes in industrial relations, and concludes with an analysis of the strengths and weaknesses of long wave theories.

Long waves in the economy

The burgeoning literature on long waves has centred on three key questions: (1) do long waves exist at all or are they merely a statistical or methodological artefact? (2) what are the most appropriate indicators to use in measuring their duration, international scope and turning points? (3) what are the mechanisms responsible for their existence and their periodicity? Table 6.1 depicts the now conventional dating system for long waves, based mainly on price, output and innovation data, but incorporates Silver's (1992) notion of transition periods.

Upswings were defined by Mandel (1975: 126–127) as periods of sustained economic growth with only occasional years of stagnation or decline, whilst downswings were periods of sporadic growth accompanied by more frequent and sustained bouts of stagnation or decline. Economies do grow during downswings, but more slowly and fitfully than in upswings. Upswings and downswings do not succeed one another neatly and swiftly but give way to one another through a transition period of change. The table presents approximate dates for upswings and downswings because precise dating is rendered difficult by international differences in the onset of long waves, by the variety of results available depending on the measures used, by gaps in the data for the earlier periods and by the problem of how to incorporate the world wars into the long wave framework. The exact dates given for transition periods (from Silver 1992) should therefore be treated circumspectly. For example, there is broad agreement that the world capitalist economy entered an upswing in the 1840s, but Gordon *et al.* (1982) proposed the 'mid 1840s', Kondratieff (1979) suggested 1844–1851, Mandel (1995) plumped for 1847 and Van Duijn (1984) went for 1845.

84

Table 6.1 Long waves in the world economy

Upswings	Downswings	Transition periods
Late 1840s–early 1870s		1870–1875
	Early 1870s–early 1890s	1890–1896
Early 1890s–World War One		1914–1920
	World War One–World War Two	1939–1945
World War Two–early 1970s		1967–1975
	Early 1970s–present	1990s?

Sources: Goldstein (1988: 67), Gordon *et al.* (1982: 9), Lembcke (1992) and Silver (1992: 285)

Goldstein (1988) presented the most exhaustive account of the variety of methods and data used to establish the existence of long waves, and more recent work has been summarized in Kleinknecht *et al.* (1992). Broadly speaking, Kondratieff waves are most readily apparent in price data, although they can also be found in production data (Menshikov 1992; Metz 1992) and rate of profit data (Shaikh 1992). On the other hand several authors have demonstrated long wave fluctuations in price data as far back as the fifteenth century, which, if true, would call into question the link between long waves and capitalist production (Goldstein 1988: 72–74).

On the question of mechanisms there are three broad schools of thought which identify fluctuations in investment, innovation and class struggle respectively as the motors of change. Cycles of investment was Kondratieff's (1979) own solution to economic periodicity, but why should investment rates follow a long and regular cycle? One answer led to the second theory of long waves based on clusters of innovations – steam power, electricity, nuclear power and micro-electronics. These new developments in products and processes opened up profitable new lines of investment and thus stimulated economic upswings. But this argument also fails to answer the question of why innovations should cluster at regular intervals. Marxist theorists have tried to link the investment and innovation behaviour of capitalists to the rhythms of class struggle and their impact on rates of profit, the ultimate motor of capitalist activity. For Mandel (1995) it is an endogenous mechanism – the rising organic composition of capital – which curtails each long upswing but transition out of the ensuing downswing is thought to depend on exogenous factors such as major working-class defeats. (For critical reviews of all these debates see Delbeke 1984; Goldstein 1988: Chapters 3 and 4; Gordon 1989; Mandel 1992, 1995; Nolan and Edwards 1984; Norton 1988; Tylecote 1991: Chapter 1.)

The question of periodicity has received the least attention in the literature, and has been addressed most explicitly by Lembcke (1992) and Screpanti (1989). Both argued that the twenty-five year periodicity corresponds approximately to the time-span of one generation and suggested various mechanisms that could link generational change in the labour force with shifts in economic and industrial relations behaviour, a theme to which I return later in the chapter. In summary, the literature on long waves in the economy shows a tendency for empirical evidence to outstrip theory, and it is the absence of any well-defined mechanism for generating such waves that perhaps accounts for the continued scepticism about their existence.

Long waves and industrial relations

A number of writers have analysed the implications of long wave theory, both for industrial relations in general (e.g. Jacobi 1986, 1988) and for specific behaviours, such as strike action (e.g. Cronin 1979; Gordon *et al.* 1982; Hobsbawm 1952). Although none of them has used mobilization theory it is possible to provide an account of long waves in industrial relations as alternating periods of worker mobilization and employer and state counter-mobilization. The core argument can be expressed in general terms as follows: each turning point between upswing and downswing is associated with an upsurge of worker mobilization, epitomized by heightened strike activity. This in turn triggers off a period of counter-mobilization by employers and the state, and out of this inten-sified period of class struggle emerges a more or less far reaching reconstruction of the relations between labour, capital and the state. Once the new phase of the long wave (upswing or downswing) gets under way, new patterns of industrial relations are gradually, if unevenly, consolidated until the next transition. During long downswings these patterns are likely to reflect the interests of employers as they exploit slack labour markets in order to consolidate their power and hege-mony, but the situation during long upswings is not so clear cut. For long wave theorists it is the regular and periodic ruptures in labour–capital relations that lay the foundations for the intervening periods of relative stability. I will examine the more detailed arguments later in the chapter but for the moment I want to explore some of the empirical evidence in order to establish the extent to which some key industrial relations variables are associated with long waves in the economy. I shall therefore look in turn at strikes, union membership, bargaining institutions, union organization and mergers, and employee 'involvement'. Some of these choices are sufficiently conventional as to require little justification but always what one can usefully talk about is constrained by availability of data. This is a particularly acute problem for long-wave theory because of the requirement for fairly reliable data over a time frame longer than one century.

Strikes and strike waves

Theorists in the long wave tradition have argued that the turning points between upswing and downswing are marked by unusually high levels of strike activity, particularly strike frequency, and the conclusions of these authors are set out in Table 6.2.

The methods used to establish the existence of strike waves vary enormously.

Table 6.2 International and national strike waves, 1870–1974

Author (date)	Country/ies	1870s	Early 1890s	1910–1920	Late 1930s–late 1940s	1968–1974
Boll (1985)	Britain, France, Germany, Italy, USA, Russia	Yes (not Italy, USA or Russia)	Yes (not Italy or Russia)	Yes	N/A	N/A
Brecher (1972)	USA	Yes	Yes	Yes	Yes	No
Cronin (1985)	UK, France, Germany	Yes	Yes	Yes	N/A	N/A
Cronin (1979)	UK	Yes	Yes	Yes	No	Yes
Dunlop (1948)	USA	Yes	Yes	Yes	Yes	N/A
Gattei, in Mandel (1995)	UK, Italy, France, USA, Germany	Yes	Yes	Yes	Yes	Yes
Goldstein (1988)	World	Yes	No	Yes	No	Yes
Gordon et al. (1982)	USA	Yes	Yes	Yes	Yes	Yes
Hobsbawm (1952)	Mainly UK	Yes	Yes	Yes	No	N/A
Mandel (1995)	Europe	Yes	No	Yes	Yes	Yes
Screpanti (1987)	UK, Italy, France, USA, Germany	Yes	No	Yes	No	Yes
Shorter and Tilly (1974)	France	Yes	Yes	Yes	Yes	Yes
Silver (1992)	World	No	Yes	Yes	Yes	No

Brecher (1972) and Cronin (1979) relied merely on visual inspection, as did Jackson and Sweet (1979) writing about the 1968–1974 strike wave. It is therefore difficult to tell from this 'method' whether Britain, for instance, experienced three strike waves between 1910 and 1926 or one continuous wave punctuated by the First World War and by postwar slump. In addition Cronin identified a strike wave lasting from 1957–1962, something reported by none of the other authors (although Franzosi (1995: 7) argued that there was a strike wave in Italy between 1959 and 1963). Silver (1992) used reports of any type of labour unrest appearing in the London *Times* and the *New York Times* from 1870, a data set that would seem particularly sensitive to journalistic, proprietorial and policy-makers' definitions of what was newsworthy. Goldstein (1988) did not use any direct evidence, but inferred strike waves from annual aggregate movements in real wages, a procedure that seems unsatisfactory although it generated similar results to those obtained with more sensible methods. Shorter and Tilly defined a strike wave as occurring when both the mean number of strikes and strikers in a given year exceeded the previous five-year averages by more than 50 per cent (1974: 106–107). But by measuring a strike wave in terms of an *annual* figure Shorter and Tilly counted each separate annual peak as a discrete strike wave and therefore ended up with an astonishing number of 'waves' – thirteen in all – between 1872 and 1968.

Screpanti (1987) used the most rigorous criteria, rightly insisting that strike waves must display significant departures from trend levels of strike activity. In addition, if we assume that Kondratieff waves reflect contradictions in the capitalist mode of production then they should be international in scope as capitalist economies experience similar sets of contradictions, and they should be synchronized because of the trading and investment links between national economies (Nolan and Edwards 1984: 203). Screpanti's measure of strike activity combined the three common indicators of frequency, workers involved and days lost into a composite variable of strike acuteness. He then used principal components analysis to separate out 'true' Kondratieff waves from nationally-specific strike peaks, demonstrating the existence of three such waves in the advanced capitalist world:[2] the early 1870s, the period either side of the First World War, roughly 1910–1920, and the period 1968–1974.[3] The results from this rigorous method are very similar to those obtained by less sophisticated methods. As with transition periods, the start and end points of a strike wave are both approximate, and variable across countries (Jackson and Sweet 1979). Silver (1992) is the only author not to record a strike wave in the early 1870s but since she had no pre-1870 data with which to compare, we should probably discount her result as a methodological artefact. There is some variation among authors in the precise dating of the second strike wave, with starting dates between 1906 and 1917, but there is consensus on 1920 as the end point and consensus also on 1968 and 1974 as the outer limits of the most recent wave. We can be especially confident about these three waves since they have been confirmed by those authors who have used international rather than national data sets and employed the most rigorous statistical criteria for wave identification, viz. Goldstein (1988) and Screpanti (1987).

These three waves have one vital feature in common, which is that all of them occurred at or near the peak of Kondratieff upswings as the world economy passed from a period of sustained economic growth into a long period of recession. For two authors – Goldstein (1988) and Screpanti (1987) – these are the only strike waves identified, but it is clear from Table 6.2 that every other author claims to have found a strike wave at the end of at least one Kondratieff downswing, either in the early 1890s, in the late 1930s/early 1940s, or both. If we examine the early 1890s there is strong evidence of a significant increase in strike frequency and numbers of strikers in the UK (1889–1890) and the USA (1889–1891); a significant increase in striker days in Italy (1893); and increases in all three measures of strike activity in France in 1893 (see Gordon *et al.* 1982: 98; Screpanti 1987: 101–102, 113; Shorter and Tilly 1974: 112–114).

The picture for the end of the next great downswing is rather more confused. There were upsurges of strike activity (strikes and strikers) in France (1936 and again in 1947 and 1948: Screpanti 1987: 101–102). Dunlop (1948) and Screpanti (1987: 101–102) both argued that the USA experienced two big strike waves, from 1933 to 1937 and again during the war, from 1941 to 1945–1946, whilst Thompson reported a strike wave in Canada beginning in the late 1930s (1993: 94). Mandel (1995: 39) suggested there was an upsurge of strike frequency across Europe starting in the late 1930s and lasting well into the late 1940s.[4] There were also strike 'surges' in the late 1940s in Australia, Germany, Ireland, Italy, Japan and the Netherlands (O'Lincoln 1985: 53; Visser 1992b: 327; von Prondzynski 1992: 84).

There are two interpretations of this evidence, the first of which follows Screpanti in suggesting that the strike activity observed at the end of downswings reflects 'national peculiarities'. This view is neither plausible nor parsimonious. Strike activity, on one or more measures, seems to have risen significantly in virtually all of the advanced capitalist countries for which we have data towards the end of and shortly after the Second World War.[5] An alternative view is that there are significant increases in strike frequency, workers involved and/or days lost at the end of long downswings, as capitalist economies move back into the upswing. However, compared with the end of upswing strike waves, this pattern of strike action shows more variability in intensity, timing and duration across the capitalist world. Overall then it can be argued that there are major strike waves towards the end of Kondratieff upswings (1869–1875, 1910–1920, 1968–1974) and minor strike waves towards the end of Kondratieff downswings (1889–1893, 1935–1948).

Trade union membership and density

Even the most cursory inspection of British trade union membership and density statistics shows that the periods of dramatic union growth seem to have coincided exactly with the major and minor strike waves. One way of examining the association between Kondratieff waves, strike waves and union membership is to cross-tabulate data on the latter against an historical periodization based on the former. There is merit in looking at both membership and density, and it seems sensible to follow conventional practice and record average annual changes in these two variables for the different historical periods. Two questions then arise: which countries should we include, and what should we expect to find? Ideally we need data over a long period from all those countries where the capitalist mode of production has been predominant for some time. In practice we are heavily constrained by the availability of data. Time-series evidence for most of the twentieth century on strike activity and union membership can be found for most of Western Europe and a number of other countries, viz. Great Britain, the USA, France, Italy, Germany, Australia, Austria, Canada, Denmark, Finland, Japan, the Netherlands, Norway, Sweden and Switzerland.[6] In terms of the core argument set out earlier, the most straightforward hypothesis is that union membership and density will grow fastest during strike waves, followed in turn by upswings and downswings respectively.

The broad picture (see Tables 6.3 and 6.4) turns out to be remarkably clear in the five major capitalist countries: unions recorded dramatic rises in membership and density during strike waves, modest rises (occasionally none) during

Table 6.3 Annual trade union membership changes during Kondratieff waves and strike waves 1894–1989 (five major capitalist countries, '000s)

Period	Character	GB	USA	France	Italy	Germany[a]
1894–1909	Upswing	52[b]	130[c]	N/A	N/A	165
1910–1920	Major strike wave	543	254	140	N/A	709
1921–1934	Downswing	−265	−120	−29	N/A	−348[g]
1935–1948	Minor strike wave	327	802	201	N/A	N/A[h]
1949–1967	Upswing	30	213	−36	−111[f]	138
1968–1974	Major strike wave	218	152 or 585[d]	114	474	138
1975–1989	Downswing	−71	−390	−121	144	43

Sources: GB and USA: Bain and Price 1980: Tables 2.2 and 3.1 (BLS series) for 1894–1974; Edwards *et al.* 1992: Table 1.4 for 1989 (GB) and Visser 1992a: Table 1.1 for 1989 (USA); France and Italy: Visser 1989: Tables FR 1/1 and 1/2 for 1913–1985 and IT 1/2 for 1950–1985; Visser 1992a: Table 1.1 for 1989; Germany/West Germany: Bain and Price 1980: Table 6.1, Col. 6 and Table 6.2, Col. 7 for 1894–1974; Visser 1992a: Table 1.1 for 1989

Notes:
[a]Becomes West Germany from 1949
[b]All figures rounded to nearest thousand
[c]Data begin in 1897
[d]The method of counting membership was changed in 1968 and two figures are quoted by Bain and Price (1980) for each year from 1968 to 1976. Since each gives a radically different estimate of growth rates for the period 1968 to 1974, I have quoted both figures
[e]Data start in 1913
[f]Data start in 1950
[g]Data for 1921–1931
[h]Data for 1947–1948 show an annual rise of 936,050

Table 6.4 Union density changes during Kondratieff waves and strike waves 1894–1985[a]
(five major capitalist countries, percentage points per annum)

Period	Character	GB	USA	France	Italy	Germany
1894–1909	Upswing	0.21	0.48[b]	N/A	N/A	1.03[g]
1910–1920	Major strike wave	3.09	0.71	N/A	N/A	3.25
1921–1934	Downswing	−1.74	−0.62	0.00[d]	N/A	−1.92[h]
1935–1948	Minor strike wave	1.51	1.56	2.60[e]	N/A	N/A[i]
1949–1967	Upswing	−0.14	−0.16	−1.28[f]	−1.20	0.15
1968–1974	Major strike wave	0.97	+0.14 or −0.33[c]	0.26	2.74	0.21
1975–1985	Downswing	−0.59	−0.99	−0.75	0.29	−0.03

Sources: GB: Bain and Price 1980: Table 2.1, Col. 9 for 1894–1977 and Waddington 1992: Table 1, Col. 5 for 1985; USA: Bain and Price 1980: Table 3.1, Col. 7 for 1897–1974 and Kumar 1993: Table 1 for 1974–1985; France and Italy: Visser 1989: Tables FR 4/1 and 4/2, Col. 6 and Table IT 4/2, Col. 5 respectively; Germany: Bain and Price 1980: Tables 6.1 and 6.2, Col. 9 for 1894–1977 and Visser 1989: Table GE 4/2, Col. 5 for 1978–1985

Notes:
[a]Reliable density data are available only until 1985
[b]Data from 1897
[c]See note d, Table 6.3
[d]1921–1931
[e]1931–1946
[f]1946–1967
[g]Data starts in 1895
[h]Data ends in 1931
[i]Density rose by 5.30 percentage points per annum 1947–1948

upswings, and lost membership and density during downswings.[7] There were exceptions to this pattern, as the tables also reveal: German union membership and density increased no faster during the 1968–1974 strike wave than in the preceding upswing; American union density actually fell during the same strike wave despite an historically high rate of membership growth. Italian union membership continued to rise during much of the present downswing but this trend conceals a substantial growth of union pensioners and an actual decline of membership amongst the employed (Ferner and Hyman 1992: Table 16.2).

Data from ten other capitalist countries is shown in Tables 6.5 and 6.6 and reveals rather more variation in union membership patterns. Evidence from Australia, Canada, Denmark, Finland, Japan, Norway and Sweden broadly conforms to expectation with dramatic membership and density rises during strike waves as compared to periods of upswing. Growth rates during these latter periods have been much more modest and in the cases of Australia and Japan union density actually declined during the long postwar boom. Downswings reveal a pattern of continued union growth in the Scandinavian countries compared with sharp falls in density or membership in Australia, Canada and Japan. As with the major capitalist countries, there are findings that do not

Table 6.5 Annual trade union membership changes during Kondratieff waves and strike waves 1894–1989 (other capitalist countries, '000s)

Character	Upswing	Major strike wave	Down-swing	Minor strike wave	Upswing	Major strike wave	Down-swing
Period	1894–1909	1910–1920	1921–1934	1935–1948	1949–1967	1968–1974	1975–1989
Australia	14	37	6	50	37	89	42
Austria	N/A	123[a]	−27	327	12	10	4
Canada	N/A	32[b]	−5	56	63	78	78
Denmark	N/A	30[c]	5	18	23	31	51[d]
Finland	N/A	N/A	N/A	43[e]	17[f]	75[g]	36
Japan	N/A	N/A	N/A	446[h]	218[i]	244[j]	−26
Netherlands	N/A	58[k]	6	25	23	19	−3
Norway	N/A	11[l]	2	20	15	19	22
Sweden	9	29	22	55	40	87	62
Switzerland	N/A	27	4	18	8	6	4

Sources: Australia: Bain and Price 1980: Table 5.1 for 1894–1974 and Visser 1992a: Table 1.1 for 1989; Austria, Denmark, Netherlands, Norway and Switzerland: Visser 1989: Tables AU 1/1 and 1/2, DE 1/1 and 1/2, NE 1/1 and 1/2, NO 1/1 and 1/2 and SZ 1/2 respectively for 1913–1985; Visser 1992a: Table 1.1 for 1989; Canada: Bain and Price 1980: Table 4.1 for 1911–1974 and Visser 1992a: Table 1.1 for 1989; Finland: Lilja 1992: Table 6.1; Japan: Kuwahara 1993: Table 10.1; Sweden: Bain and Price 1980: Table 7.1 for 1894–1974 and Visser 1992a: Table 1.1 for 1989

Notes:
[a]Data from 1914
[b]Data from 1911
[c]Data from 1913
[d]Data end 1988
[e]1944–1950
[f]1950–1965
[g]1965–1975
[h]1935–1949
[i]1950–1965
[j]1965–1975
[k]Data from 1913
[l]Data from 1913

conform to expectations: union membership has shown remarkable resilience in several countries, rising steadily in Canada and Finland and quite strongly in Denmark, Norway and Sweden; conversely, Norwegian union density declined during the 1968–1974 world strike wave (despite a rise in membership) whilst Danish union density rose only modestly. Even more intriguing are developments in Austria, the Netherlands and Switzerland where annual union growth rates have declined in each successive Kondratieff period since the minor strike wave of 1935–1948.

How can these unexpected results be accounted for within the long wave framework? One possible explanation can be derived from the institutional forms of industrial relations across the capitalist world (Crouch 1992: 179–183; 1993:

Table 6.6 Union density changes during Kondratieff waves and strike waves 1894–1985[a]
(other capitalist countries)

Character	Upswing	Major strike wave	Down-swing	Minor strike wave	Upswing	Major strike wave	Down-swing
Period	1894–1909	1910–1920	1921–1934	1935–1948	1949–1967	1968–1974	1975–1985
Australia	N/A	1.96[b]	−0.49	1.37	−0.16	0.31	−0.91[c]
Austria	N/A	4.85[d]	−1.58[e]	N/A[f]	−0.13	−0.54	−0.06
Canada	N/A	N/A	−0.15[g]	1.10[h]	0.22	0.33	0.26[i]
Denmark	N/A	3.60[j]	−0.50	0.73	0.58	0.44	1.65[k]
Finland	N/A	N/A	N/A	N/A[l]	0.47[m]	3.20[n]	0.70[o]
Japan	N/A	N/A	N/A	3.49[p]	−1.31[q]	−0.04[r]	−0.55
Netherlands	N/A	2.70[s]	−0.24	0.59	−0.01	−0.24	−1.05
Norway	N/A	1.28	0.16	1.85	0.76	−0.50	0.33
Sweden	0.64	1.51	0.79	1.99	0.19	1.27	1.13
Switzerland	N/A	N/A	0.06	0.95	−0.44	−0.27	0.03

Sources: Australia: Bain and Price 1980: Table 5.1, Col. 7 for 1911–1976 and Visser 1992a: Table 1.1, Col. 9 for 1989; Austria, Denmark, Netherlands and Switzerland: Visser 1989: Tables AU 4/1 and 4/2, DE 4/1 and 4/2, NE 4/1 and 4/2 and SZ 4/1 and 4/2 Col. 5; Canada: Bain and Price 1980: Table 4.1, Col. 11 for 1921–1974 and Kumar 1993: Table 1 for 1974–1985; Finland: Lilja 1992: Table 6.2; Japan: Kuwahara 1993: Table 10.1; Norway: Bain and Price 1980: Table 9.1 for 1910–1920 and Visser 1989: Tables NO 4/1 and 4/2, Col. 5 for 1920–1985; Sweden: Bain and Price 1980: Table 7.1 for 1894–1912 and Visser 1989: Tables SW 4/1 and 4/2, Col. 5 for 1913–1985

Notes:
[a]There are no reliable density data after 1985
[b]Data from 1911
[c]Data end 1989
[d]Data for 1919 and 1920 only
[e]1921–1933
[f]Density rose by 7.10 points per annum during 1946–1948
[g]1921–1931
[h]1931–1948
[i]Data may not be comparable with earlier periods
[j]1913–1920
[k]Data end 1984
[l]Density rose by three points per annum during 1944–1950
[m]1950–1965
[n]1965–1975
[o]1975–1985 and data may not be comparable with earlier periods
[p]1935–1949
[q]1949–1965
[r]1965–1975
[s]Data from 1913

Chapters 6 and 7). A number of countries have evolved highly centralized, corporatist systems of industrial relations involving powerful unions – the labour-dominant systems of Denmark, Norway, Sweden and more recently Finland. It is in this type of system that union membership levels have held up during the recent downswing, partly because of below-European average levels of unemployment (for the relevant figures see Ferner and Hyman 1992: Table A.7). By contrast, in those countries which came to develop employer-dominant corporatist systems – the Netherlands and Switzerland and to a lesser extent Austria – union growth has proved feeble even during the postwar upswing and the subsequent world strike wave that began in the late 1960s. One reason for this lack of significant growth (at least in Austria and Switzerland) may be that the incidence of strike activity, and thus of worker mobilization, barely changed at all in the late 1960s and 1970s (Traxler 1992: Table 8.7; Hotz-Hart 1992: Table 9.3; Shalev 1992: Table 3.1).[8] It is those countries with the least developed forms of corporatism, whether labour- or employer-dominant, that have displayed the most pronounced fluctuations in levels of union membership across the phases of the Kondratieff cycle – Great Britain, the USA, France, Italy, Australia and Japan.

Another way of examining the relationship between strike activity and union membership is to look at the association between annual changes in both series. That exercise shows that strike frequency and union membership changes went hand in hand (up or down together) in 70 per cent of the years from 1889 to 1993 in Great Britain. None of this evidence necessarily vindicates long wave theory because there could be other periodizations of the data which might prove even more illuminating than those used here. Moreover, it would be possible to acknowledge that there was an empirical association between trends in union membership and strike activity but to reject long waves as the underlying mechanism. Nonetheless, the evidence does at the very least suggest that the theory is worth taking seriously.

Other industrial relations indicators

Extensive data is available from 1900 on union mergers and formations in three countries, Britain, Sweden and the Netherlands. In Britain mergers have been concentrated in three periods of intense activity: 1918–1924, 1944–1948 and 1966–1987 (Waddington 1995: 21), and there were similar merger waves in Sweden and the Netherlands at about the same periods (Sweden: 1902–1921, 1934–1957 and 1968–1977; Netherlands: 1908–1926, 1941–1950 and 1966–1979; Visser and Waddington 1996: 43–44). Each of the first two merger periods was synchronized with the later stages of strike waves (both upswing and downswing) and with the turning points in the Kondratieff cycle. The formation of new unions has displayed a similar pattern with peaks around 1920 in Britain, the Netherlands and Sweden, the mid-1940s to the mid-1950s (Sweden) and the late 1960s to the late 1970s (Britain and the Netherlands) (Visser and Waddington 1996: 35–36). If Waddington's analysis is updated, and we assume that by the mid-1990s we are nearing a new turning point between downswing and upswing, then as expected, a recent surge of merger activity can be detected in a number of countries. Britain has witnessed the creation of a series of large unions since the late 1980s: NUCPS (1987), MSF (1988), GMB-APEX (1989), NUKFAT (1990), RMT (1990), GPMU (1991), BECTU (1991), AEEU

(1992), UNISON (1993), CWU (1995), PTC (1996) and more in the pipeline. The annual rate of mergers has also risen sharply in both Canada and the USA since 1990 following a slow and steady increase throughout the postwar period (Chaison 1996: Tables 3, 4 and 6).[9] Yet it might be just as plausible to suggest that what has occurred (at least in Britain) is not a recent merger wave but a near continuous thirty-year surge of merger activity, beginning in 1966. On that view the link between mergers and long waves in the economy, at least in Britain, might then be called into question (see Undy 1996 and Waddington 1997).

Comparative time-series data on bargaining coverage is practically non-existent (Golden and Wallerstein 1996: 11), although Milner has collected evidence for Britain, shown in Table 6.7. The picture is similar to that for union membership and density, with dramatic increases in coverage during strike waves, modest or no increases during upswings and significant declines during downswings.

Radical changes in the structure of bargaining have also been associated with long waves and strike waves and can best be illustrated with British data. Towards the end of the First World War the government-created Whitley Committee of Inquiry recommended the creation of Joint Industrial Councils across private manufacturing industry and in the public sector, and many of the latter still exist today. The resurgence of the shop stewards' movement with the 1930s economic recovery laid the foundation for a system of workplace bargaining, initially in engineering, that would spread across industry throughout the whole postwar period. The 1980s downswing has witnessed a dramatic decentralization of collective bargaining as employers have abandoned multi-employer agreements and sought to establish greater control over their own bargaining structure, processes and outcomes (Clegg 1985; Purcell 1991; Terry 1983).

Changes in union organization can be illustrated from the British case for each of the major and minor strike waves on which we have data, beginning with

Table 6.7 Collective bargaining and statutory pay coverage in Britain 1895–1985

Period[a]	Character	Average annual change in coverage (percentage points)[b]
1895–1910	Upswing	+0.50 to +0.56
1910–1925	Major strike wave	+2.56 to +2.81
1925–1935	Downswing	−1.55 to −2.00
1935–1950	Minor strike wave	+1.94 to +2.19
1950–1965	Upswing	−0.25 to 0.00
1965–1975	Major strike wave	+1.18 to +1.55
1975–1985	Downswing	−2.31 to −2.44[c]

Source: Milner 1995b: Figure 1 and Table 2

Notes:
[a]Milner's periods correspond approximately, but not exactly to the wave dating system I have used earlier
[b]Milner's data contain range estimates of coverage so I have calculated range values of change
[c]Figures for collective bargaining only

1889–1893. This wave witnessed major advances in the organization of semi- and unskilled workers (the so-called New Unionism) and laid the foundations of what were later to become the country's two major general unions, the TGWU and the GMB. As the strike wave abated however, some of the major employers, particularly in engineering, sought to recoup some of the ground they had lost and the result was a series of lockouts and strike defeats, as well as judicial actions culminating in the engineering lockout of 1897 on the one hand, and on the other the Taff Vale judgement of 1901. The strike wave of 1910–1920 was associated with the growth of rank-and-filist ideologies such as syndicalism, which laid the foundations for an enduring politicization of the shop steward movement in manufacturing industry, under the sway of Communist Party organization. In the escalating wave of industrial action from 1910 there was growing agitation for trade union unity and a process of mergers and amalgamations on a scale that would not be seen again until the 1970s (see above). The same pressures towards unity resulted in the formation of the TUC General Council as an executive body of the whole trade union movement, empowered to call industrial action (a power used with disastrous results in 1926). The minor strike wave of 1935–1948 inaugurated the distinctly modern shop steward form of organization, now commonplace in unionized settings, based on local bargaining with front-line supervisors and high levels (often 100 per cent) of workplace union density. Unionization spread to the new industries manufacturing consumer durables, particularly motor vehicles, with dramatic consequences for postwar industrial relations, both in cars and throughout the economy as a whole. Finally the strike wave of 1968–1974 was associated with the spread of shop steward organization into the public sector, most notably with the adoption of this system by NUPE and NALGO at their 1974 conferences. Multiplant shop steward (combine) committees also grew rapidly in numbers in this period and the first Workplace Industrial Relations Survey showed that 60 per cent of the manual combines existing in 1980 were less than ten years old (the figure for non-manual committees was 72 per cent) (Cronin 1984; Hinton 1983; Terry 1985: 363–364).

British developments in patterns of worker participation in company decision-making have also displayed a strong cyclical pattern with waves of interest in both financial and decision-making forms, in the periods 1865–1873, 1889–1892, 1908–1909, 1912–1914, the First World War, the Second World War, and 1964–1976 (Ramsay 1977: 483–485, 489–490, 493–494). Ramsay argued that employers' interests reflected shifts in the balance of power that were themselves the result of labour shortages, state involvement in labour markets, and industrial unrest. These periods all coincided with strike waves, starting somewhat earlier than the major strike waves (in 1865, 1908 and 1964) but more or less coterminous with the minor waves (1889 and 1939).[10]

There is, in my view, enough empirical evidence to show that the Kondratieff economic turning points are associated with major upheavals in industrial relations, and these can be discerned through patterns of union membership and density, strike activity, union mergers, collective bargaining coverage and a variety of other institutional changes. It is to the explanation of what I shall call these long wave 'ruptures' that I now turn.[11]

The mechanisms of long wave ruptures

There is no agreed model or even framework for thinking about the levels and forms of worker mobilization (as well as state and employer counter-mobilization) observed during long wave ruptures. The literature contains so many scattered observations and suggestions it is difficult even to produce a meaningful short list of alternative approaches, let alone a consensus. What criteria, then, must be met by a satisfactory account? First, the mechanisms must be derived from basic features of capitalist production, such as contradictions in the process of labour exploitation. Contingent properties of capitalist societies will almost certainly be unable to account for the regularity and international scope of long wave ruptures. Second, any mechanisms must operate across the capitalist world. Features unique to particular countries will be unable to account for the international character of long waves, although they may be very important in helping us understand the timing, duration, intensity and outcomes of long wave ruptures in different countries (Nolan and Edwards 1984; Norton 1988). Third, a satisfactory account of national aggregate trends should be able to offer at least some insights into disaggregated variation. The most detailed empirical attempt to dissect the underlying mechanisms is to be found in Cronin's (1979) account of British strike waves, although he offers no formal theory or set of propositions, and the argument of his book has to be pieced together with some care. I shall therefore draw on Cronin, but will cast his account within the framework of mobilization theory. As a consequence the following sections will be rather slanted towards strike waves and towards British experience, but will embrace other industrial relations phenomena and other countries where data (and space) permit. It is also important to distinguish the dynamics of upswing and downswing ruptures for reasons that will become clear shortly.

Upswing ruptures: mobilization and counter-mobilization 1968–1974[12]

In general terms it is the pattern of interactions between workers and employers over the duration of the upswing that seems to prepare the way for the ruptures at the upswing peak. Mobilization theory would suggest that we focus on the actions of employers and their impact on workers' sense of injustice or illegitimacy. From there we would need to assess changes in worker mobilization and the opportunities for collective action, particularly as they are affected by the balance of power and by the actions of the state. Finally, as we are investigating long-run changes in mobilization we should also explore the significance of changes in the composition of the workforce.

Employer actions

First, it has been argued that employers, particularly in manufacturing, experience declining rates of profit towards the tail end of a long upswing and attempt to restore profitability in ways that impinge either directly on workers' living standards (through wage controls or wage cuts, intensification of labour or labour shedding) or indirectly, by raising prices to customers. British manufacturing net profit rates fell between 1955 and 1958 (from 18.8 per cent to 15.4 per cent) and then began a particularly steep fall in 1964, plunging from 14.0 per cent to 9.6 per cent in 1970 before crashing to 1.7 per cent in the depths of the recession (1981) (Armstrong *et al.* 1984: 464). (US manufacturing profit rates fell over the same period from 35.7 per cent (1965) to 17.7 per cent (1970) and then to 10.7 per cent in 1981. French and German profit rates declined more slowly and steadily until the mid-1970s but Japanese profit rates were high and stable until 1975 (Armstrong *et al.* 1984: 464).) As a result of labour shedding, unemployment in Britain began to rise in 1965 and climbed steadily from 1.5 per cent, hitting a new postwar peak of 3.8 per cent in 1972 (Cronin 1979: 229). Similar trends occurred elsewhere so that by 1970 unemployment levels were higher than five years previously in virtually all of the major capitalist countries (Italy and Japan were the exceptions: Bamber and Whitehouse 1993: 284). Finally there was a surge in retail prices throughout the advanced capitalist world, from the late 1960s, as manufacturers sought to protect declining profit rates (Jackson and Sweet 1979: 47).

Injustice

Employers' attempts to restore profitability, however, generated a growing sense of injustice on the part of workers. Rising inflation, coupled with increased taxation (and in Britain compounded by state incomes policies) had checked the growth of real earnings in many capitalist countries despite increases in labour productivity (Jackson and Sweet 1979: 48). On the threshold of the 1968–1974 strike wave the percentage of wage strikes in Britain was running at about 45 per cent; within seven years it had climbed to almost 66 per cent as workers sought to restore the annual increases in real wages to which they had become increasingly accustomed throughout the postwar upswing (Cronin 1979: 213–214). Across the capitalist world the average annual percentage of strike days lost in pay disputes was 53 per cent between 1951 and 1968 but this figure rose sharply to 76 per cent over the subsequent six years (Jackson and Sweet 1979: 49). Beyond specific concerns about wages, many commentators such as Phelps Brown (1986), Cronin (1979), Flanders (1970) and Screpanti (1984) detected a general increase in worker expectations of employment, a factor they attributed to the long years of full employment whose corrosive effects on workplace discipline were predicted as early as 1943:

the *maintenance* of full employment would cause social and political changes which would give a new impetus to the opposition of business leaders. Indeed, under a regime of permanent full employment, 'the sack' would cease to play its role as a disciplinary measure. The social position of the boss would be undermined and the self-assurance and class consciousness of the working class would grow. Strikes for wage increases and improved conditions of work would create political tension.

(Kalecki 1943: 326)

But if rising expectations of employment are a necessary precursor to collective action they are not sufficient. According to mobilization theory the failure of employers to satisfy worker expectations will culminate in such action only if workers come to believe they are the victims of injustice.

Workforce composition and generational change

How do large numbers of workers come to feel similarly aggrieved at about the same time? One answer, suggested by a number of writers (though rejected by Cronin) is generational change, an idea already referred to in the discussion as to why long waves appear to be of fifty years' duration. Phelps Brown (1986) argued that workers' expectations of employment are largely determined by the state of the labour market at the time of their entry into the labour force, though subsequent events can also make a difference. In fact the trade unions in early post-Second World War Britain were led by men who had started work shortly before the major strike wave of 1910–1920 but who eventually came to possess what Cronin (1979: 138) called a 'depression mentality' (see also McIlroy 1997: 118–119). That, and the pervasive anti-communism of the upper echelons of British trade unionism in the 1940s and 1950s, resulted in a willingness to compromise with employers that proved increasingly unacceptable to the growing cohorts of shop stewards and branch officers who had known only full employment and regular increases in pay and living standards. By the late 1960s, according to Phelps Brown, this new generation of union activists had become a 'critical mass', sufficiently numerous and influential to force radical shifts in union policy and workers' militancy, albeit after long and often bitter factional struggles inside almost every one of Britain's largest unions (see Undy *et al.* 1981: Chapter 4). More recent research has confirmed the significance for collective bargaining demands of generational differences among full-time union officers (Kelly and Heery 1994: 139–140, 198–203), but important questions remain unanswered. How does one constitute a 'generation' conceptually and empirically (Braungart and Braungart 1987)? Are workers' expectations largely shaped by economic factors, as Phelps Brown contends, or do political agencies (militant shop stewards, politicians, employers) also play a role as mobilization theory suggests (cf Darlington 1994 on militant shop stewards; Fishman 1995 on the British

Communist Party)? How are generational differences in expectations affected by the institutional and other means available for their expression? And how do generational changes amongst employers and state officials alter the dynamics of industrial relations in the upswing?

Balance of power

The fourth factor in the dynamics of long wave ruptures is the balance of power. Most writers assume that under conditions of full employment workers have more 'defensive' *and* 'offensive' power: they are better able to resist employer attacks on their conditions (compare the pathbreaking 1956 BLMC strike against redundancies in the car industry with the absence of such action in the preceding downswing), and they are more capable of imposing their own demands on employers by threatening to strike and by actually doing so (Lyddon 1996: 191–192). It is true, however, that few writers on long waves have moved beyond these broad generalizations on union power of the sort that I strongly criticized in Chapter 2, not least because of the problem of accounting for exceptions. Japanese workers for instance failed to benefit from low levels of postwar unemployment and instead suffered a series of major defeats in key industries (cars, coal, steel and paper) that induced a long period of labour quiescence (Armstrong *et al.* 1984: 190–191; Beale 1994: 24–30). Similarly Franzosi (1995) observed that levels of strike activity in Italy in the 1950s were lower than expected from economic theory because of the depressive effects of employer victimization of communist trade unionists. It is also important to note that the genesis of collective action is affected by what Tilly calls the 'opportunity structure', the vulnerability of the ruling class to new claims. Such vulnerability may in turn be the product of a political crisis within the ruling class as in France 1968 (Tilly 1978: 55).

Worker mobilization

Discontent is translated into collective action only through organization (trade unions, workplace branches, mass meetings, etc.) and through mobilization by shop stewards, union officials and other activists (Batstone *et al.* 1977; Kelly and Heery 1994; and Chapters 3 and 4 above). Employer and state concerns with profitability and their resistance to worker demands, workers' increased sense of grievance, generational shifts in the workforce, a shift in the balance of power towards workers and increased worker mobilization: it is the gradual confluence of these five factors that leads to the upsurge of strike activity at the tail end of Kondratieff upswings. If we go back briefly to the 1910–1920 strike wave we can find evidence on strike activity and strike outcomes (the latter is not available for the 1968–1974 period) which demonstrates the virtuous circle that is then set in motion (Table 6.8).

Table 6.8 shows that strike frequency climbed rapidly until 1913, falling back

100

Table 6.8 Strike frequency, strikers involved, union membership and strike outcomes 1908–1920

Year	Number of strikes	Strikers involved (000s)	Percentage of worker defeats	Union membership (000s)
1908	399	224	43	2,485
1909	436	170	46	2,477
1910	531	385	37	2,565
1911	903	831	32	3,134
1912	857	1,233	30	3,416
1913	1,497	516	25	4,135
1914	972	326	33	4,145
1915	672	401	37	4,354
1916	532	235	26	4,644
1917	730	575	22	5,494
1918	1,165	923	23	6,533
1919	1,352	2,401	23	7,926
1920	1,607	1,779	32	8,348

Source: Cronin 1979: Tables B.1, B.2, B.5, B.10

during the war but surging again from 1917. The figures for worker mobilization (strikers involved), union membership and strike outcomes followed a similar trajectory. From the annual aggregate figures therefore it appears that unions became the beneficiaries of a virtuous circle of effectiveness and membership. As the scale of strike activity increased, so did the win rate, and as the win rate increased, bargaining coverage rose, more workers perceived unions to be effective and joined them, which in turn enabled more strikes to be called . . . and so on.[13]

State and employer counter-mobilization

The rising tide of worker mobilization which peaked between 1968 and 1974 generated a predictable counter-mobilization by the state and the employers and we can use Tilly's framework (Chapter 3 above) to categorize their forms. Both Labour and Conservative governments of that period attempted to persuade workers they had common interests with employers in boosting productivity and competitiveness and curbing wage demands. Bodies such as the National Board for Prices and Incomes were created (in 1965) to monitor pay settlements and try to link them to productivity. The Royal Commission on Trade Unions and Employers' Associations (1965–1968) focused many of its enquiries and recommendations on union organization, particularly at workplace level, and sought the closer integration of shop stewards into union structures. Both governments tried to repress the growing level of worker mobilization for strikes by legal measures, and to change the forms of collective action through the use of 'cooling off' periods and secret ballots. Finally, governments also created opportunities for union involvement in corporatist decision-making structures and thereby sought to reduce the incentives for unions to take industrial action (Maguire 1996; Taylor 1993: Chapters 5, 6 and 7).

Employers meanwhile were deeply divided over how best to counter the power of organized labour. Some of the motor industry employers supported legal curbs on unions, whilst others believed that the Donovan route of formalized industrial relations and productivity bargaining was the sensible response to worker power (Strinati 1982). Only with the dismissal of the chief shop steward from one of the country's best organized plants in 1979 (the BL, now Rover plant in Birmingham) did a growing number of employers start to embark on far-reaching changes within their own plants: closures and redundancies, cutbacks in union facilities, more flexible work practices and labour intensification, contracting out of functions and (from about 1988) overt derecognition of unions (Smith and Morton 1993). Sporadic defeats of traditionally well-organized workers, usually involving a coalition of the state and employers, also contributed to the long period of employer ascendancy after 1979: printers 1983, miners 1985, printers (again) 1987, school teachers 1987 and dockers 1989.

Downswing ruptures (1889–1893, 1935–1948)

The explanation for downswing ruptures is more complex and difficult because the impact on workers of long periods of employer power is less clearcut. Employers' profit rates will have recovered during the long years of downswing in the wake of company liquidations, rationalization of production and product and process innovations that will have cheapened commodities and opened up new markets. Enhanced profitability could allow employers to concede to the rising demands of their workforce (let us assume for the moment they are rising), but by the same token it could also facilitate resistance to those demands by providing employers with a profits 'cushion' in the event of a costly dispute(s). Hence the well-established difficulty of predicting whether profits should correlate negatively or positively with strike frequency, and the familiar (and connected) finding that the coefficient on the profit variable in strike frequency regression equations is usually small and non-significant (cf Ashenfelter and Johnson 1969).

Workers' sense of injustice is equally difficult to conceptualize. On the one hand it is plausible to suggest that the process of restructuring which so effectively raises profitability also generates a growing volume of employee grievances, as the wage–effort exchange is shifted in the employers' favour. Evidence on employee complaints brought to the Citizens' Advice Bureaux (reported in Chapter 4 above) shows their number rising from over 400,000 in 1983 to almost 900,000 by 1993 (NACAB 1993). The longevity and bitterness of major downswing strikes, such as the 1984–1985 miners' strike in Britain, suggests that the intensity of grievances may also be affected by prolonged recession (Screpanti 1984). The strike waves of 1889–1893 and 1935–1948 involved significant, though not dramatic, increases in the percentage of wage strikes, as workers tried to recover ground lost during the wage cutting of the downswing years (Cronin 1979: 213).

On the other hand the workforce that emerges from downswing is significantly different in composition from the one that entered the downswing, twenty to twenty-five years earlier. If Phelps Brown is right that worker expectations of employment are formed at the time of entry to the labour force, this means that the downswing workforce increasingly comprises people with expectations of employment lowered because of the context of mass unemployment and therefore less susceptible to feelings of grievance or injustice than workers with more labour market experience. Quite how these two lines of argument can be reconciled is not clear, not least because of other factors, such as the politics of labour movement leaderships. In the early 1990s British trade unions were staffed by about 3,000 full-time officers whose average age was between 40 and 50 and who first entered the labour force in the 1960s, towards the peak of the previous upswing and around the time of the last great strike wave. There is evidence that this generation of officers was significantly more militant (in a variety of ways) than their counterparts of a previous generation, and that they sought to impart their values to existing union members (Kelly and Heery 1994: 113–118, 139–141). On the other hand it is probably also true that national union leaderships witnessed a shift towards moderation as seen in their promotion of various forms of class collaboration such as 'social partnership' (cf TUC 1994 and Kelly 1996).

As the economy moves back into a Kondratieff upswing the level of unemployment falls and *ceteris paribus* the balance of power shifts back in favour of workers. Before it does so employers are likely to exploit their power advantage at the workplace, shifting the wage–effort exchange in their favour, and trying to incorporate, marginalize or eliminate union organization through derecognition (Smith and Morton 1993). The impact of these measures on union membership, combined with the effects of mass unemployment, in turn stimulates union merger activity. A shift in the balance of power means that the opportunities for mobilization become more frequent if only because the constraint of perceived job insecurity gradually lessens. Since mobilization requires the presence of activists then the persistence of shop steward organization (as in the 1975–1990s downswing) or its swift regeneration (as at the tail end of the inter-war downswing) is vital, especially in decentralized systems of industrial relations such as the British and American.

Towards the end of long upswings it is highly plausible to argue that the factors we have looked at are mutually reinforcing and serve to generate an escalating level of worker mobilization. The situation at the end of long downswings is far less clearcut since these factors may reinforce one another to trigger off growing mobilization, but they do not necessarily do so. Hence the observation made earlier that minor (downswing) strike waves are more variable in duration, intensity and timing compared with major strike waves. More broadly, the pattern of class relations arising out of downswing ruptures is also highly variable. The British 'postwar settlement' and US postwar pattern bargaining both reflected class compromises in which organized labour secured significant concessions from their respective ruling classes: state commitment to full employment, welfare state programmes, and employer toleration of collective bargaining. By contrast Japanese employers embarked on a series of lockouts and disputes with organized labour throughout the 1950s so that 'By the close of the decade militant trade unionism had been literally eradicated in the private sector' (Armstrong *et al.* 1984: 190). In Italy the level of worker mobilization in the 1950s was lower than predicted by econometric models because 'The structure of labour relations was paternalistic at best, and most likely very repressive and authoritarian, in a general political climate very unfavourable to the working class' (Franzosi 1995: 254).

Implications and conclusions

Long wave theory is sometimes criticized as a mechanical notion which exaggerates historical continuity and repetition at the expense of change. At the end of his study of long waves of strike activity Cronin firmly rejected this view:

> social conflict is not the manifestation of some fixed and undifferentiated quantum of discontent. . . . Rather, social and industrial conflict are the means used by ordinary working men and women to assert their changing needs and aspirations. . . . The strike itself therefore changes its form and meaning as society and economy alter; and because the latter have developed so fast and in such diverse ways over the past hundred years, the nature of industrial conflict has been transformed dramatically as well. The only two constants in all this are the basic division of labour that gives rise to conflict, and the persistent function of the strike as the fundamental statement of the humanity and intelligence of the working class.
>
> (Cronin 1979: 195)

A number of authors have documented more than enough variation in the causes, demands, politics and protagonists of strike activity, both over time and internationally, to confirm that long wave theory can readily 'accommodate' historical variety and change. What are its other strengths? First, the theory does not simply illuminate one particular facet of industrial relations activity, but accounts for fluctuations in a wide range of variables: union membership and density, union mergers, bargaining coverage, strike activity and employer policies on worker participation. Not only that, but the theory is international in scope, at least for some variables (e.g. strike frequency). The theory specifies relationships between variables so that union membership and strike activity, for instance, are portrayed as components of a virtuous circle mediated by strike effectiveness. Second, a large amount of evidence, both from Britain and other countries, shows significant differences in a variety of industrial relations indicators between the upswing, downswing and transition components of Kondratieff waves. The transition periods between Kondratieff waves are also the turning points for union growth, strike activity, union mergers and bargaining coverage, variables on which, in Britain at least, there is fairly reliable time-series data for most of this century, and in some cases a little beyond. What is even more striking is that the turning points in the Kondratieff cycle, both upswing to downswing and vice versa, are associated with dramatic ruptures to the prevailing patterns of industrial relations. British union membership, for instance, has grown during strike waves at between *five* and *ten* times the growth rates recorded during long upswings (see Table 6.3 above). The theory is a valuable corrective to institutionalist approaches which tend to skirt around these 'exceptional periods'. Bain and Price's (1983) essay on British union membership, for instance, simply failed to mention that the most dramatic periods of union growth coincided with strike waves – though Price observed the coincidence in a later publication (1991).

Long wave theory is anchored in Marxist analyses of the capitalist employment relationship and therefore emphasizes the conflicts of interest between labour and capital deriving from the latter's exploitation and domination of the former. In addition to the abstract concepts bequeathed by Marxism, I have used a series of intermediate concepts in order to grasp the ways in which upswing–downswing transitions (and vice versa) impact on industrial relations, viz. employer policies, worker expectations, generational change, the balance of power and worker mobilization. Broadly speaking, it is the shifting patterns of worker mobilization and state and employer counter-mobilization that generate what Screpanti (1984) described as 'recurring proletarian insurgencies' and which in turn are associated with the 'ruptures' of industrial relations.

The theory's chief strength lies in the analysis of historical and international shifts in the formation of worker organizations, in worker–employer relations and in worker mobilization. Given the underdevelopment of historical and theoretical work in industrial relations these contributions are potentially very significant (cf Arrighi 1990 and Lyddon and Smith 1996). Textbooks of industrial relations for instance tend to be highly contemporary in their focus and the lack of adequate historical analysis opens up the danger of constructing future trends by simply projecting the recent past. Long wave theory is a valuable corrective to this view by virtue of its insistence on historical ruptures and discontinuities. The theory also has weaknesses, however, and it is to these I now turn.

The existence of long waves is still a contentious topic notwithstanding the evidence in price series and in some production and innovation data (Cleary and Hobbs 1984). Despite its anchorage in Marxism the theory has in fact been criticized by a variety of Marxist and neo-Marxist writers who remain unconvinced by the empirical evidence for regular long waves or, if that is accepted, are concerned about the inadequate theoretical specification of mechanisms that could generate such predictable cycles of economic activity (Green and Sutcliffe 1987: 230–231; Harris 1988: 28–29, 39; Howard and King 1992: 311–312; Nolan and Edwards 1984; Norton 1988; Tarrow 1991: 44–45). Most of this critical literature has focused on the problem of finding mechanisms that can account satisfactorily for the repetition and synchronization of long waves. In the absence of such mechanisms long wave ruptures in industrial relations could be interpreted in a variety of ways: the contingent results of world wars, the consequences of inadequate management or union leadership, the byproducts of corporate restructuring or the unintended effects of state fiscal and incomes policies, to name but four. International variations in timing, duration and intensity of strike waves, for instance, could be elevated to the foreground and used to stress the dissimilarity of international experiences and the significance of national peculiarities. Disaggregated strike statistics could be used to emphasize the differences between countries in the groups of workers most prominent in any particular strike wave. Methodologically, it is unclear whether we should date the beginning of a strike wave using the international dating system (1910, 1935, etc.) or whether we should take account of national variations in timing. Nor is it clear which of the three conventional measures of strike activity is the most appropriate. Should we confine the level of analysis to aggregate figures or should we also look at sectoral data? And does it matter that the precise relationship between strikes and union membership varies over time and between countries? Union membership started to climb just *before* the British and French strike waves of 1889–1893 and before the British wave of 1968–1974. By contrast, union membership only began to increase *after* the 1910 strike waves in Germany and the USA. It is possible that disaggregation of the data, by industry or by month, would reveal a clearer picture, but in all probability it would reveal different dynamics across sectors and over time.

In response to these points I would argue first of all that there is more than enough evidence to demonstrate long-term fluctuations in patterns of worker mobilization and state and employer counter-mobilization. The historical turning points in industrial relations have *coincided* with Kondratieff transition periods but there could turn out to be explanations of the industrial relations phenomena that owe little or nothing to long wave theory as it is now understood. It is true there are differences between countries in the precise timing and content of industrial relations ruptures but what else would one expect? It would be an extraordinarily mechanical theory which proposed that the precise forms of mobilization or outcomes of strike waves were the same across the whole of the advanced capitalist world irrespective of differing levels of union power and variations in state and employer policies. The forms of counter-mobilization for example have almost invariably displayed remarkable heterogeneity even within a single country. Writing of the 1869–1875 strike wave in Britain, Cronin observed that,

> like later insurgencies . . . it was followed by a substantial counterattack by employers that succeeded in beating back workers' organization from its furthest and weakest extensions, but did not manage to turn the clock back to the state of organization that had existed prior to the strike wave. The modes used to reestablish order within 'the industrial relations

system' also exhibited ... an odd mix of ... attempts to inflict symbolic defeats upon key groups of workers, together with efforts on the part of union leaders, state officials and enlightened employers to elaborate restrictive conciliation schemes and procedures for resolving disputes.

(Cronin 1989: 84)

What is valuable about the idea of long waves is the analysis of industrial relations in the downswing as a period of counter-mobilization in which one or more dimensions of worker collectivism will come under attack, whether it be ideological attempts to promote redefinitions of interest, restrictions on collective organization, increased opposition to mobilization, or changes in the opportunities for collective action. The test of the framework is whether it can help us understand the varied forms of mobilization and counter-mobilization through time.

If we assume the existence of Kondratieff long waves in the economy then it can be demonstrated that the periods of upswing and downswing correspond very closely to different patterns of industrial relations and that the turning points from one to the other are associated with dramatic changes in a series of industrial relations indicators: union membership and density, union organization, union mergers, strike activity, collective bargaining coverage and employer policies on worker participation. These results are reasonably clear and consistent across strike waves and across countries although there are a number of exceptions. I drew on mobilization theory to account for the industrial relations ruptures that characterize transition periods in the Kondratieff cycle, identifying the role of state and employer policies and their links to profitability, workers' sense of injustice, generational change amongst the workforce, shifts in the balance of power and patterns of worker mobilization. These mechanisms provide a useful framework for systematically exploring contemporary changes in industrial relations and for setting them into a proper historical framework. In similar vein the theory gives us some insight into the recurring patterns of state and employer counter-mobilizations that have been set in train during long downswings in the economy. The idea of long waves of mobilization and counter-mobilization is consistent with a large body of empirical evidence from a number of countries over a long time span, although there are still problems and weaknesses to be overcome. The existence of long waves in the economy is still a matter of debate and the mechanisms of industrial relations ruptures need to be thought through in more detail. Nonetheless, the notion of long waves offers a rich agenda for research, focused around the mechanisms discussed in this chapter, and provides a broad framework for integrating a wide range of observations.

7

POSTMODERNISM AND THE END OF THE LABOUR MOVEMENT

A critique

Introduction

The idea of long waves in industrial relations focuses our attention on recurring periods of worker mobilization and state and employer counter-mobilization. With its underpinning in a Marxist analysis of labour's exploitation and domination it suggests that the class struggle between labour and capital is a perennial feature of capitalist society. By contrast the ideas of postmodernism have called into question so many of the propositions that are central to mobilization theory and to the notion of long waves in industrial relations that it is necessary to appraise them at some length. The term 'postmodernism' was virtually unknown in Britain in the early 1980s, yet today it stands at the centre of debates in the social sciences. It has commanded adherents and opponents, generated a range of texts, both expository and critical, but has, to date, made virtually no impact whatever on the field of industrial relations. The core of 'postmodernism' is the idea that the advanced capitalist countries are passing through one of those rare periods of history marked by a sea-change in people's attitudes and behaviours and in the institutions through which they act. In the sweeping language so popular in this literature, the modernist era of mass production industries, class politics and the organized labour movement is giving way to a new era of post-Fordist production, social movement politics and the decay of the labour movement as a major political actor. The verities of the modernist era, such as faith in scientific and technological progress and in social and economic planning are being displaced by postmodernist uncertainty and disillusion. Postmodernists have poured scorn on Marx's dictum that the aim of science is to change the world, not just understand it, arguing that even to understand the 'postmodern' world is well-nigh impossible.

There is no single version of the 'postmodernist' argument, not even an agreed definition of the term. Some postmodernists are vigorously anti-Marxist (Crook *et al.* 1992) but there are postmodern Marxists (Harvey 1989 for instance) and

Marxist anti-postmodernists (Callinicos 1989 is the prime example). There is disagreement as to whether postmodernism is a new stage of capitalism (Jameson 1989), a form of post-industrialism (Crook *et al.* 1992), or a continuation of modernism (Harvey 1989). Some writers are happy with the concept of a 'modernist era', whilst others want to divide modernism into 'heroic' and 'stable' phases, or to distinguish the progressive modernism of the left from the reactionary modernism of the extreme right. There is also disagreement as to whether changes in, say, the cultural sphere of society necessarily entail changes in the economy (such as post-Fordism) or whether the postmodernist label conceals a set of coincidental trends lacking any coherence or unifying logic. Perhaps, as one commentator wrote, 'The only general point of agreement is that something significant has changed in the way capitalism has been working since about 1970' (Harvey 1989: 173).

Postmodernist theory is potentially very relevant to industrial relations. It provides a broad conceptual framework in which contemporary changes in society (including the sphere of industrial relations) are analysed as the expressions of a qualitative and historic transformation in the capitalist system of production. Moreover, through its analysis of the economic, political and social preconditions of the 'old, adversarial' industrial relations it presages their demise and the emergence of a variety of new forms of labour–employer relations. Postmodernism therefore bears directly on the British and American debates about continuity and transformation of industrial relations and on the central problems of industrial relations identified earlier. In this chapter I propose to break down the postmodernist argument into three sets of propositions, dealing respectively with philosophy, economics, and culture and politics. I shall first set out what I take to be the principal postmodernist arguments and then examine them critically.

Postmodernist arguments

Philosophy

On the subject of philosophy postmodernist writers have advanced two distinct claims. The first is that we cannot adjudicate between competing theories by appealing to an independent (theory-neutral) world of 'facts'. For postmodernists there is either no such world or, if there is, we have no way of knowing it because we have no direct access to 'reality'. All we know is language, and they argue both 'theory statements' and 'factual statements' are best understood as linguistic expressions, not reflections of an external reality. Hence the tendency for postmodernist writers to redescribe scientific or theoretical debates as 'language games', and to state, or imply, that there is no sure foundation, in an objective reality, for 'testing' different theories. Presumably therefore either one theory is as good as any other, or is to be preferred to its rivals on non-epistemological grounds (see Harvey 1989: 46–47; Hassard 1993: 17–18; McLennan 1992: 331–333).

The second claim is that 'grand theory', such as Marxism or Freudianism ('meta-narratives' in the language of postmodernism) is particularly objectionable because of its allegedly undesirable political consequences. Marxism oversimplifies a 'complex' and 'fluid' reality and therefore misrepresents it to such a degree that the theory is seriously misleading. Consequently the Marxists who held state power in Eastern Europe forced 'reality' to fit the theory by means of coercion and terror. Since Marxism is taken to be the archetypal meta-narrative of the modernist era it has been claimed by some postmodernist writers that state terror represents the inexorable logic of meta-narrative. 'Genocide turned out to be the destiny of Stalinist Communism . . . the revolutionary belief in a single set of universal principles . . . turned out to be profoundly dangerous' (Mulgan 1989a: 382; see also Harvey 1989: 52; Hebdige 1989: 80; Thompson 1992: 229; Thompson 1993: 194–196).

There are two implications of these arguments for the study of industrial relations. The first is that academics should abandon the pretence of developing scientific theory to study an objective reality and resign themselves to the idea that scientific debate is merely one language game amongst many. More specifically we should be particularly wary of Marxism and of Marxists because of the intellectual and political dangers inherent in its 'totalizing drive' to construct an all-embracing grand theory. The same warning applies to the labour movement, and in particular to those movements in countries such as France and Italy which have been deeply influenced by Marxist ideas.

Economics

There are two central claims in postmodernist analyses of the economy; first that it is entering a distinct new stage, most commonly described as post-Fordist, and second that within society the social and economic 'significance' of production is declining whilst that of consumption is rising. Each of these claims is complicated and entails a large set of auxiliary propositions, so let us take them in turn. It is common amongst postmodernist writers to characterize the advanced capitalist economies of the twentieth century as 'Fordist' and to argue that Fordism has now exhausted its economic potential and is therefore being displaced by new forms of economic organization (see Allen 1992a, b; CPGB 1989; Crook et al. 1992; Lash and Urry 1987; Murray 1989; Piore and Sabel 1984). We should note at this stage that the term 'Fordism' has been used in a variety of quite different (though not necessarily inconsistent) ways. There is Fordism as a particular type of mass production labour process; Fordism as an economy dominated by mass production sectors such as motor vehicles; Fordism as a form of industrial organization based around large, vertically-integrated companies; and finally Fordism as a 'mode of regulation' (or a regime of accumulation) comprising the whole set of postwar institutions and practices that coordinated production and consumption and underpinned the postwar economic boom (Boyer 1990; Hyman 1991; Sayer and Walker 1992: 194). I am here mainly interested in Fordism as a labour process, although some of the other components of the term will be examined from time to time as appropriate. The term post-Fordism is common but not universal and there are other terms in use, some of which are very similar in meaning e.g. flexible specialization (Piore and Sabel 1984), but some of which are broader, embracing political as well as economic themes, e.g. disorganized capitalism (Lash and Urry 1987). (The parallel debates about 'lean production' (Womack *et al.* 1990) and 'Japanization' are examined shortly.) The core of the postmodernist analysis of the labour process is set out in Table 7.1.

The giant mass production plant, with its standardized products, dedicated equipment, narrow job descriptions and semi-skilled workers is said to be giving way to a quite different type of workplace – smaller in size, with small runs of customized products manufactured by multi-skilled workers (or indeed by robots) using flexible equipment.

The flavour of some of the post-Fordist analyses is best captured by quotations:

> Work is being reorganized around new technology. Traditional demarcation lines between blue and white collar, skilled and unskilled are being torn down in the wake of massive redundancies in manufacturing. In future, work in manufacturing will be about flexible team working within much smaller, more skilled workforces.
>
> (CPGB 1989: 7)

> Bureaucratic hierarchies dissolve as owners and workers work at the same desk or workstation . . . the power of owners is constrained by the possibility of workers withdrawing their skills and knowledge and transferring them to other organizations.
>
> (Crook *et al.* 1992: 38)

> As for production the keyword is flexibility – of plant and machinery, as of products and labour. Emphasis shifts from scale to scope, and from

Table 7.1 Fordism and post-Fordism

	Fordism	*Post-Fordism*
	Mass production	Small scale/batch production
	Standardized products	Customized products
	Semi-/unskilled workers	Multi-skilled workers
	Fixed job descriptions	Flexible work roles
	Moving assembly lines	Robots, computerization and work teams
	Large plants	Small–medium plants

Source: Adapted from Murray (1989)

cost to quality. Organizations are . . . seen as frameworks for learning as much as instruments of control. Their hierarchies are flatter and their structures more open.

(Murray 1989: 47; and see also Allen 1992b; Mulgan 1989b;
Piore and Sabel 1984)

A related account of labour process changes can be found in Womack *et al.*'s (1990) study of Japanese car production in which they coined the term 'lean production' to designate a wide-ranging policy of eliminating waste from the labour process. The principles of 'lean production', sometimes described as 'Toyotaism' after the company that originated them (see Wood 1991) are shown in Table 7.2.

The implications of lean production for the workforce were spelled out by Womack and his colleagues: 'it . . . provides workers with the skills they need to control their work environment and the continuing challenge of making the work go more smoothly' (Womack *et al.* 1990: 101).

Common to post-Fordist and lean production arguments is the notion that work for many employees will become more skilled, more involving and presumably more fulfilling. The implications of these claims for industrial relations are not quite so straightforward, and it is possible to trace one main line of argument and two sets of qualifications. The core argument is that since post-Fordist work will be relatively skilled then the experience of alienation induced by Fordist assembly line work will become significantly less common. Insofar as this sense of alienation lies at the root of labour–management conflict, then the post-Fordist labour process should be far less prone to industrial conflict. Under post-Fordism there exists, in other words, a much firmer basis than in the past for a mutuality of interests between labour and management.

The first set of qualifications to this argument revolves around the role of institutions. Piore and Sabel noted that the industrial relations institutions found in different capitalist countries could influence the degree to which post-Fordist labour processes took root, as well as their form. In Japan it was the weakly unionized smaller firms that were said to be leading the way in labour process innovations; in Germany it was the heavily unionized big companies that first

Table 7.2 The principles of 'lean production'

Just-in-time production
Multi-skilled workers
On-the-job worker participation
Zero defects
High intensity effort
Simplified product designs
Employment security

Source: Adapted from Womack *et al.* (1990)

began experimenting with 'new production concepts'; whilst in America labour process reorganization has been pursued both through union–management cooperation programmes and vigorous union-busting (1984: 223–226, 229–234, 240–250). The precise implications of labour process change will therefore vary between national settings because of institutional differences in union density, bargaining coverage and union protection. Though Piore and Sabel were not themselves postmodernists in any sense of the word their writings have exerted a profound influence over some of the most well-known postmodernist texts, e.g. Crook *et al.* 1992: 187–188; Harvey 1989: 189–190; Hassard 1993: 17; and Murray 1989: 42–48. The second group of qualifications lays more stress on employer policies at company or workplace level. For Womack *et al.* 'lean production' will be associated with more cooperative industrial relations only where employers seek to enhance the status and well-being of their workforces through participative decision-making, guarantees of job security and single-status benefits and conditions.

Not only is the workplace said to be changing, but its significance in the economy and society is also said to be dwindling in comparison with the sphere of consumption. The argument here is that consumption has become more significant in the economy as a source of wealth and employment, a reflection according to some writers, of the shift to a service, or post-industrial economy in which a growing proportion of the workforce supplies services directly to consumers (Crook *et al.* 1992: 120–121). Consumption is thus thought to figure much more in people's everyday lives than in the past and its main features were well summarized by Harvey:

> The mobilization of fashion in mass as (opposed to elite) markets provided a means to accelerate the pace of consumption not only in clothing, ornament, and decoration, but also across a wide swathe of life-styles and recreational activities. . . . A second trend was a shift . . . into the consumption of services – not only personal, business, educational and health services, but also into entertainments, spectacles, happenings and distractions. . . . the primary effect has been to emphasise the values of instantaneity (instant and fast foods, meals, and other satisfactions) and of disposability.
>
> (Harvey 1989: 285–286)

Why has consumption become a more significant part of people's lives? Lash and Urry (1987: 228) gave four reasons: the steady increase in average disposable income over the postwar period, the reduction in working time, the vastly increased range of goods and services available for consumption and the opportunities (through late night shopping and more leisure time) to purchase and consume them. Whilst the giant car assembly plant was the archetypal institution of the modernist era, symbolizing the centrality of production, it is the giant shopping mall that has captured the imagination of postmodernists and which many of them regard as the icon of the postmodernist era (see for instance the cover of Crook *et al.* 1992).[1] Why are these trends in the spheres of production and consumption so important? For postmodernists they both reflect and enforce a shift in the primary social context in which people's identities are forged. The class-based division of labour, characteristic of Fordism, when coupled with mass housing, the presence of trade unions and occupational communities, generated a strong and widespread sense of *class* identity (Leadbeater 1989). The significance of changing patterns of consumption is that they are said to allow people more choice in the construction of a diverse range of lifestyles and of associated identities. Although these choices are influenced by social class (because of differences in income), the constraints and ties of social class are thought to be less compelling than in the past. As the postmodernists would say, people of all social classes can spend their leisure time in the shopping malls of the postmodernist age (Crook *et al.* 1992: 120–121; Mort 1989).

Culture and politics

In the modernist era social class was all pervasive: it showed through in your occupation, educational qualifications, residential area, type of residence, union membership, party voting and lifestyle. The modernist individual, or subject, was thus described as 'unified' because these various components of identity derived from a common source (Hall 1992). In the postmodern era this 'unified' subject is said to be disintegrating under the impact of post-Fordist changes at the workplace and new patterns of consumption. The 'postmodern' subject has an identity that is 'diverse and fragmented', 'fluid and unstable', based on gender, race, age, disability, lifestyle as well as social class (Brunt 1989; Hall 1992: 276–277; Thompson 1992: 229). Postmodern writers have often cited affluence as a mechanism that facilitates greater choice in lifestyles and consequently in identities, an argument that parallels the claims of Phelps Brown (1990 and see Chapters 3 and 4 above) about the decline in worker collectivism.[2] Other writers have referred to the easing of social constraints, the decline in deference to authority, the growth of informality in social life and the breakup of occupational communities as factors that have opened up more choices in lifestyles for more people (Lash and Urry 1987). One of the putative consequences of greater diversity and fragmentation in lifestyles and identities is that social class ceases to become the main line of division in society. A whole range of divisions is then opened up as potential foci for collective action and conflict so that the politics of the postmodern era becomes increasingly diverse and fragmented (CPGB 1989: 14–15; Hearn and Parkin 1993).

The first expression of this transformation has been the decline in trade union membership, density and influence across the capitalist world. Under the conditions of post-Fordism it is said, 'the great industrial classes are beginning to merge rather than polarize – a process specifically manifested in the decline of labour unionism' (Crook *et al.* 1992: 38).

Most writers accept that there are short-term, or conjunctural factors at work here, but they are also keen to stress the impact of longer-term shifts in the composition of the working class. The absolute or relative decline in numbers of male, manual, full-time industrial workers and the rise of female, non-manual, part-time and service workers has been said to represent a long-term erosion of the traditional base of the labour movement (CPGB 1989: 7; Urry 1989). Second, the scale of collective action by trade unions has declined since 1980 and although some industrial conflict is expected to continue in the future, it has been suggested that this will increasingly take the form of 'status action' by discrete groups, rather than large-scale mobilizations by an organized labour movement (Crook *et al.* 1992: 122–123; Lash and Urry 1987: 108–109).

Third, it has been predicted that the trade union movement will continue to decline as a unified political actor which seeks to represent the interests of more or less class conscious members alienated from society by relative deprivation and lack of skills (Crook *et al.* 1992: 122–123; Held 1992: 34; Urry 1989). It will function instead as a federation of status and special interest groups no longer unified by an overarching class identity or inspired by an ideological vision of socialism. Some writers have been more circumspect and foresee different options for the trade union movement, depending on its capacity to expand its membership base and/or forge alliances with 'new social movements', but on the whole these more nuanced views have come from beyond the mainstream of postmodernist writing (e.g. Goldthorpe 1984; Offe 1985: 857–868; Touraine *et al.* 1987: 286–294). Fourth, the transition to postmodernism is said to imply the decline of the class-based, two (occasionally three-) party political system. One piece of evidence cited in support of this claim is the declining association between class location (manual or non-manual) and voting behaviour in Britain since the 1960s. The decomposition of the traditional political system also showed up in the loss of membership and votes for the major class parties, and the concurrent rise of nationalist parties and the centre party. Elsewhere in Europe it has been the extreme right, green parties and regional parties that have challenged socialist–conservative hegemony. As Benton put it, 'The political party as we have known it is an anachronism' (1989: 333; see also Scott 1992: 141–147).

Finally, politics in the postmodernist era is thought to centre much more around social movements than political parties, particularly the so-called 'new social movements' of women, peace campaigners and environmentalists that came to prominence from the late 1960s (Crook *et al.* 1992: 138–142). These movements have often been described as *new* in order to distinguish them from modernist political parties and from the traditional labour movements of advanced capitalism, and their novelty is thought to reside in five features: the pursuit of universal rather than class or sectional values; the preference for direct action over institutional action; the antagonism to the state; their emphasis on cultural and lifestyle changes; and their dependency on the mass media (Crook *et al.* 1992:148; Offe 1985: 828–832; Scott 1992: 141–147). The new movements draw their support primarily from the younger generations of 'new middle' (or service) class employees (Inglehart 1990), and for some writers they reflect a concern with the creation and development of personal identity *rather* than being instrumental means for achieving certain goals (cf Cohen 1985). This counter-position of 'new' to 'old' social movements was expressed historically by Hall who argued that the rise of the new social movements, 'reflected the weakening, or break-up of class politics, and the mass political organizations associated with it, and their fragmentation into various and separate social movements' (1992: 290).

Summary: postmodernism and industrial relations

Postmodernist work has six substantive implications for the field of industrial relations. First, it conveys a powerful sense that the world is undergoing a fundamental transformation, and that contemporary change in industrial relations is deep-seated and not simply conjunctural. Second, the transformations identified by the postmodernists are not confined to this or that sphere of society but are comprehensive, touching the economy, politics and culture. The shifting patterns of industrial relations are located on a broad canvas and comprise just one component of a whole mosaic of change. Because the changes in politics, economy and culture are interconnected and mutually reinforcing, the shifts we observe in the world of industrial relations are likely to prove more durable than would otherwise be the case.

Third, conflict at the workplace is likely to diminish (or to remain at historically low levels) because its Fordist roots have been attenuated or removed. Work in the future will be more skilled, more flexible and more challenging, a far cry from the alienating rhythms of the assembly-line. Consequently there will be fewer issues that divide workers and employers and provide the fuel for conflict, and more interests in common as employers come to value the contributions of a skilled and committed workforce. Even where conflicts of interest do occur, the skills possessed by such workers will allow them to move around the labour market in search of better opportunities. Fourth, as the roots of conflict wither then so too will the perceived necessity by employees to join trade unions. Union membership and density is therefore unlikely to recover to its late 1970s levels. Lowered levels of membership and density will be reinforced by changes in the composition of the workforce away from those traditionally well-organized groups (full-time male manual workers in manufacturing) and towards groups that have proven historically to be difficult to organize and sometimes unreceptive to trade unionism (part-timers, women, non-manuals, service workers). Fifth, the trade union 'movement' will gradually cease to represent a distinct working-class constituency based in Fordist industry and will more and more consist of a collection of discrete interest groups lacking the cohesion that stems from a common class identity or a shared set of deprivations within and beyond work. As a result the union 'movement' will find it increasingly difficult to aggregate the interests of its heterogeneous membership and speak to governments with one voice. Its role as a major political actor is therefore likely to diminish so that the notion of a workers' (or labour) *movement* will become purely vestigial. Finally, the prospect of a resurgence of the trade union movement, implicitly held out by long wave writers, is decisively ruled out by postmodernists.

Problems of postmodernism

The postmodernist argument, taken as a whole, has two obvious strengths.[3] First, its empirical foundations cover a wide range of familiar landmarks: the crisis of Marxist theory and Marxist states, the decline of old industries, the reorganization of work, the slump in union membership and political influence, the proliferation of new social movements, and the shift from high street stores to out-of-town shopping malls-cum-leisure centres. Some (though by no means all) of the evidence laid out by the postmodernists is beyond dispute and this fact alone lends their argument an air of plausibility. Second, and more significantly, the postmodernists offer a seemingly coherent and sweeping vision of contemporary change, pointing to connections between a wide range of apparently disparate phenomena. The sheer scale and breadth of postmodernist theory is perhaps part of its appeal, and legitimately so because, other things being equal, a theory with greater scope *should* be preferred to narrower rivals.

As we shall see the *ceteris paribus* condition does not hold and the postmodernist argument suffers from a series of major problems and limitations: important facts are ignored, contradictions are downplayed, trends are exaggerated, and some of the 'evidence' is dubious if not wrong. I shall first look critically at each of the three areas of philosophy, economics, and culture and politics before then drawing on mobilization theory and long waves in industrial relations to offer an alternative interpretation of the current period.[4]

Philosophy

There is a striking division between postmodern sociologists and postmodern philosophers. Whilst some of the latter have inveighed against meta-narratives and grand theorizing, their sociological colleagues have been busy constructing grand theory in a manner that makes Marx look like an esoteric specialist. Crook and his colleagues (1992) have used postmodernism as an overarching category to capture change in almost every sphere of society, whilst Lash and Urry (1987) used Offe's (1985) term, 'disorganized capitalism' to label the many social, economic and political changes currently under way. If meta-narrative is so objectionable, then the categories of 'disorganized capitalism', and perhaps even postmodernism, should also be done away with. On the other hand, if these categories are acceptable ways of analysing a particular trajectory of societal evolution, then one of the objections to Marxist theories of historical change must fall (Jameson 1989; McLennan 1992: 343; Thompson 1993: 197).

The relativist notion of social scientific theory as a linguistic game has been adequately dealt with by Sayer (1992: 72–79) and I will not repeat his arguments here. One point worth stressing, however, is that the absence of any *absolute* foundation for knowledge does not mean there are no foundations and that all theoretical and empirical statements are equally valid.[5] Sayer lays emphasis on the notion of 'practical adequacy' in adjudicating between theories. In other words, to what extent do different theories help us intervene in the social world to bring about change?

Economics

The problem with postmodernist claims about the economy does not lie in their veracity as such, since much of what they describe is true: labour processes are being reorganized, workers and equipment are more flexible and average plant size is smaller than in the recent past. The problems turn on whether they have offered a representative or a partial account of economic trends; whether they have properly estimated or exaggerated the trends; and whether they have drawn the appropriate inferences about relations between workers and employers. Let us take the references to multi-skilled workers and the revival of craft production. For Murray (1989) and Piore and Sabel (1984) it is the changes to the *manufacturing* workplace that command their attention and provide the empirical foundation for their optimistic vision of a more skilled workforce. But the millions of low paid and unskilled workers doing menial jobs in the service sector hardly figure in their future projections. The authors might object that they only intended to write about manufacturing and that it is illegitimate to complain about their omission of the service sector. But the fact is that the concepts of 'flexible specialization' and 'post-Fordism' have come nonetheless to inform general debates about the future of work, employment and industrial relations. The authors themselves can hardly complain about this development since despite their focus on manufacturing, they did set out with general aims – to produce 'strategies for relaunching growth in the advanced countries' (Piore and Sabel 1984: 6) and to analyse 'the dominant form of twentieth century production' (Murray 1989: 38).

If we look more closely at some of the employment trends described by postmodernists we find that the expansion of women's employment and service sector employment are long-run trends dating back at least to the start of the century, whilst the growth of self-employment, contracting-out and temporary working are all more recent phenomena. The latter *might* prove to be long-run trends, then again they might not, but neither Crook *et al.* (1992) nor Lash and Urry (1987) offer any grounds for believing they will be the former not the latter. In other words the postmodernists have too readily lumped together a number of trends in employment that certainly differ in longevity and quite possibly therefore in causation. They have also assumed, without clear justification, that these (possibly heterogeneous) trends will continue into the future and are unlikely to decelerate or reverse.

If we turn now to industrial relations it will become clear that the postmodernist case for a sustained diminution of industrial conflict is less than convincing. Their first argument was that the average skill level of work is increasing and that this upgrading of the content of work erodes the basis for industrial conflict. There is certainly a considerable volume of recent national survey data which shows that the majority of British employees are likely to report that their own work is more skilled now than it was five or ten years ago. The 1986–1987 Social Change and Economic Life Initiative study of six local labour markets found 52 per cent of employees reported their jobs were more skilled than in the past, whilst the 1992 Employment in Britain survey reported a figure of 63 per cent (Gallie 1994; Gallie and White 1993: 22). These figures change very little when you control for promotion or job mobility so they probably do reflect changes in job content. Moreover the *stock* of skilled jobs, defined as those requiring some entry qualification, appears to be increasing and now comprises about 70 per cent of all jobs compared with 60 per cent in 1986 (Gallie and White 1993: 21). However the 'skilled content' of new manufacturing jobs or service sector employment can easily be exaggerated. Work in Japanese manufacturing transplants for instance is better noted for its intensity of work and its tight specification of work methods and standards than for its enrichment (Berggren 1993; Fucini and Fucini 1990: Chapter 9; Garrahan and Stewart 1992; Graham 1995: Chapter 4). The fastest growing segment of the labour force since 1983 has been part-time women workers, many of whom are still concentrated in low paying, relatively unskilled service sector employment (Nolan and Walsh 1995: 57). Overall then it is more accurate to refer to a polarization of skill levels in the labour market rather than a simple upgrading (Gallie 1994; Noon and Blyton 1997: 99–116).

In any case the proposed connection between high level skill and lowered conflict is open to serious doubt. Occupational analysis of British strike activity since 1968 has shown a remarkable expansion of industrial conflict from manual industrial workers to white collar workers in the private and especially the public sectors (Durcan et al. 1983). Recent evidence suggests this shift in strike pattern has endured and in the late 1980s and early 1990s the public sector (both white collar and manual) accounted for the majority of strikes and days lost through strikes in Britain (Dickerson and Stewart 1993: 274; Edwards 1995c: 442). Nor can we derive the prediction of lowered conflict from the spread of job security and worker participation. If anything the trend discerned by postmodernists themselves is towards *less* security of employment, except for small groups of core workers (Crook et al. 1992: 176; Lash and Urry 1987: 282–283).[6] Evidence of significant worker participation in decision-making, at least in Britain, is mixed: on the one hand a national survey in 1992 found that 44 per cent of employees said they had a lot of influence over their jobs. On the other hand this figure dropped to 30 per cent when employees were asked about changes to their jobs (Gallie and White 1993: 37, 40), and there is evidence that more employers are closing down potential channels of employee influence, such as collective bargaining, through derecognition (Claydon 1996; Millward 1994: 33; Smith and Morton 1993).

If postmodernist assessments of production change and industrial relations are open to doubt, what of the idea that people's lives are now more influenced by consumption than by production? This somewhat ill-defined notion is akin to the older sociological concept of work (or leisure) as a 'central life interest' and in the light of that earlier debate and of recent evidence, there are two points to make. First, the categories of production and consumption are intimately linked by the employee's wage or salary. The most consumption-oriented employee is necessarily concerned with his/her level of earnings, even if nothing else at the workplace touches them, a finding reported almost thirty years ago by Goldthorpe and his colleagues (1968) in their study of the consumption-oriented affluent worker. But other issues *will* affect them, whether it is organizational change, lack of participation or job insecurity, to mention just three. Second, if we try to measure the significance of production (or work) there are two principal indices that are readily available. One is commitment to employment, where recent British survey evidence suggests that far from declining, as some postmodernists might have expected, it has actually risen. Asked whether they would continue in employment if there were no financial necessity to do so, 68 per cent of men and 67 per cent of women said yes in 1992, significantly greater than the figures fifteen years earlier (60 per cent and 61 per cent respectively) (Gallie and White 1993: 18). If we consider hours of work as a measure of commitment, then the much vaunted historical decline in the basic working week, often now just 35–37 hours for full-time workers, still means a five-day working week with just two days off.

Culture and politics

What of the argument about the declining significance of social class in the formation of people's identities and in shaping contemporary politics? In order to underline the novelty of postmodernism, Hall (1992) contrasted the 'fragmented subject' of the postmodernist era with the 'unified' class subject of the past. This is a curious procedure because there is a substantial literature, from Marx and Engels up to the present day, which has explored the lack of (predicted) class consciousness amongst the working class. Discussion has taken in racism, sexism, nationalism and religion; the role of dominant ideologies; the practices of labour movement leaders; the strategies of employers and the state; and the ways in which the operation of a market economy induces a 'false consciousness' amongst its participants, obscuring the operation of capitalist power (see Kelly 1988: 76–78, 128–146). The longevity, scope and vitality of these debates suggests that the idea of a 'unified class subject' may have been an aspiration amongst Marxists but (unlike Hall) they rarely confused aspiration with reality. In the literature on trade unionism, for instance, one of the most frequent complaints by writers and activists, from the Webbs (1920) onwards, has been the lack of interest in branch affairs by the rank-and-file membership and the chronically low level of attendance at union meetings.

It would be more accurate to say that for much of the twentieth century a working-class identity was widely subscribed to by many people (and still is) but this was for the most part a rather diffuse and passive identification which had few direct implications for people's behaviour at the workplace or in the political sphere. Class identity could be 'switched on' by activists from time to time but mobilization of workers on the basis of such an identity was never easy even in the most highly organized workplaces, as Beynon's (1984) study of Ford Halewood showed so clearly. It may be true, as Phelps Brown (1990) suggested, that class identification at the workplace was reinforced by external circumstances such as occupational communities and class-segregation of housing areas. But unionism and collective action became increasingly common amongst residentially-dispersed white-collar workers, so these external factors appear neither necessary nor sufficient for the appearance of 'class subjects'.

It is true that the recent decline of trade union membership correlates with many recent industrial and employment changes lumped together under the rubrics of post-Fordism and postmodernism. But that is about as far as postmodernist writers ever get, and there is certainly no attempt in the literature to discover whether the degree of membership loss correlates with the degree of postmodernization. More to the point is the fact that union membership losses have occurred during the long downswings of capitalism in almost all those countries for which we have data, as the previous chapter showed. It may be that the causes of the recent decline are different from those in the past, and although some postmodernists have implied this is the case, the reasoning is neither clear nor explicit.

Hall's caricature of the 'unified' Fordist worker does however have a serious purpose, and that is to heighten our sense of difference between the present and the past, so as to reinforce the notion of a sea change in society, a shift to postmodernism. As always with postmodernist arguments there is a grain of truth in Hall's depiction of the 'postmodern subject'. There does exist today a greater range of 'identities', measured by the evidence of the number and variety of interest groups seeking to legitimate and promote their particular claims, such as lesbian, gay, black and disabled groups, as well as the 'new' social movements: the women's movement, and peace and environment campaigners. If this were all that Hall was saying it would be an uncontentious empirical observation, but the real force of his argument is that these 'new' identities and movements somehow compete with and weaken class identity and class movements, and that as a result the latter are now more 'fragmented'.

There are interesting questions here about the inter-relations of different types of social movements and identities but Hall's bipolar categories of old vs new social movements and unified vs fragmented identities hinder rather than help our understanding. Melucci (1988) for instance has argued persuasively that the category of 'new social movements' (NSMs) is incoherent. Of the three movements conventionally and most frequently placed under the NSM umbrella, the peace movement dates back to the early part of the century, the women's movement has displayed a pronounced cyclical pattern for almost a century, whilst the environmental, or green, movement is the only one of the three that can genuinely claim to be new. Whilst the most recent renaissance of the women's movement in Britain coincided with the resurgence of the labour movement in the strike wave of 1968–1974 (Coote and Campbell 1982), the other two flourished somewhat later. The peace movement in Britain built strong links with the trade unions, securing affiliations from thirty-four unions by 1993, but the environmental groups had far fewer union connections.[7] The environmental and peace movements displayed some of the characteristics of NSMs listed by Crook *et al.* (1992) such as a preference for direct action but the women's movement by contrast displayed a wide range of organizational forms and modes of action, both conventional and unconventional. Some of the features of some NSMs, e.g. loose organization and direct democracy, are probably life-cycle effects common to all new organizations including trade unions (see the Webbs 1920; and Held 1992: 37; Scott 1992: 150–154; Tarrow 1991). Other features, such as reliance on direct (as opposed to constitutional) action are common to old *and* 'new' social movements during what Tarrow (1994: Chapter 9) called 'cycles of protest'. Factory occupations and sit-ins for instance became popular forms of union protest in Britain during the strike wave of 1968–1974 (Klandermans and Tarrow 1988; Tarrow 1994).

On the topic of class and non-class identities let us take the recent proliferation of sexual identities through the lesbian and gay movements as a case in point. Some sections of these movements are primarily concerned with lifestyle issues that are far removed from, if not independent of, unions and political parties. Some are antithetical to or highly critical of unions but there are also gay and lesbian employees who have defined these components of their identity as compatible with class identity. As a result they have joined unions and sought to create gay and lesbian sections within them (LRD 1991). For them, the politics of sexuality enriches rather than divides the trade union movement and their class identity. At the height of the 1984–1985 British miners' strike, for instance, there were ten local branches of a national organization called Lesbians Against Pit Closures. As three of its members wrote,

> who can think of a more unlikely alliance? But of course the strike was about the coal which fuelled the lights we sat under, it was about jobs, not just the miners', it was about a fight back against the government no less.
>
> (Vittorini *et al.* 1986: 142–143)

There is no sign here of any *fragmentation* of identity but of a *fusion* of identities – as consumer, worker and lesbian – focused on the class struggle between the miners and the state. The whole issue of the inter-relations between different facets of identity and different social movements is far more complex than suggested by Hall's simple nostrums about 'unified' and 'fragmented' subjects, or old and new movements. Whether the mislabelled 'new' movements and identities will strengthen or reinforce the older movement of trade unionism is an open question, depending in part on the ideological messages and mobilizing tactics of union leaders (Touraine *et al.* 1987: 286–290).

Finally, it is worth commenting in more global terms on the supposed decline of class politics in the postmodernist age. Labour unions across the advanced capitalist world, but particularly in the UK and the USA, have been the subject of a concerted employer and state offensive which can quite properly be described as class war. Its main features and forms have been referred to in previous chapters but they include the avoidance of unions, the derecognition of unions, the marginalization of workplace representatives, the repudiation of collective agreements, cutbacks in wages, intensification of work, large-scale redundancies and a general reassertion of employer prerogatives in the workplace. Yet you can read some of the standard postmodernist sociology and be entirely unaware of this many-faceted class struggle. Perhaps the crude and forceful reassertion of class power at the point of production sounds too much like the class politics from an era that is supposed to be disappearing before our eyes?

Is the current period of change unique?

Consider the following account of the interwar Depression in Britain. In the realm of political philosophy the 'meta-narrative' of Marxism was subject to vigorous attack from right-wing philosophers, and the principal Marxist organization at the time – the Communist Party – subjected to bans and proscriptions within the labour movement. (Across the rest of Europe the fate of communist parties was more drastic and often violent, as in Germany and Austria.) In the economy, there was a steep decline in the output and employment of the old industries, such as clothing, cotton, steel and coal mining. New industries emerged, symbolized by the opening of Ford's Dagenham car plant in 1929 and by the expansion of the engineering industry in London and the West Midlands. Large numbers of people left the depressed areas of Scotland, Wales and the North of England and travelled to the Midlands and the South in search of work. The suburbs of older towns expanded significantly as the greatest house building boom in British history got under way (Bourke 1994: 15, 84). Cultural change was enormous: radio, unknown before the First World War, was ubiquitous by the eve of the Second. Many new cinemas opened up in the 1930s following the first 'talking' movie in 1927, and mass circulation newspapers, precursors of the modern tabloids, first made an appearance. The nature of class identity was the subject of intense debate amongst intellectuals following a series of major political events: the debacle of Labour's election defeat in 1931 (and again in 1935), the 1928 enfranchisement of women under the age of 30, the rise of German nationalism and the weakness of the left in Britain despite mass unemployment and the threat of fascism. By 1933 the trade union movement had lost almost half of its 1920 membership and density had slumped from 45.2 per cent to 22.6 per cent over the same period. The General Strike of 1926 had been defeated, anti-union legislation then enacted and in 1928 the total number of strikes reached an all time low of just 302.

There is an uncanny resemblance between the nature and scale of the changes that took place in the interwar period and those depicted by the postmodernists. Naturally enough there are differences but the similarities seem to me sufficiently striking to suggest that the current period may not after all be unique. It may, as the previous chapter suggested, be better understood as a period of economic restructuring and state and employer counter-mobilization of the type which has occurred at regular intervals throughout the history of capitalism. The most compelling account of the political economy of the current era is that of the Marxist geographer David Harvey (1989) whose argument, reduced from its vast complexity to bare essentials, is as follows.[8] From 1973 the advanced capitalist economies slid into an economic crisis from which they have been struggling ever since to extricate themselves. The earliest signs of this crisis were growing rigidities in technology, labour markets and the labour process, coupled with a shift in the balance of power towards organized labour. These rigidities increasingly hindered the twin pillars of capitalism, the extraction of surplus value in the production process (hence the falling rate of profit) and the realization of surplus through high levels of demand. There are familiar and well-documented state and employer policies for dealing with the first problem, and Harvey mentions mass unemployment, the weakening of trade unions, wage cuts, changes in technology and in working practices and the reorganization of the workforce around a skilled core and a less skilled (often unskilled) periphery. Whilst some firms in some sectors and countries have switched over to 'flexible specialization', others have pursued more flexible forms of mass production to achieve economies of scale *and* scope (cf Sorge and Streeck 1988 on 'diversified quality production').

The problem of realization of surplus value has also been addressed in a variety of ways, but perhaps most significantly by a tremendous reduction in the circulation time of commodities. Physical goods are repeatedly redesigned and updated and advertising encourages the replacement of old (unfashionable) items with more up-to-date models, a process facilitated by the easy availability of credit and the extended opening hours of shops. The service industries, particularly leisure and tourism, offer an ever-expanding range of experiences and locations, the latter made possible by long-haul jets and the economies of Third World countries eager to receive an influx of First World tourists. The normal, steady changes in patterns of production and consumption are greatly speeded up during Kondratieff downswings of the present type and in a context of economic insecurity (because of mass unemployment) and political uncertainty (because of the defeats suffered by organized labour), these rapid changes give rise to the so-called 'postmodernist' moods of disillusion and to the sense of pervasive and ceaseless change which postmodernists have sought to articulate.

Harvey's account differs from those offered by non-Marxist postmodernists in six main ways. First, his argument is *historical* because he sees periods of economic restructuring as *recurring* features of the capitalist mode of production. The period from the 1970s to the present therefore has parallels with similar developments in the 1840s and with events during the early years of this century (1989: 306–307). Second, the argument is grounded in an analysis of the conflicting interests of labour and capital and is thus able to avoid some of the more naive ideas about labour–management cooperation that lurk in the postmodernist literature. Third, whilst assuming the future vitality of the labour movement, it leaves open the issue of how the social movements of recent times will relate to the labour movement. Fourth, it constructs an account of the present period that starts from the twin imperatives of enhancing and realizing surplus value and it thus rejects the fashionable lack of interest in production and the equally fashionable penchant for consumption and culture. Fifth, unlike so many postmodernist arguments, it uses and looks at evidence and does so in the light of theory, rather than drowning the reader in a sea of selected facts and figures designed to show that everything is in flux. Last, it accounts for the moods and feelings of insecurity and change which postmodernist intellectuals have articulated into an entire theory of transition to a new era.

Conclusions

The postmodernist account of the current decline of the labour movement has focused mainly on historical changes in worker definitions of their interests and on the rise of a more cooperative industrial relations. Despite the grand sweep of postmodernist theory and the presentation of large quantities of empirical evidence the end result is unconvincing. What we have been offered is an untenable philosophical relativism; an incoherent attack on meta-narratives; a view of the decline of mass production that does not accord with the evidence; ideas about consumption and production that lose sight of the intimate links between the two; a vision of the manufacturing workplace of the future that sounds more like a unitarist fantasy than a well-grounded depiction and which is practically silent on the new found power of the employer; a portrayal of modern and postmodern identities that owes more to caricature and assertion than to evidence; claims about the decline of the labour movement that take no account of historical precedents; and assertions about 'new social movements' and the end of class politics based on superficial and incoherent categories and on sloppy use of evidence. There are so many holes in the postmodernist case that there is a genuine puzzle as to why it was ever taken so seriously. Its prognosis for the labour movement is not only bleak (that at least would be a legitimate point of view), but it is ill-informed in the extreme.

8

CONCLUSIONS

Mobilization theory

In this study I have brought the insights of mobilization theory to bear on what I have taken to be the central problems in the field of industrial relations. Whether we are interested in the alleged decline of worker collectivism, the prospects for the labour movement, the exercise of power at the workplace or the mobilization of workers for collective action, the theory offers a conceptual framework for thinking about these issues and for generating testable propositions. In broad terms, mobilization theory has three major advantages over rival approaches. First, it helps us construct a very different intellectual agenda for the field of industrial relations. Instead of starting from the employers' needs for cooperation and performance or from the general problem of 'getting work done', it begins with the category of *injustice*. Workers in capitalist societies find themselves in relations of exploitation and domination in which many of their most significant interests conflict with those of the employer. The individual's need to be in paid employment and hence for economies to operate at full employment conflicts with the capitalist requirements for periodic job-destructive reorganization and for a labour surplus. Hence the fact that even the British capitalist economy, one of the wealthiest in the world, has achieved full employment in only thirteen of the eighty-five peace-time years in the twentieth century. From the vantage point of mobilization theory it is the perception of, and response to, injustice that should form the core intellectual agenda for industrial relations.

Second, the achievement of the theory as developed and expounded in this book is to provide a framework for helping us think rigorously and analytically about the many particular questions entailed by that agenda. The framework does not rely on broad and ill-defined concepts of 'collectivism' and 'individualism' but distinguishes between collective interest definition, collective organization, mobilization, opportunities for, and barriers to, action and the different forms of collective action. Mobilization theory treats as problematic what previous industrial relations research often took for granted, namely the awareness by workers of a set of common interests opposed to those of the employer. The theory locates the emergence of this consciousness in employer violations of laws, conventions or 'consensual social values' that are seen as unjust. Such awareness may arise from direct experience or may be vicarious, passed on within social and family networks as appropriate attitudes towards employers. Whilst the roots of collective interest definition lie in perceived injustice, it is crucial that workers *attribute* their problems to an agency which can be held responsible either for causing their problem or for ameliorating it (or both). Normally this agency would be the employer, although it might also be the state. Such attributions of blame both derive from and reinforce a sense of distinct group *identity*, founded on interests that are common to the group but opposed to those of the employer and often described in everyday terms as a sense of 'them and us'. For mobilization theorists it is this core set of concepts – injustice, attribution and identity – which provides the means for understanding the emergence (or not) of collective interest definition and for mapping changes over time.

Collective interest definition in turn provides the basis for collective organization and for mobilization. The transformation of a set of individuals into a collective actor is normally the work of a small but critical mass of activists whose role in industrial relations has been seriously understated. A key part of such work involves promoting a sense of grievance amongst workers by persuading them that what they have hitherto considered 'normal' or 'acceptable' is in fact unjust. Activists are also required to sustain or create a high degree of group cohesion, to urge the appropriateness of one or more forms of collective action and to legitimate such action in the face of counter-mobilization by the employer. The arguments and discussions that take place amongst activists, fellow workers and employers in what McAdam calls the 'micromobilization context' involve debates about the most appropriate ways of 'framing' issues and problems. In other words they are debates about the most appropriate linguistic categories to use in describing and accounting for employers' actions or inactions, and study of the day-to-day language, or discourses of industrial relations is therefore of major significance. Whether such research necessarily requires the collection of qualitative data through case studies is an interesting question. In theory one could measure variables such as social identity through the use of standardized questionnaires administered to large samples, as indeed is the common practice in mainstream social psychology. But some of the most illuminating studies of collective interest definition and mobilization have consisted of case studies relying either exclusively on qualitative data, e.g. Fantasia (1988) or on a combination of quantitative and qualitative data, e.g. Kelly and Breinlinger's (1996) study of women's collective action. In its emphasis on group identity and collective definitions of interest, mobilization theory contrasts with one of the most widely discussed approaches to collective action, namely the work of Olson. His *Logic of Collective Action* is in the tradition of economic theorizing centred on the decision-making of rational individuals seeking to maximize personal gains whilst minimizing costs. But a detailed critique of Olson's theory demonstrated both the narrowness and implausibility of the underlying assumptions and its inability to account satisfactorily for any of the industrial relations issues addressed in *The*

Logic of Collective Action: the emergence of trade unions, their survival and growth and the organization of collective action.

Mobilization theory does not simply offer a way of analysing workplace relations over the short run, but can be extended to generate an historical account of long waves in industrial relations. The turning points between Kondratieff long waves in the economy appear to have coincided with historic high water marks of worker mobilization, measured in particular by strike rates and by surges in union membership: hence the great world strike waves of the 1870s, 1910–1920 and 1968–1974 and the minor waves of the early 1890s and the late 1930s to late 1940s. The major strike waves have invariably occurred towards the tail end of long economic upswings because of a conjuncture of circumstances. Employers faced with declining profit rates have sought to intensify the labour process and/or to curb the growth of wages, often in conjunction with or through the medium of the state. These measures however impact on a workforce that has become accustomed to steady or at least frequent rises in living standards during the years of economic upswing, thereby fuelling a sense of injustice. The presence of militant activists willing to organize collective action in a labour market where some groups of workers have become relatively powerful adds the final ingredient to the potent mixture that results in periodic eruptions of acute class struggle. During the ensuing downswings employers and the state typically embark on a wide ranging series of counter-mobilizations against organized labour to restore both their profitability and their control of the labour process. Such measures are likely to target all of the dimensions of collectivism: definition of interests, organization, mobilization, the costs and benefits of action and the various forms of action.

Third, mobilization theory is particularly valuable in helping us think about the central problems in industrial relations. How do workers come to develop a sense of collective interest which pits them against their employer and requires the creation of collective organization? The literature on this issue has largely focused on why workers join unions rather than examining the formation of interests and even then has concentrated on a rather narrow set of variables, notably job dissatisfaction and union instrumentality. By contrast, mobilization theory focuses our attention on processes that are largely absent from this literature: how do workers come to define dissatisfaction as injustice? How do they come to acquire a shared identity with their fellow employees that divides them from their employer? How do they acquire the conviction that the employer is to blame for their problems? The debates about an alleged decline of worker collectivism have been unsatisfactory because they have not paid sufficient attention to the ways in which workers come to define their interests in collective terms. But they have also displayed a lack of conceptual sophistication that mobilization theory helps overcome by virtue of its distinctions between interest, organization, mobilization, opportunity and forms of action. Whilst it is clear that the period since 1979 has witnessed a decline in the incidence of collective action and organization amongst workers (more so in the private sectors of the capitalist economies than the public), it is not clear that there has been a corresponding decline in collective interest definition.

On the subject of power, the theory shifts our focus in two very different directions. On the one hand it points to the significance of legitimacy in the maintenance of employer rule and reinforces the value of investigating the arguments and counter-arguments amongst workers and managers about day-to-day workplace issues that contribute to the reproduction or erosion of employer authority. This line of research is not original since it can be found in some of the more sophisticated workplace case studies in the past such as Armstrong *et al.* (1981), as well as in more recent case study research such as Darlington (1994) and Scott (1994). Nonetheless, this type of investigation would be even more illuminating if it were cast within a well-developed theoretical framework. Mobilization theory also alerts us to a different facet of employer power, namely the coercive practices which include various forms of repression, victimization and blacklisting. The malign face of employer power has received remarkably little attention in recent years despite the presence of favourable conditions for its emergence (in Britain at least) such as mass unemployment, right-wing government and a battery of anti-union laws. Quite why researchers should have proved so eager to write about 'human resource management' rather than employer authoritarianism is an interesting question in its own right. Within the framework of mobilization theory we can think about many of the employer practices of the 1980s and 1990s as forms of counter-mobilization against organized labour. The idea that workers have collective interests separate from and opposed to those of the employer has been sharply criticized within several variants of HRM. The employee is constructed in some of this literature as the employer's most valued asset whose talents and motivation can be harnessed to corporate goals that will benefit both parties to the employment relationship. In this world view, ideas of conflicting interests are rhetorically castigated as old-fashioned and irrelevant throwbacks to the past. Collective organization has come under attack through employer decisions to reduce the numbers of, and facilities for, union stewards and in the extreme case to derecognize unions for collective bargaining. Anti-union laws have hindered the mobilization of workers for collective action as well as the effectiveness of any action that does get organized. The concept of counter-mobilization actually conveys the antagonistic relationship of employers towards collective organization and action amongst their own labour forces and is therefore a valuable corrective to the ideologically-loaded and obfuscating category of HRM. In similar vein the capitalist state is understood primarily, though by no means exclusively, as a class agency whose chief function is to maintain and reproduce the conditions for capital accumulation. In so doing the state acts as a key agent of counter-mobilization against organized labour, particularly through its repressive organs such as the police, the army and the intelligence services. This critical perspective is a far cry from the anodyne formulations of the state as legislator, as employer and as economic manager.

Finally, by locating contemporary industrial relations developments in historical perspective the theory provides a valuable antidote to the ahistorical pessimism which informs some of the arguments in support of 'social partnership' and 'labour–management cooperation for mutual gain'. Some of these policy prescriptions in the industrial relations literature flow from inadequately theorized assumptions about the attitudes and values of contemporary workers and about the current state of labour movements in the advanced capitalist world. A number of sociologists have presented reasonably coherent accounts of the decline of the 'workers' movement' as an expression of the transition to a postmodern society and economy. But the panoramic sweep of such theorizing is vitiated by fundamental conceptual and empirical flaws. Postmodernist writers have frequently set out projections of a post-Fordist future centred around skilled and rewarding work performed within relatively harmonious employment relations by workers with only a weak sense of traditional collectivism. Such scenarios are contrasted with the Fordist past where the key sectors of industry comprised large concentrations of unionized, class-conscious workers alienated from their work and locked in adversarial patterns of industrial relations with their employers. Both accounts are based on flimsy and partial evidence, sloppy conceptualization (of terms such as collectivism) and a limited appreciation of the many similarities between contemporary events and previous periods of capitalist restructuring. Mobilization theory, by contrast, suggests that periods of employer and state counter-mobilization, such as the present downswing, are a normal and familiar feature of capitalist economies. During such periods both the organization and mobilization of workers are eroded and the ideologies of the labour movement are subjected to assault from a variety of sources. At the same time the different forms of economic restructuring help to create the basis for a new period of worker mobilization because of their adverse impact on workers' sense of justice. The composition of the workforce emerging out of the long downswing is very different from the one that entered it: there are far more women and part-timers and far fewer industrial workers. The grievances they raise may well differ from those which dominated industrial relations in the long postwar boom. But on all past experience and in the light of mobilization theory, we would predict that the long period of employer and state counter-mobilization and of labour weakness will not last. As the next long economic upswing gathers momentum then so too should the organization and mobilization of workers across the capitalist world.

The field of industrial relations

Industrial relations was traditionally defined as the study of rules and rule-making (or job regulation to use Flanders' term). In theory this definition encompassed a variety of rule-making processes but in practice it was displaced by a narrower, operating definition of the field which centred around collective bargaining and trade unions. Once these institutions began to decline across parts of the advanced capitalist world it was only a matter of time before the focus on bargaining and trade unionism was called into question. The most radical challenge to the field emerged from the study of what became known as human resource management, although it can also be found amongst those who wanted to reorient academic industrial relations towards a focus on labour–management cooperation (e.g. Beaumont 1995 in the UK; Kaufman 1993 and Kochan and Osterman 1994 in the USA). In an era of 'global competition' it has become fashionable to argue that firms can only survive through labour–management cooperation whose study should thus comprise a major part of the industrial relations research agenda. Far from saving the field of industrial relations by adapting it to contemporary 'realities', this strategy will succeed only in liquidating industrial relations as a distinct area of research by subsuming it into the study of management (Hyman 1989a). The emerging intellectual problems in the field – issues such as how to improve work motivation, labour utilization and employee commitment – will increasingly come to reflect the economic and political priorities of employers and the state. The subordination of intellectual work to particular class interests is also apparent from the way in which the employers' term, human resource management, has entered the discourse of industrial relations as if it were a bona fide theoretical construct rather than an ideologically loaded category (such criticisms have been made by a number of researchers: see the contributions in Blyton and Turnbull 1992b and Legge 1989, 1995a, b).

A second response to the current plight of industrial relations has been to define the field in terms of *processes* rather than institutions. For Edwards, industrial relations is the study of 'the ways in which the employment relationship is regulated' (1995c: 5). Labour power hired by the employer has to be turned into labour in a process of negotiation whose output is some degree of social order based on rules. Collective bargaining is seen as simply one method, not *the* method, of regulation amongst many and the analysis of the employment relationship can therefore embrace a variety of institutions, settings and practices. Because such analysis (sometimes called a 'labour regulation approach': Edwards *et al.* 1994) is not tied to any particular set of institutions, then the decline of unions and collective bargaining and the rise of 'human resource management' do not pose any insuperable intellectual problems (see also Adams 1993 and Milner 1995a for related views). 'Negotiation' in some form can therefore be discerned and explored even in the most despotic locations. By contrast, a traditional focus on bargaining institutions might well overlook the subtle and oblique challenges to authority and the real but subterranean haggling that occurs even in such inhospitable settings.

Despite its valuable emphasis on social processes the 'labour regulation' approach suffers from two drawbacks. First, in conditions of employer ascendancy and world recession there is a real danger that a focus on the negotiation of order to 'get work done' cedes intellectual priority to the employer's agenda of labour utilization and control. It is true that sociological workplace studies have often explored both the negotiation of order *and* the forms of conflict between workers and managers, so one could argue that there is no necessary incompatibility between these two research foci. But it is also true that the principal focus of one's research *does* make a difference: to the types of questions that are asked, to the theoretical frameworks that are employed and to the interests that are served by the research findings. To define the heart of industrial relations research as injustice and the ways in which workers define and respond to it is therefore a very different intellectual agenda from a focus on 'how work gets done'.

The second difficulty derives from the pervasive use of the term 'negotiation' to cover everything from well-organized strikes through to devices such as 'irony, humour and flirting' (Haiven *et al.* 1994: 279). One consequence is that important differences between settings can all too easily be obscured. Chung's (1994) account of 'negotiation' in a Singaporean electronics plant for instance downplayed the *repressive* context of labour relations, including the past imprisonment of militant union leaders and the legal suppression of most forms of collective action (Leggett 1993: 224–226). Likewise, in postwar Italy there was undoubtedly 'negotiation' in many engineering plants but we can easily overstate its significance if we lose sight of the wide-ranging repression directed against communist militants throughout that period (Franzosi 1995).

The field of industrial relations will not be preserved as a valuable area of study unless it takes its distance from the intellectual agenda of dominant class interests and becomes far more self-consciously theoretical. Mobilization theory satisfies both of these requirements. It is firmly anchored in Marxist accounts of the employment relationship as an unequal and exploitative exchange and is thus well-protected against the zeitgeist of 'human resource management' and labour–management cooperation. At the same time it provides a framework of well-developed concepts that has significantly increased our understanding of a wide range of social movements and whose application to industrial relations could prove invaluable.

NOTES

2 THE FIELD OF INDUSTRIAL RELATIONS

1 The ten major textbooks of British Industrial Relations are: Beaumont (1990), Blyton and Turnbull (1994), Edwards (1995a, successor to Bain 1983), Farnham and Pimlott (1995), Gospel and Palmer (1993), Hyman (1975, 1989c), Jackson (1991), Kessler and Bayliss (1995), Rollinson (1993) and Salamon (1992). In addition there are a number of introductory books, viz. Burchill (1997), Goodman (1984) and Keenoy (1985), as well as the more applied text by Towers (1992).

2 Brown and Wright (1994) also wrote a valuable defence of the 1970s case study research but their list omitted Lane and Roberts, Nichols and Armstrong, Nichols and Beynon and Pollert. It should also be noted that case studies were not the exclusive preserve of sociologists as some very influential cases were written up by Brown (1973) in his study of shop steward principles and piecework bargaining, and by Boraston, Clegg and Rimmer (1975) in their study of full-time union officers and workplace organization. It was arguably the worldwide upsurge of strikes from 1968 and the associated revival of Marxism as an intellectual and political force that renewed academic interest in the politics of workplace trade unionism and its anti-capitalist potential.

3 They also serve to refute Cappelli's claim that, 'The weakness of case studies is that they do not provide adequate *tests* of theories because sample sizes are small (e.g. a single case) and the results therefore lack external validity' (1985: 92). Propositions about social influence, mobilization or systems of argument can be, and have been, tested in many single cases as the burgeoning literature on social movements amply demonstrates (see Morris and Mueller 1992). If particular cases have failed to produce generalizable results, this is a failure of research design not an inherent limitation of the case study method.

4 Edwards prefers to use the term 'structured antagonism' rather than interest, his main objections to the latter being as follows (Edwards 1986: 27–28, 55, 77; 1990: 139–140; Edwards and Scullion 1982: 7–8). Insofar as it is based on Marxism it implies that workers have an overriding interest in the overthrow of capitalism, an idea which overlooks the many specific and contradictory interests workers actually possess. On the other hand, if the idea of real interests is not anchored in the Marxist concept of capitalist exploitation then there is no obvious justification for using the term at all. Finally, the concept can wrongly imply that interests are unproblematically translated into conflictual behaviours and that conflict is therefore an enduring and pervasive feature of industrial relations. Edwards therefore prefers to talk about a relationship of 'structured antagonism' based on capitalist exploitation and domination of labour. Quite *which* Marxists have ever advocated these positions is unclear since Edwards does not mention anyone by name. Indeed, contrary to his own claims, Marxists have no

difficulty in recognizing that workers' interests are contradictory (cf the debates on sectionalism: see Kelly 1988: Chapter 6) and that the link between conflicts of interest and conflict behaviours is complex, even though the nature of these links is still not well understood. Indeed, in his later essay Edwards seems to accept the force of such points and simply argues that 'Potential confusions will be reduced' if the concept of interests is jettisoned (1990: 140). Stripped of its curious and resolute ambition to be non-Marxist, Edwards' work is extremely valuable.

5 There was a debate in the 1970s about the balance of power between the social classes as part of the intellectual struggle between industrial relations' pluralists and Marxists. Disagreement turned *inter alia* on the question as to whether pluralists assumed there was a balance of power between labour and capital (cf Clegg 1975, 1979; Fox 1973, 1974; Goldthorpe 1977; Hyman 1978). This was the claim advanced by Fox (1974) and Hyman (1978) who argued that pluralists were led to this erroneous conclusion because of their focus on a narrow range of contested issues at the workplace. A broader study of labour and capital would show that capitalists rarely needed to deploy their full repertoire of power resources – control of property, access to the state and ideological hegemony. Were they to do so, it would 'destroy[ing] at once the illusion of a power balance' (Fox 1974: 280). Critics of pluralism are right to argue that a focus on contested issues in the bargaining arena will overstate the power of workers vis-à-vis their employers, a point thoroughly documented by Edwards and Heery's (1989) study of coal mining. On the other hand there is a corresponding danger in focusing on the undoubtedly immense power resources of capitalists and stressing the great imbalance of power between labour and capital. For if there is indeed such a power disparity it is hard to understand why workers ever succeed in winning disputes with their employers.

Hyman's (1975) discussion of power, by contrast, is far more sophisticated though considerably briefer than that of his radical colleague, Alan Fox. He acknowledged and took seriously the dependency of employers on workers, as well as vice versa; showed that ideological power resources were available to both social classes; and conveyed a much sharper sense of a class struggle than did Fox whose account of power imbalances is at times almost Marcusian in its one-sidedness.

6 Union density is equally problematic, not least because its stability over the period 1945–1968 suggests the implausible result that there was no postwar rise in union power at all until after 1968, a position occasionally argued by Flanders (Flanders and Fox in Flanders 1970: 244; but see Flanders 1961: 19, 21; 1965: 106, 111–112; 1966: 134, all in Flanders 1970, for the more conventional view that with full employment, unions (or at least their shop stewards), *were* more powerful than in the past). Moreover, a union could be well-organized, with close to 100 per cent density and yet its members might be unwilling to take union action (the footwear industry would be a good example). Conversely a union may have only low or moderate density but its members may be highly willing to act, perhaps because they occupy a strategic position in a firm's labour process (e.g. warehouse staff and delivery drivers employed by supermarket chains).

7 It is also possible to take a more differentiated approach to union power and distinguish between national and local levels of union organizations. Martin (1992: 173–177) for instance argued that national union officials had experienced a much sharper decline in power than workplace organizations (though he noted that the fate of workplace union power was quite variable).

8 The material in this section is a short summary of parts of Kelly (1996).

9 The term 'institutionalism' has also been used in a misleading way as a synonym for research that is descriptive and insufficiently analytical. But an interest in institutions does not logically entail a proclivity for description, as Flanders' (1970) analyses of

collective bargaining demonstrated, and nor does descriptive research entail a focus on institutions: you can describe attitudes, behaviours or events, for example.

10 According to Edwards (1995b), however, the case study approach has not atrophied but evolved: the focus has shifted towards management and there is greater methodological sophistication in both the collection and interpretation of data. Semi-structured interviews are more common now, findings are contextualized and their generalizability more adequately discussed. I agree with these observations but I would still maintain that the most valuable feature of the 1970s cases was their social process orientation around the central issues of interest definition and mobilization. Since this was lost from their 1980s successors it is more accurate to use the critical term 'eclipse', rather than the neutral-sounding category 'evolution'.

11 In 1979 the CBI created its Pay Databank Survey and the following year saw the first Workplace Industrial Relations Survey (WIRS1) (Daniel and Millward 1983) as well as the Department of Employment's survey of women workers (Martin and Roberts 1984). In 1983 there was Batstone's (1984) survey of 133 large manufacturing companies and the first of the annual *British Social Attitudes* surveys (Jowell *et al.* 1984). The following year (1984) saw WIRS2 (Daniel 1987; Millward and Stevens 1986) as well as Paul Edwards' (1987) survey of factory managers and Batstone and Gourlay's (1986) survey of unions and new technology. The company level supplement to WIRS2 was conducted in 1985 and written up three years later by Marginson and his colleagues (1988). In 1990 there was the workplace survey carried out by Gregg and his colleagues (Gregg and Yates 1991; Gregg and Machin 1991) as well as WIRS3 (Millward *et al.* 1992; Millward 1994) and the first of a series of management surveys conducted by Cranfield (Brewster 1995). WIRS4 was conducted in 1997. The other major, regular survey is the Labour Force Survey which actually began in 1973.

12 The obvious exceptions to these strictures are, for different reasons, the surveys by Batstone (1984) and Edwards (1987). Batstone used his own data in conjunction with *Changing Contours* and WIRS1 to mount an extensive and critical assessment of the strengths and weaknesses of unitarist, pluralist and radical analyses of the Donovan reforms to collective bargaining. Edwards (1987) *inter alia* used some of his data to contribute to the debate on unions and productivity which took off following the publication in 1984 of Freeman and Medoff's *What Do Unions Do?*

13 Hendy's (1993) work is an exception to this stricture. He has located the anti-union laws as part of a drive by the British capitalist state to cut labour costs and restore profitability through the weakening of organized labour in a programme inspired by the right-wing neo-liberal Friedrich von Hayek.

14 In the same way that Dunlop's concept of an Industrial Relations System has left its imprint on the structure of textbooks, the 'pluralism debate' has established itself as the staple fare of most Introductory or Overview chapters dealing with the nature of the field (Burchill 1997: Chapter 1; Clegg 1979: Chapter 11; Farnham and Pimlott 1995: Chapter 1; Goodman 1984: Chapter 3; Hyman 1975: Chapter 1; Jackson 1991: Chapter 1; Gospel and Palmer 1993: Chapter 1; Salamon 1992: Chapter 2). But a careful reading of these texts quickly establishes an important point: once the abstract debates about conflict and cooperation have been rehearsed and the unitary, pluralist and radical/Marxist perspectives have been described, they are whisked off stage and rarely used to organize any subsequent discussions or generate ideas: Gospel and Palmer (1993) and Hyman (1975) are the exceptions. (Gospel and Palmer (1993) used the categories to describe management approaches to industrial relations whilst Hyman (1975) explicitly set out to defend Marxist theory against pluralism and to show up the limitations of the latter.) Batstone (1984, 1988a) is the only substantial attempt to use the ideas of unitarism, pluralism and radicalism as theoretical frameworks in his study of the outcomes of the 1960s and 1970s reforms to industrial

relations. Where the unitarist/pluralist/Marxist categories are used in industrial relations textbooks it is purely for the classification of writers or more commonly policy measures, such as the Conservative anti-union laws (unitarist) or different varieties of human resource management (unitarist and pluralist). But it takes little ingenuity to 'locate' legal or other policies under their appropriate theoretical (or perhaps we should say, ideological) headings, and the effortless ease of the classificatory exercise testifies to its intellectual emptiness.

15 Although Flanders used the distinctive term 'job regulation' it is clear from his acknowledgement of Dunlop's influence that he shared the latter's understanding of industrial relations as a process of rule-making (Flanders 1965: 86).

16 One reason for this dearth of theoretically-inspired research was identified by Poole (1984: 60) in his evaluation of Flanders' work:

> *Precisely formulated* models of trade union action and behaviour, however, seldom appeared in Flanders' theoretical writings. . . . What we have . . . is largely a set of exploratory dimensions which . . . have no special weights attached to designate their relative significance . . . and clearly constituting something of a 'check-list'.

In fact Flanders' unpublished writings on trade union growth, dating from the late 1950s, contain a fairly elaborate and well worked out theory (see Kelly forthcoming).

17 The Kochan *et al.* model is not as dissimilar from Dunlop's industrial relations systems as their text suggests. Dunlop was aware that industrial relations systems changed and that a satisfactory theory needed to account for such changes (Dunlop 1958: 16–17, 61, page references are to the 1993 edition). Hence his discussion of the impact of economic factors, changes in the organization of the actors and in the ideology underpinning the system (ibid.: Chapters 7 and 8), a discussion that Kochan *et al.* chose to ignore. What can be said is that the general tenor of *Industrial Relations Systems* conveyed a sense of stability in industrial relations, even if its formal theory acknowledged the possibility of change.

3 MOBILIZATION THEORY

1 Tilly actually used the term model rather than theory even though his work embodies the main components of theory discussed by Bain and Clegg (1974) viz. specification of dependent and independent variables, and the relationships between these variables; identification of the relevant mechanisms or processes; and the generation of testable hypotheses. I have therefore taken to describing his ideas as a theory.

2 Edwards' theory of collective action comprised three dimensions of variation in workers' approaches and organization: militant or acquiescent orientation to the employer, individual or collective orientation and the degree of collective organization (1986: 226). The latter two dimensions correspond to Tilly's categories of interests and organization. The first can be thought of in terms of worker views about the legitimacy of employer rule and is an important topic discussed more fully below.

3 Semi-collective refers to individual interests, such as a grievance about promotion, pursued through collective means, e.g. pressure on management from a local union organization.

4 In similar vein Edwards (1992: 367–368) has criticized Korpi and Shalev's political economy model of strikes for failing to address the issue of how workers are mobilized for action in the first place.

5 Tilly's approach to these issues begins with a problem. Should we conceptualize people's interests, as liberal theorists propose, on the assumption that individuals are the best judges of their own interests and therefore take their own views at face value? Or should we start, as many Marxists contend, with the view that interests are shaped by one's position in the social structure and that individuals may have a distorted picture of those interests (Balbus 1971; Lukes 1974)? Tilly argues, I think rightly, that this is a pseudo-choice. You can construct a theory of interests, derived from social position and a theory of the conditions under which people will realize those interests and then proceed to test it, thereby combining notions of objective and subjective interests.

6 Ferree and Miller (1985) proposed that collective action to resolve grievances will arise only when people make stable, external attributions, i.e. when they 'blame the system' rather than attributing blame to their lack of effort (internal, unstable), to chance (external, unstable) or to some fixed, personal characteristic (internal, stable) (cf also Klandermans 1988). However, as they themselves pointed out, 'blaming the system' is a broad category of attribution which may derive from a wide range of ideologies and include factors such as poor equipment, badly-trained colleagues, inadequate procedures, the general economic situation, etc. Ferree and Miller's 'blaming the system' is therefore only one instance of a much wider category of external attributions, many of which will have *no* implications for collective action. This is because some of these attributions refer to a *situation* rather than to an *agency* against whom collective action would be appropriate. This distinction informed some recent research into employee reactions to job insecurity (van Vuuren *et al.* 1991). The authors divided external attributions into those which were controllable (such as management decision-making) and those which were uncontrollable (such as the economic situation, automation and low product demand). They showed that employees' willingness to engage in collective action to deal with job insecurity was significantly and positively associated with the former but not the latter (van Vuuren *et al.* 1991: 94, 99). Armstrong *et al.* (1981: 187–194) suggested it may be sufficient for collective action that workers blame a particular manager for wrong-doing, but Cunnison found that such individual attributions could divide the workforce amongst itself as well as unite it against management (1966: 249).

7 The stronger the identification with your own group (the union, for instance) the more likely you are to show hostility to relevant outgroups, such as management, especially in cultures encouraging inter-group competition (Hinkle and Brown 1990).

8 Beynon (1984: 245) reported that one of the key stewards at the Ford Halewood plant was widely regarded as a 'charismatic leader'.

9 There are of course exceptions to this stricture, most notably the work of Claydon (1989, 1996), Gall and McKay (1994) and Smith and Morton (1993, 1994), but quite why the benign face of employer power should have proved a more attractive research area than the malign face is an interesting question in its own right.

4 MOBILIZATION AND INDUSTRIAL RELATIONS

1 The theme of declining worker collectivism is not especially new and easily predates the 1980s. In an assessment of Labour's 1959 electoral defeat Abrams and Rose (1960: 119) wrote that:

> Support . . . for its class appeal is being undermined because the working class itself . . . is emerging from its earlier unhappy plight; manual workers are gradually moving over into the white-collar category . . . and many, particularly among the young, are now crossing the class frontiers into the

middle class. The ethos of class solidarity is beginning to crumble in the face of the new fluidity of our society, the new opportunities for advancement through individual effort.

2 There are other conceptualizations of collectivism apart from that of Phelps Brown. Hofstede (1984) defined the concept as a cultural value having three facets: collective self-reliance, collective goals taking precedence over personal goals, and a strong sense of ingroups and outgroups. He measured collectivism through a questionnaire survey of over 116,000 IBM employees in 1967 and 1973 and was able to rank order the 40 participating countries on the collectivism–individualism scale. Despite the sophisticated conceptualization there was actually very little correlation between country collectivism scores and trade union density. Moreover, it is not clear how the relative stability of national collectivism scores helps us understand the sudden changes in trade union density in the capitalist world in the early 1980s (for similar conceptualization see Triandis 1989, and for criticism see Kagitcibasi 1994).

3 Case studies of large non-union companies are not peculiar to the 1980s since Flanders carried out an influential study of the John Lewis Partnership in the mid-1960s (Flanders et al. 1968).

4 A similar picture emerges from comparative time-series data on job satisfaction between 1985 and 1995. In the International Survey Research study of seven major European countries it was British workers who showed the steepest decline in overall job satisfaction, from 64 per cent satisfied in 1985 to 53 per cent in 1995 (ISR 1995: Figure 4).

5 The 1992 *Employment in Britain* survey reported that just 32 per cent of employees believed they would have a 'great deal' or 'quite a lot' of say in decisions about the way they did their job (Gallie and White 1993: 38).

6 Officially the Communist Party 'transformed' itself in 1991 into a new type of organization called Democratic Left, but since this is little more than a loose federation of discussion circles with a total membership in the hundreds, the term 'demise' is more accurate.

7 Contrary to Ram, there is no reason to think that the presence of *any* negotiation at all is sufficient to question the analytical relevance of the category 'autocracy'. Primo Levi's (1987) graphic accounts of daily life in the Nazi concentration camps showed that even in the paradigm case of a 'total institution', ruled by terror, there was room for negotiation.

8 An earlier generation of industrial relations writers devoted considerable attention to the union–Labour Party link and to labour movement politics (see Clegg 1954: Part IV; Flanders 1952: Chapter VII; Roberts 1962: Chapter IV).

9 The existence of factions and factional rivalry amongst similar groups of workers casts doubt on the fashionable idea that particular types of occupation, say professional non-manuals for instance, are prone to certain kinds of trade unionism. Further doubt emerges when we consider the existence of competitive unionism. School teachers, for instance, can join the traditionally militant NUT, or the increasingly militant but less factionalized NAS/UWT, or the right-wing, anti-strike PAT. Clearly, teachers as an occupational group display a wide range of political orientations and it is this political diversity, rather than Brown's narrow instrumentalism, that is so striking to an observer.

10 Hyman (1986) wrote an analytical essay on the miners' strike in the *Socialist Register 1985/86* and there are brief discussions of picketing in Farnham and Pimlott (1995) and Salamon (1992).

11 This section is a shortened version of Kelly (1996).

5 OLSONIAN THEORY AND COLLECTIVE ACTION

1 *The Logic of Collective Action* was first published in 1965 but my references are to the slightly expanded 1971 edition.

2 Some writers are committed to the view that most of the behaviour we want to explain can be accounted for within the framework of rational choice theory whereas for others rational choice is just a sensible starting point: 'even if rationality often is unimportant or absent, or unstable, there is a hard core of important cases where the rational-choice model is indispensable. I argue, furthermore, that this model is logically prior to the alternatives' (Elster 1979: 116; see also Abell 1991: xi; Sandler 1992: 62).

The differences amongst rational choice theorists were brought out clearly and succinctly by Abell (1991). If the standard assumptions lead to faulty predictions, he suggests progressively relaxing them until a fit is discovered. So for instance you can drop the assumption of self-interest and treat agents as capable of altruism. In this way a 'narrow' rational choice model can be broadened step by step. There is also a distinction between 'thin' and 'thick' models of rationality. According to the thin model an action is rational if it is consistent with the agent's beliefs but the nature and sources of those beliefs (and preferences) are immaterial in the determination of rationality. The broad theory however stipulates that the beliefs themselves must conform to some notion of rationality, or as Elster put it, 'Substantively rational beliefs are those which are grounded in the available evidence' (Elster 1983: 2).

3 Explanations of this type are often contrasted with accounts that refer to past experiences, e.g. norms, values, traditions, etc. as determinants of current action.

4 Another way of adjudicating between competing claims of rationality is to generate an external, objective criterion. Elster proposed that 'The substantive rationality of beliefs concerns the relation between the beliefs and the *available evidence*, not the relation between the world' (1983: 16, my italics, and see also Elster 1989b: 4).

In the earlier example the evidence available to miners pondering strike action might have included *inter alia* the degree of support for strike action, the resources of their opponents, the likely impact of the strike and the degree of solidarity from the rest of the trade union movement. Any one of these topics would prove difficult to think about. How much solidarity action, for example, could have been anticipated from other groups of workers? The 'available evidence' of recent disputes, legal constraints and unemployment levels might have suggested very little. On the other hand a miner might have reasoned that the scale of job losses was so enormous and the government's problems so severe that predictions derived from older and different circumstances were no longer valid. Would this have been careful and detailed rational thought or irrational wishful thinking? Any answer to this question is bound to involve assumptions about the impact of unemployment on solidarity action, the significance of coal miners in public consciousness and the balance of power resources between the parties. Only by making such assumptions can we generate the criteria to distinguish between rational thought and wishful thinking. In other words, judgements of the rationality of other people's actions are not made on objective criteria but on the basis of theoretical assumptions about what it is possible for agents to achieve given the constraints and opportunities of their situation.

5 Marwell *et al.*'s empirical refutation of large-scale free-riding needs to be treated cautiously. Their studies all used student subjects who have been shown in Gordon *et al.*'s (1984) research on collective bargaining to be strongly disposed towards norms of fairness as compared with 'real-world' negotiators.

6 Barry (1978: 178) and Sandler (1992: 62) offered similar assessments, whilst Zeckhauser (1987) was more critical.

7 One defence of Olson's argument about group size claims that whilst unions *appear* to be large groups, subject to the logic of free-riding, they are in fact *federal* groups that are immune to its logic. Olson defined the latter as

> a group divided into a number of small groups, each of which has a reason to join with the others to form a federation representing the large group as a whole . . . they may be induced to use their social incentives to get the individuals belonging to each small group to contribute towards the achievement of the collective goals of the whole group.
> (1971: 63; see also Barbalet 1991: 454–455; Crouch 1982: 65–67; Sandler 1992: 11)

This is all that Olson says by way of definition so it is not at all clear precisely what he meant by a federal group, but on the most sensible interpretation of his remarks federal groups are the exception rather than the rule. First, the groups into which national unions are divided, the geographical or workplace branches, are very rarely small groups in any meaningful sense. Olson himself was unclear on the point at which a 'small' group ceased to be small so it is hard to tell whether any particular group is acting as Olson would predict. All he said on this question was that, 'Ordinarily no union local with thousands or *perhaps even hundreds* of members can be an effective social unit' (1971: 74, italics added).

Since most trade union branches in Britain and the US do have hundreds and sometimes thousands of members this would seem to imply that they are too large to function as small group members of a federation. But there is a second reason for doubting whether Olson intended the federal group to be anything other than an exceptional case and this has to do with the structure of large organizations. Every large social movement organization is 'divided up' into branches. Now if such division was sufficient to create a federal group that could then free itself from Olsonian logic, the social world would consist almost entirely of federal groups and Olsonian logic would be largely irrelevant. This cannot be what Olson meant and we therefore have to conclude that most large groups, including trade unions, are *not* federal groups.

8 Some post-Olsonians have tried to rescue the theory by invoking self-interested 'political entrepreneurs' who have a 'preference' for organizing. According to Hardin these are 'people who, for their own career reasons, find it in their private interest to work to provide collective benefits to relevant groups' (1982: 35).

The career advantages of being blacklisted for union organizing are not immediately obvious. The labour economist Alison Booth was much nearer the truth when she said 'the economics of the trade union has little to say about the formation and growth of unions' (1995: 73).

6 LONG WAVES IN INDUSTRIAL RELATIONS

1 One of the chief protagonists in this discussion was Trotsky (1921a, b, 1922, 1923) whose first writings slightly predate Kondratieff's. There is in fact some debate as to when long waves were discovered (or invented) and by whom. The Dutch economist van Gelderen first wrote about them in 1913, ten years before Kondratieff, but Mandel claims the Russian economist Parvus analysed them in the mid-1890s, whilst Tylecote gives credit to Jevons, writing in the 1880s (see Mandel 1975: 122–124; Tinbergen 1984; Tylecote 1991: 10–11). Kondratieff was arrested in 1930 as the head of the illegal (and non-existent) 'Peasants' Party'. He stood trial in 1931 and was not heard of again (Jasny 1972: 158).

2 What is to count as 'the advanced capitalist world' is a difficult problem. The five countries selected by Screpanti (partly on grounds of data availability) would probably be accepted by most observers as a reasonable approximation for the 1870s. By the early twentieth century however the Scandinavian countries as well as Austria, Belgium, the Netherlands, Australia and Canada could all lay reasonable claim to inclusion. By the late twentieth century we could add Ireland and Japan.

3 Data for the period prior to the early 1870s are rudimentary and unreliable and have therefore been excluded.

4 The European postwar strike wave was perhaps not detected by Screpanti because there were no strike figures for Italy between 1923 and 1948, for Germany from 1933 until 1949 and for France between 1939 and 1945, and for all of these years he therefore recorded values of zero in his statistical analysis (1987: 118).

5 Some writers, e.g. Goldstein (1988), have suggested the world wars need to be incorporated into long wave theory because of their proximity to one and possibly two strike waves. I remain slightly sceptical of this idea because the relevant strike waves began some years before the world wars. On the other hand, the political consequences of the wars, and particularly the radicalization of the workers' movement, may well have interacted with the internal dynamics of the ongoing strike waves, amplifying their intensity, scale and/or duration. For a detailed account of the relationship between party politics, worker mobilization and strike action see Claudin (1975).

6 According to Visser (1989: 11) there is no reliable time-series data on union membership for Belgium and Ireland or for the former authoritarian states of Spain, Portugal and Greece.

7 It could be argued that the periodization used in Tables 6.3 onwards conflates the impact of Kondratieff transition periods with world wars. To test this possibility I divided the first two twentieth-century strike waves into war years (1915–1918, 1940–1945) and non-war years (1910–1914, 1919–1920, 1935–1939, 1946–1948) and recalculated separate rates of union membership and density change for the two sets of years. The annual rate of membership and density change was not significantly different in the war years of the strike waves as compared with the non-war years.

8 The Austrian case does not fit easily into this schema because its labour movement is not as weak as the Dutch or the Swiss but not as strong as the Scandinavian (see Crouch 1992: 181).

9 Recent rises in merger rates in Australia and New Zealand owe more to legislative curbs on the rights of small unions (Chaison 1996: 123–125, 147–149).

10 The concept of 'cycles of control' has recently been criticized by Marchington *et al.* (1992) because it suggests an automatic repetition of employer interest in worker participation and fails to capture the dynamics of employee involvement at enterprise level (see also Ackers *et al.* 1992). This line of attack is both mistaken and confused: mistaken because there is nothing in Ramsay's analysis to suggest automaticity rather than strong probability; and confused because the cycles concept is an historical construct designed to capture long-term fluctuations, not an organizational concept intended to capture enterprise dynamics.

11 I have taken over the term 'ruptures' from Jacobi (1986).

12 I shall omit earlier strike waves of 1869–1875 and 1910–1920 because of the lack of reliable data on many key variables.

13 Astonishingly, there is no reliable data on strike outcomes in Britain after 1935.

7 POSTMODERNISM AND THE END OF THE LABOUR MOVEMENT

1 Or, as one colleague of mine graphically said, the mode of production gives way to the mode of shopping!

2 This is a familiar and long-standing theme in British sociology, from Abrams and Rose's (1960) argument that affluence was eroding Labour's electoral support to Phelps Brown's (1990) complaint that it was undermining solidarity and class identity. Negative empirical evidence, from the Affluent Worker study onwards, seems incapable of damaging this tenaciously held belief (see Goldthorpe *et al.* 1968, 1969).

3 There is a third strength, according to Callinicos, which is that postmodernism offers solace and justification to disillusioned ex-radicals and socialists.

> The discourse of postmodernism is best seen as the product of a socially mobile intelligentsia in a climate dominated by the retreat of the Western labour movement and the 'over-consumptionist' dynamic of capitalism in the Reagan-Thatcher era . . . [it is the] means . . . [by] which this intelligentsia has sought to articulate its political disillusionment and its aspiration to a consumption-oriented lifestyle.
>
> (Callinicos 1989: 170–171)

Rustin (1989: 311–312) advanced a similar though less cynical analysis.

4 Inevitably many specific postmodernist claims and propositions will be examined only cursorily, if at all. For instance there is an argument that the transition to a post-Fordist economy was triggered by market saturation in the consumer goods produced by Fordist industry (Piore and Sabel 1984: 183–187). This argument has been clearly refuted by a number of writers who have pointed to the continuing expansion of Japanese and South East Asian mass production up until the present day, the creation of new consumer products and the opening up of new markets in parts of the 'Third World' and the former Eastern bloc (Allen 1992a: 248: Brenner and Glick 1991; Sayer and Walker 1992: 196–198; Williams *et al.* 1987).

5 Sayer's (1992) book is an excellent and critical analysis of some fashionable ideas in the philosophy of science.

6 There is now considerable debate about trends in job insecurity and it is clear that the concept is not easy to define or measure (see OECD 1997: Chapter 5; Spencer 1996).

7 Information on union affiliations to the Campaign for Nuclear Disarmament was supplied by CND's then Union Organizer, Jimmy Barnes.

8 A similar argument, sketched more briefly, can be found in Rustin (1989: 307–311).

BIBLIOGRAPHY

Abell, P. (1991) 'Introduction', in P. Abell (ed.) *Rational Choice Theory*, Aldershot: Edward Elgar.

Abrams, M. and Rose, R. (1960) *Must Labour Lose?*, Harmondsworth: Penguin.

Ackers, P., Marchington, M., Wilkinson, A. and Goodman, J. (1992) 'The use of cycles? explaining employee involvement in the 1990s', *Industrial Relations Journal* 23, 4: 268–283.

Adams, R. J. (1991) 'Introduction and overview', in R. J. Adams (ed.) *Comparative Industrial Relations: Contemporary Research and Theory*, London: HarperCollins.

—— (1993) '"All aspects of people at work": unity and division in the study of labor and labor management', in R. J. Adams and N. M. Meltz (eds) *Industrial Relations Theory: Its Nature, Scope and Pedagogy*, Metuchen, NJ: IMLR Press.

Ahlstrand, B. (1990) *The Quest for Productivity*, Cambridge: Cambridge University Press.

Akerlof, G. A. (1980) 'A theory of social custom, of which unemployment may be one consequence', *Quarterly Journal of Economics* 94, 4: 749–775.

Allen, J. (1992a) 'Post-industrialism and post-Fordism', in S. Hall, D. Held and T. McGrew (eds) *Modernity and its Futures*, Oxford: Polity Press.

—— (1992b) 'Fordism and modern industry', in J. Allen, P. Braham and P. Lewis (eds) *Political and Economic Forms of Modernity*, Oxford: Polity Press.

Allen, V. L. (1971) *The Sociology of Industrial Relations*, London: Longman.

Anderson, P. (1967) 'The limits and possibilities of trade union action', in R. Blackburn and A. Cockburn (eds) *The Incompatibles: Trade Union Militancy and the Consensus*, Harmondsworth: Penguin.

Armstrong, K. J., Bowers, D. and Burkitt, B. (1977) 'The measurement of trade union bargaining power', *British Journal of Industrial Relations* 25, 1: 91–100.

Armstrong, P., Glyn, A. and Harrison, J. (1984) *Capitalism Since World War II*, London: Fontana.

Armstrong, P. J., Goodman, J. F. B. and Hyman, J. D. (1981) *Ideology and Shop-floor Industrial Relations*, London: Croom Helm.

Arrighi, G. (1990) 'Marxist century, American century: the making and remaking of the world labour movement', *New Left Review* 179: 29–63.

Ashenfelter, O. and Johnson, G. E. (1969) 'Bargaining theory, trade unions and industrial strike activity', *American Economic Review* 59, 1: 35–49.

143

Axelrod, R. and Hamilton, W. D. (1981) 'The evolution of cooperation', *Science* 211: 1390–1396. Reprinted in P. Abell (ed.) *Rational Choice Theory*, Aldershot: Edward Elgar.

Bach, S. and Winchester, D. (1994) 'Opting out of pay devolution? The prospects for local pay bargaining in UK public services', *British Journal of Industrial Relations* 32, 2: 263–282.

Bacon, N. and Storey, J. (1996) 'Individualism, collectivism and the changing role of trade unions', in P. Ackers, C. Smith and P. Smith (eds) *The New Workplace and Trade Unionism*, London: Routledge.

Baddon, L., Hunter, L., Hyman, J., Leopold, J. and Ramsay, H. (1989) *People's Capitalism? A Critical Analysis of Profit-Sharing and Employee Share Ownership*, London: Routledge.

Bailey, R. (1996) 'Public sector industrial relations', in I. Beardwell (ed.) *Contemporary Industrial Relations: A Critical Analysis*, Oxford: Oxford University Press.

Bain, G. S. (ed.) (1983) *Industrial Relations in Britain*, Oxford: Blackwell.

Bain, G. S. and Clegg, H. A. (1974) 'A strategy for industrial relations research in Great Britain', *British Journal of Industrial Relations* 12, 1: 91–113.

Bain, G. S. and Elsheikh, F. (1976) *Union Growth and the Business Cycle: an Econometric Analysis*, Oxford: Blackwell.

Bain, G. S. and Price, R. (1980) *Profiles of Union Growth*, Oxford: Blackwell.

—— (1983) 'Union growth: dimensions, determinants, and destiny', in G. S. Bain (ed.) *Industrial Relations in Britain*, Oxford: Blackwell.

Balbus, I. (1971) 'The concept of interest in pluralist and Marxian analysis', *Politics and Society* 1, 2: 151–177.

Bamber, G. J. and Whitehouse, G. (1993) 'Appendix: Employment, economics and industrial relations: comparative statistics', in G. Bamber and R. D. Lansbury (eds) *International and Comparative Industrial Relations* 2nd edn, London: Routledge.

Barbalet, J. M. (1991) 'Class and rationality: Olson's critique of Marx', *Science and Society* 55, 4: 446–468.

Barling, J., Fullagar, C. and Kelloway, E. K. (1992) *The Union and its Members: a Psychological Approach*, New York: Oxford University Press.

Barnes, J. (1995) Personal correspondence.

Barry, B. (1978) *Sociologists, Economists and Democracy*, Chicago: University of Chicago Press.

Bassett, P. (1986) *Strike Free: New Industrial Relations in Britain*, London: Macmillan.

—— (1988) 'Non-unionism's growing ranks', *Personnel Management* March: 44–47.

Bassett, P. and Cave, A. (1993) *All for One: the Future of the Unions*, London: Fabian Pamphlet 559.

Batstone, E. (1984) *Working Order: Workplace Industrial Relations Over Two Decades*, Oxford: Blackwell.

—— (1988a) *The Reform of Workplace Industrial Relations*, Oxford: Clarendon.

—— (1988b) 'The frontier of control', in D. Gallie (ed.) *Employment in Britain*, Oxford: Blackwell.

Batstone, E. and Gourlay, S. (1986) *Unions, Unemployment and Innovation*, Oxford: Blackwell.

Batstone, E., Boraston, I. and Frenkel, S. (1977) *Shop Stewards in Action*, Oxford: Blackwell.

Batstone, E., Boraston, I. and Frenkel, S. (1978) *The Social Organization of Strikes*, Oxford: Blackwell.

Batstone, E., Gourlay, S., Levie, H. and Moore, R. (1987) *New Technology and the Process of Labour Regulation*, Oxford: Clarendon.

Beadle, R. (1995) 'Opting out of pay devolution? the prospects for local pay bargaining in the UK public services: a comment', *British Journal of Industrial Relations* 33, 1: 137–142.

Beale, D. (1994) *Driven By Nissan? A Critical Guide to the New Management Techniques*, London: Lawrence and Wishart.

Bean, R. (1994) *Comparative Industrial Relations* 2nd edn, London: Routledge.

Beaumont, P. B. (1987) *The Decline of Trade Union Organisation*, London: Croom Helm.

—— (1990) *Change in Industrial Relations*, London: Routledge.

—— (1995) *The Future of Employment Relations*, London: Sage.

Beaumont, P. B. and Harris, R. I. D. (1990) 'Union recruitment and organising attempts in Britain in the 1980s', *Industrial Relations Journal* 21, 4: 274–286.

Beetham, D. (1991) *The Legitimation of Power*, London: Macmillan.

Benton, S. (1989) 'The decline of the Party', in S. Hall and M. Jacques (eds) *New Times*, London: Lawrence and Wishart.

Berggren, C. (1993) 'Lean production – the end of history?', *Work, Employment and Society* 7, 2: 163–188.

Beynon, H. (1984) *Working for Ford* 2nd edn, Harmondsworth: Penguin.

—— (ed.) (1985) *Digging Deeper: Issues in the Miners' Strike*, London: Verso.

Bigoness, W. (1990) 'Comment on Peterson', in J. Chelius and J. Dworkin (eds) *Reflections on the Transformation of Industrial Relations*, Metuchen, NJ: IMLR Press.

Blain, A. N. J. and Gennard, J. (1970) 'Industrial relations theory – a critical review', *British Journal of Industrial Relations* 8, 3: 389–407.

Blanchflower, D. G. and Freeman, R. B. (1992) 'Unionism in the United States and other advanced OECD countries', *Industrial Relations* 31, 1: 56–79.

Block, R. N. (1990) 'American industrial relations in the 1990s: transformation or evolution?', in J. Chelius and J. Dworkin (eds) *Reflections on the Transformation of Industrial Relations*, Metuchen, NJ: IMLR Press.

Blyton, P. and Turnbull, P. (1992a) 'HRM: debates, dilemmas and contradictions', in P. Blyton and P. Turnbull (eds) *Reassessing Human Resource Management*, London: Sage.

—— (eds) (1992b) *Reassessing Human Resource Management*, London: Sage.

—— (1994) *The Dynamics of Employee Relations*, London: Macmillan.

Boll, F. (1985) 'International strike waves: a critical assessment', in W. J. Mommsen and H-G. Husung (eds) *The Development of Trade Unionism in Great Britain and Germany 1880–1914*, London: Allen & Unwin.

Booth, A. (1985) 'The free rider problem and a social custom theory of trade union membership', *Quarterly Journal of Economics* 100, 1: 253–261.

—— (1995) *The Economics of the Trade Union*, Cambridge: Cambridge University Press.

Boraston, I., Clegg, H. A. and Rimmer, M. (1975) *Workplace and Union*, London: Heinemann.

Bourke, J. (1994) *Working Class Cultures in Britain 1890–1960: Gender, Class and Ethnicity*, London: Routledge.

Boyer, R. (1990) *The Regulation School: A Critical Introduction*, New York: Columbia University Press.

145

Braungart, R. G. and Braungart, M. M. (1987) 'Generational politics', *Annual Review of Political Science* 2: 34–83.

Brecher, J. (1972) *Strike!*, Boston: South End Press.

Brenner, R. and Glick, M. (1991) 'The regulation approach: theory and history', *New Left Review* 188: 45–119.

Brewer, M. B. and Schneider, S. K. (1990) 'Social identity and social dilemmas: a double-edged sword', in D. Abrams and M. A. Hogg (eds) *Social Identity Theory: Constructive and Critical Advances*, Hemel Hempstead: Harvester Wheatsheaf.

Brewster, C. (1995) 'HRM: the European dimension', in J. Storey (ed.) *Human Resource Management: A Critical Text*, London: Routledge.

Brown, H. P. (1986) *The Origins of Trade Union Power*, Oxford: Oxford University Press.

—— (1990) 'The counter-revolution of our time', *Industrial Relations* 29, 1: 1–14.

Brown, R. K. (1988) 'The employment relationship in sociological theory', in D. Gallie (ed.) *Employment in Britain*, Oxford: Blackwell.

—— (1992) *Understanding Industrial Organisations*, London: Routledge.

Brown, R. (1978) 'Divided we fall: an analysis of relations between sections of a factory workforce', in H. Tajfel (ed.) *Differentiation Between Social Groups*, London: Academic Press.

—— (1988) *Group Processes: Dynamics Within and Between Groups*, Oxford: Blackwell.

Brown, W. (1973) *Piecework Bargaining*, London: Heinemann.

—— (ed.) (1981) *The Changing Contours of British Industrial Relations*, Oxford: Blackwell.

—— (1993) 'The contraction of collective bargaining in Britain', *British Journal of Industrial Relations* 31, 2: 189–200.

Brown, W. and Walsh, J. (1991) 'Pay determination in Britain in the 1980s: the anatomy of decentralization', *Oxford Review of Economic Policy* 7, 1: 44–59.

Brown, W. and Wright, M. (1994) 'The empirical tradition in workplace bargaining research', *British Journal of Industrial Relations* 32, 2: 153–164.

Bryman, A. (1992) *Charisma and Leadership in Organizations*, London: Sage.

Brunt, R. (1989) 'The politics of identity', in S. Hall and M. Jacques (eds) *New Times*, London: Lawrence and Wishart.

Buchanan, A. (1979) 'Revolutionary motivation and rationality', *Philosophy and Public Affairs* 9, 1: 59–82.

Bunyan, T. (1977) *The History and Practice of the Political Police in Britain*, London: Quartet.

Burawoy, M. (1979) *Manufacturing Consent*, Chicago: University of Chicago Press.

—— (1985) *The Politics of Production*, London: Verso.

Burchill, F. (1997) *Labour Relations* 2nd edn, London: Macmillan.

Callinicos, A. (1982) 'The rank-and-file movement today', *International Socialism* 17: 1–38.

—— (1987) *Making History: Agency, Structure and Change in Social Theory*, Oxford: Polity Press.

—— (1989) *Against Postmodernism: a Marxist Critique*, Oxford: Polity Press.

Cappelli, P. (1985) 'Theory construction in IR and some implications for research', *Industrial Relations* 24, 1: 90–112.

Carter, B. (1997) 'Adversity and opportunity: towards union renewal in Manufacturing, Science and Finance?', *Capital and Class* 61, Spring: 8–18.

Cave, A. (1994) *Managing Change in the Workplace*, London: Kogan Page.

Cavendish, R. (1982) *Women On The Line*, London: Routledge and Kegan Paul.

Chadwick, M. (1983) 'The recession and industrial relations: a factory approach', *Employee Relations* 5, 5: 5–12.

Chaison, G. N. (1996) *Union Mergers in Hard Times*, Ithaca, NY: ILR Press.

Chung, Y. K. (1994) 'Conflict and compliance: the workplace politics of a disk-drive factory in Singapore', in J. Belanger, P. K. Edwards and L. Haiven (eds) *Workplace Industrial Relations and the Global Challenge*, Ithaca, NY: ILR Press.

CIR, *Reports*, various years, London: Commission on Industrial Relations.

Clark, J., McLoughlin, I., Rose, H. and King, R. (1988) *The Process of Technological Change*, Cambridge: Cambridge University Press.

Clarke, T. and Clements, L. (eds) (1977) *Trade Unions Under Capitalism*, London: Fontana.

Claudin, F. (1975) *The Communist Movement: from Comintern to Cominform*, Harmondsworth: Penguin.

Claydon, T. (1989) 'Union derecognition in Britain in the 1980s', *British Journal of Industrial Relations* 27, 2: 214–224.

—— (1996) 'Union derecognition: a re-examination', in I. Beardwell (ed.) *Contemporary Industrial Relations: a Critical Analysis*, Oxford: Oxford University Press.

Cleary, M. N. and Hobbs, G. D. (1984) 'The fifty year cycle. A look at the empirical evidence', in C. Freeman (ed.) *Long Waves in the World Economy*, London: Frances Pinter.

Clegg, H. A. (1954) *General Union: A Study of the National Union of General and Municipal Workers*, Oxford: Blackwell.

—— (1975) 'Pluralism in industrial relations', *British Journal of Industrial Relations* 13, 3: 309–316.

—— (1976) *Trade Unionism Under Collective Bargaining*, Oxford: Blackwell.

—— (1979) *The Changing System of Industrial Relations in Great Britain*, Oxford: Blackwell.

—— (1985) *A History of British Trade Unions Vol. 2: 1911–33*, Oxford: Oxford University Press.

Coates, D. (1975) *The Labour Party and the Struggle for Socialism*, Cambridge: Cambridge University Press.

—— (1980) *Labour in Power?*, London: Longman.

—— (1989) *The Crisis of Labour: Industrial Relations and the State in Contemporary Britain*, Oxford: Philip Allan.

Coates, K. and Topham, T. (1986) *Trade Unions and Politics*, Oxford: Blackwell.

Cochran, B. (1977) *Labor and Communism: The Conflict That Shaped American Unions*, Princeton, NJ: Princeton University Press.

Cohen, J. L. (1985) 'Strategy or identity: new theoretical paradigms and contemporary social movements', *Social Research* 52, 4: 663–716.

Cohn, S. (1993) *When Strikes Make Sense – And Why: Lessons From Third Republic French Coal Miners*, New York: Plenum Press.

Coleman, J. S. (1986) 'Social theory, social research and a theory of action', *American Journal of Sociology* 91, 6: 1309–1335.

Collard, R. and Dale, B. (1989) 'Quality circles', in K. Sisson (ed.) *Personnel Management in Britain*, Oxford: Blackwell.

147

Coote, A. and Campbell, B. (1982) *Sweet Freedom: the Struggle for Women's Liberation*, London: Picador.

CPGB (1989) *Manifesto For New Times*, London: Communist Party of Great Britain.

Cregan, C. and Johnston, S. (1990) 'An industrial relations approach to the free rider problem: young people and trade union membership in the UK', *British Journal of Industrial Relations* 28, 1: 84–104.

Cressey, P. and MacInnes, J. (1980) 'Voting for Ford', *Capital and Class* 11: 5–33.

Crick, M. (1984) *Militant*, London: Faber & Faber.

Cronin, J. E. (1979) *Industrial Conflict in Modern Britain*, London: Croom Helm.

—— (1984) *Labour and Society in Britain 1918–1979*, London: Batsford Academic.

—— (1985) 'Strikes and the struggle for union organization: Britain and Europe', in W. J. Mommsen and H-G. Husung (eds) *The Development of Trade Unionism in Great Britain and Germany 1880–1914*, London: Allen & Unwin.

—— (1989) 'Strikes and power in Britain, 1870–1920', in L. H. Haimson and C. Tilly (eds) *Strikes, Wars, and Revolutions in an International Perspective*, Cambridge: Cambridge University Press.

Crook, S., Pakulski, J. and Waters, M. (1992) *Postmodernization: Change in Advanced Society*, London: Sage.

Crouch, C. (1982) *Trade Unions: the Logic of Collective Action*, London: Fontana.

—— (1986) 'The future prospects for trade unions in Western Europe', *Political Quarterly* 57, 1: 5–17.

—— (1992) 'The fate of articulated industrial relations systems: a stock-taking after the neo-liberal decade', in M. Regini (ed.) *The Future of Labour Movements*, London: Sage.

—— (1993) *Industrial Relations and European State Traditions*, Oxford: Clarendon.

Cunnison, S. (1966) *Wages and Work Allocation*, London: Tavistock.

Daniel, W. W. (1987) *Workplace Industrial Relations and Technical Change*, London: Frances Pinter/PSI.

Daniel, W. W. and Millward, N. (1983) *Workplace Industrial Relations in Britain*, London: Heinemann.

Darlington, R. (1993) 'The challenge to workplace unionism in Royal Mail', *Employee Relations* 15, 5: 3–25.

—— (1994) *The Dynamics of Workplace Unionism*, London: Mansell.

—— (1995) 'Restructuring and workplace unionism at Manchester Airport', *British Journal of Industrial Relations* 33, 1: 93–115.

Delbeke, R. (1984) 'Recent long-wave theories. A critical survey', in C. Freeman (ed.) *Long Waves in the World Economy*, London: Frances Pinter.

Deshpande, S. P. and Fiorito, J. (1989) 'Specific and general beliefs in union voting models', *Academy of Management Journal* 32, 4: 883–897.

Dickerson, A. P. and Stewart, M. B. (1993) 'Is the public sector strike prone?', *Oxford Bulletin of Economics and Statistics* 55, 3: 253–284.

Dickson, T., McLachan, H. V., Prior, P. and Swales, K. (1988) 'Big Blue and the unions: IBM, individualism and trade union strategies', *Work, Employment and Society* 2, 4: 506–520.

Disney, R. (1990) 'Explanations of the decline in trade union density in Britain: an appraisal', *British Journal of Industrial Relations* 28, 2: 165–177.

Dunleavy, P. (1991) *Democracy, Bureaucracy and Public Choice*, Hemel Hempstead: Harvester Wheatsheaf.

Dunlop, J. T. (1948) 'The development of labor organization: a theoretical framework', in R. A. Lester and J. Shister (eds) *Insights Into Labor Issues*, New York: Macmillan.

—— (1993) *Industrial Relations Systems* rev. edn, Boston: Harvard Business School Press.

Dunn, S. (1990) 'Root metaphor in the old and new industrial relations', *British Journal of Industrial Relations* 28, 1: 1–31.

Dunn, S. and Gennard, J. (1984) *The Closed Shop in Britain*, London: Macmillan.

Dunn, S. and Metcalf, D. (1996) 'Trade union law since 1979: ideology, intent, impact', in I. Beardwell (ed.) *Contemporary Industrial Relations*, Oxford: Oxford University Press.

Dunn, S. and Wright, M. (1993) 'Managing without the closed shop', in D. Metcalf and S. Milner (eds) *New Perspectives on Industrial Disputes*, London: Routledge.

Durcan, J. W., McCarthy, W. E. J. and Redman, G. P. (1983) *Strikes in Post-War Britain*, London: Allen & Unwin.

Edwards, C. (1978) 'Measuring union power: a comparison of two methods applied to the study of local union power in the coal industry', *British Journal of Industrial Relations* 16, 1: 1–15.

—— (1983) 'Power and decision making in the workplace: a study in the coal mining industry', *Industrial Relations Journal* 14, 1: 50–69.

Edwards, C. and Heery, E. (1989) *Management Control and Union Power: A Study of Labour Relations in Coal Mining*, Oxford: Clarendon.

Edwards, P. K. (1977) 'A critique of the Kerr-Siegel hypothesis of strikes and the isolated mass: a study in the falsification of sociological knowledge', *Sociological Review* 25, 3: 551–574.

—— (1986) *Conflict at Work*, Oxford: Blackwell.

—— (1987) *Managing the Factory*, Oxford: Blackwell.

—— (1990) 'Understanding conflict in the labour process: the logic and autonomy of struggle', in D. Knights and H. Willmott (eds) *Labour Process Theory*, London: Macmillan.

—— (1992) 'Industrial conflict: themes and issues in recent research', *British Journal of Industrial Relations* 30, 3: 361–404.

—— (1994) 'A comparison of national regimes of labor regulation and the problem of the workplace', in J. Belanger, P. K. Edwards and L. Haiven (eds) *Workplace Industrial Relations and the Global Challenge*, Ithaca, NY: ILR Press.

—— (ed.) (1995a) *Industrial Relations: Theory and Practice in Britain*, Oxford: Blackwell.

—— (1995b) 'From industrial relations to the employment relationship', *Relationnes Industrielles–Industrial Relations* 50, 1: 39–63.

—— (1995c) 'The employment relationship', in P. K. Edwards (ed.) *Industrial Relations: Theory and Practice in Britain*, Oxford: Blackwell.

Edwards, P. K. and Hyman, R. (1994) 'Strikes and industrial conflict: peace in Europe?' in R. Hyman and A. Ferner (eds) *New Frontiers in European Industrial Relations*, Oxford: Blackwell.

Edwards, P. K. and Scullion, H. (1982) *The Social Organization of Industrial Conflict*, Oxford: Blackwell.

Edwards, P. K. and Terry, M. (1988) 'Conclusions: another way forward?', in M. Terry and P. K. Edwards (eds) *Shopfloor Politics and Job Controls: the Post-War Engineering Industry*, Oxford: Blackwell.

Edwards, P. K., Belanger, J. and Haiven, L. (1994) 'Introduction: the workplace and labor regulation in comparative perspective', in J. Belanger, P. K. Edwards and L. Haiven (eds) *Workplace Industrial Relations and the Global Challenge*, Ithaca, NY: ILR Press.

Edwards, P. K., Hall, M., Hyman, R., Marginson, P., Sisson, K., Waddington, J. and Winchester, D. (1992) 'Great Britain: still muddling through', in A. Ferner and R. Hyman (eds) *Industrial Relations in the New Europe*, Oxford: Blackwell.

Edwards, R. (1993) *Rights At Work: Employment Relations in the Post-Union Era*, Washington: Brookings Institution.

Elgar, J. and Simpson, B. (1993) *Union Negotiators, Industrial Action and the Law: Report of a Survey of Negotiators in Twenty-Five Unions 1991–92*, London: London School of Economics Centre for Economic Performance, Discussion Paper 171.

Elster, J. (1979) *Ulysses and the Sirens*, Cambridge: Cambridge University Press.

—— (1982) 'Marxism, functionalism and game theory', *Theory and Society* 11, 4: 453–482. Reprinted in P. Abell (ed.) *Rational Choice Theory*, Aldershot: Edward Elgar (1991).

—— (1983) *Sour Grapes*, Cambridge: Cambridge University Press.

—— (1985) *Making Sense of Marx*, Cambridge: Cambridge University Press.

—— (1986) 'Further thoughts on Marxism, functionalism and game theory', in J. Roemer (ed.) *Analytical Marxism*, Cambridge: Cambridge University Press.

—— (1989a) *The Cement of Society*, Cambridge: Cambridge University Press.

—— (1989b) *Solomonic Judgements*, Cambridge: Cambridge University Press.

Fantasia, R. (1988) *Cultures of Solidarity: Consciousness, Action and Contemporary American Workers*, Berkeley: University of California Press.

Farnham, D. and Pimlott, J. (1995) *Understanding Industrial Relations* 5th edn, London: Cassell.

Ferner, A. (1988) *Governments, Managers and Industrial Relations: Public Enterprises and Their Political Environment*, Oxford: Blackwell.

Ferner, A. and Hyman, R. (1992) 'Introduction. Industrial relations in the new Europe: seventeen types of ambiguity', in A. Ferner and R. Hyman (eds) *Industrial Relations in the New Europe*, Oxford: Blackwell.

Fernie, S. and Woodland, S. (1995) 'HRM and workplace performance: evidence using WIRS3 – a reply to McCarthy', *Industrial Relations Journal* 26, 1: 65–68.

Fernie, S., Metcalf, D. and Woodland, S. (1994) *What Has Human Resource Management Achieved In The Workplace?*, London: Employment Policy Institute.

Ferree, M. M. and Miller, F. D. (1985) 'Mobilization and meaning: toward an integration of social psychological and resource perspectives on social movements', *Sociological Inquiry* 55, 1: 38–61.

Fine, B. and Millar, R. (eds) (1985) *Policing the Miners' Strike*, London: Lawrence and Wishart.

Fireman, B. and Gamson, W. A. (1979) 'Utilitarian logic in the resource mobilization perspective', in M. N. Zald and J. D. McCarthy (eds) *The Dynamics of Social Movements*, Cambridge, Mass.: Winthrop Publishers.

Fishman, N. (1995) *The British Communist Party and the Trade Unions, 1933–45*, Aldershot: Scolar Press.

Flanders, A. (1952) *Trade Unions*, London: Hutchinson's University Library.

—— (1961) 'Trade unions in the sixties', in A. Flanders *Management and Unions*, London: Faber & Faber (1970).

—— (1965) 'Industrial relations: what is wrong with the system?', in A. Flanders *Management and Unions*, London: Faber & Faber (1970).

—— (1966) 'The internal social responsibilities of industry', in A. Flanders *Management and Unions*, London: Faber & Faber (1970).

—— (1968a) 'What are trade unions for?', in A. Flanders *Management and Unions*, London: Faber & Faber (1970).

—— (1968b) 'Collective bargaining: a theoretical analysis', in A. Flanders *Management and Unions*, London: Faber & Faber (1970).

—— (1970) *Management and Unions*, London: Faber & Faber.

Flanders, A. and Fox, A. (1970) 'Collective bargaining: from Donovan to Durkheim', in A. Flanders *Management and Unions*, London: Faber & Faber.

Flanders, A., Pomeranz, R. and Woodward, J. (1968) *Experiment in Industrial Democracy: A Study of the John Lewis Partnership*, London: Faber & Faber.

Flood, P. C. and Toner, B. (1997) 'Large non-union companies: how do they avoid a catch 22?', *British Journal of Industrial Relations* 35, 2: 257–277.

Foley, T. (1992) *A Most Formidable Union: the History of DATA and TASS*, London: Manufacturing, Science and Finance Union.

Foster, J. and Woolfson, C. (1986) *The Politics of the UCS Work-In*, London: Lawrence and Wishart.

Foulkes, F. (1980) *Personnel Policies in Large Non-Union Companies*, New York: Prentice Hall.

Fox, A. (1973) 'Industrial relations: a social critique of pluralist ideology', in J. Child (ed.) *Man and Organisation*, London: Allen & Unwin.

—— (1974) *Beyond Contract: Power, Work and Trust Relations*, London: Faber & Faber.

—— (1975) 'Collective bargaining, Flanders and the Webbs', *British Journal of Industrial Relations* 13, 2: 151–174.

Franzosi, R. (1995) *The Puzzle of Strikes: Class and State Strategies in Postwar Italy*, Cambridge: Cambridge University Press.

Freeman, R. B. (1985) 'Why are unions faring poorly in NLRB elections?', in T. A. Kochan (ed.) *Challenges and Choices Facing American Labor*, Cambridge, Mass.: MIT Press.

Freeman, R. B. and Medoff, J. L. (1984) *What Do Unions Do?*, New York: Basic Books.

Friedman, D. and Hechter, M. (1988). 'The contribution of rational choice theory to macrosociological research', *Sociological Theory* 6, 2: 201–218.

Frolich, N. and Oppenheimer, J. A. (1970) 'I get by with a little help from my friends', *World Politics* 23, 1: 104–120.

Fucini, J. J. and Fucini, S. (1990) *Working for the Japanese: Inside Mazda's American Auto Plant*, New York: Free Press.

Gall, G. and McKay, S. (1994) 'Trade union derecognition in Britain 1988–94', *British Journal of Industrial Relations* 32, 3: 433–448.

Gallie, D. (1978) *In Search of the New Working Class*, Cambridge: Cambridge University Press.

—— (1983) *Social Inequality and Class Radicalism in France and Britain*, Cambridge: Cambridge University Press.

—— (1994) 'Patterns of skill change: upskilling, deskilling, or polarization?', in R. Penn, M. Rose and J. Rubery (eds) *Skill and Occupational Change*, Oxford: Oxford University Press.

—— (1996) 'Trade union allegiance and decline in British urban labour markets', in D. Gallie, R. Penn and M. Rose M. (eds) *Trade Unionism in Recession*, Oxford: Oxford University Press.

Gallie, D. and White, M. (1993) *Employee Commitment and the Skills Revolution,* London: Policy Studies Institute.

Gamson, W. A. (1992) *Talking Politics*, Cambridge: Cambridge University Press.

—— (1995) 'Constructing social protest', in H. Johnston and B. Klandermans (eds) *Social Movements and Culture*, London: UCL Press.

Garrahan, P. and Stewart, P. (1992) *The Nissan Enigma: Flexibility at Work in a Local Economy*, London: Mansell.

Geary, R. (1985) *Policing Industrial Disputes: 1893 to 1985*, Cambridge: Cambridge University Press.

Gilbert, R. (1993) 'Workplace industrial relations 25 years after Donovan: an employer view', *British Journal of Industrial Relations* 31, 2: 235–253.

Golden, M. A. (1997) *Heroic Defeats: the Politics of Job Loss*, Cambridge: Cambridge University Press.

Golden, M. A. and Wallerstein, M. (1996) *Reinterpreting Postwar Industrial Relations: Comparative Data on Advanced Industrial Societies*, University of California at Los Angeles, Department of Political Science, Unpublished MS.

Goldfield, M. and Gilbert, A. (1995) 'The limits of rational choice theory', in T. Carver and P. Thomas (eds) *Rational Choice Marxism*, London: Macmillan.

Goldstein, J. S. (1988) *Long Cycles: Prosperity and War in the Modern Age*, New Haven, Conn.: Yale University Press.

Goldthorpe, J. H. (1977) 'Industrial relations in Great Britain: a critique of "reformism"', in T. Clarke and L. Clements (eds) *Trade Unions Under Capitalism*, London: Fontana.

—— (1984) 'The end of convergence: corporatist and dualist tendencies in modern Western societies', in J. H. Goldthorpe (ed.) *Order and Conflict in Contemporary Capitalism*, Oxford: Clarendon.

Goldthorpe, J. H., Lockwood, D., Bechhofer, F. and Platt, J. (1968) *The Affluent Worker: Industrial Attitudes and Behaviour*, Cambridge: Cambridge University Press.

—— (1969) *The Affluent Worker in the Class Structure*, Cambridge: Cambridge University Press.

Goodman, J. F. B. (1984) *Employment Relations in Industrial Society*, Oxford: Philip Allan.

Goodman, J. F. B., Armstrong, E. G. A., Davis, J. E. and Wagner, A. (1977) *Rulemaking and Industrial Peace*, London: Croom Helm.

Gordon, D. (1989) 'What makes epochs? a comparative analysis of technological and social explanations of long economic swings', in M. di Matteo, R. M. Goodwin and A. Vercelli (eds) *Technological and Social Factors in Long Term Fluctuations*, Berlin: Springer-Verlag.

Gordon, D. M., Edwards, R. and Reich, M. (1982) *Segmented Work, Divided Workers: the Historical Transformation of Labor in the United States*, Cambridge: Cambridge University Press.

Gordon, M. E., Schmitt, N. and Schneider, W. G. (1984) 'Laboratory research on bargaining and negotiations: an evaluation', *Industrial Relations* 23, 2: 218–233.

Gospel, H. F. and Palmer, G. (1993) *British Industrial Relations* 2nd edn, London: Routledge.

Gouldner, A. (1954) *Wildcat Strike*, New York: Harper and Row.

152

Graham, L. (1995) *On the Line at Subaru-Isuzu: the Japanese Model and the American Worker*, Ithaca, NY: ILR Press.

Green, F. and Sutcliffe, B. (1987) *The Profit System*, Harmondsworth: Penguin.

Green, P. (1990) *The Enemy Without: Policing and Class Consciousness in the Miners' Strike*, Milton Keynes: Open University Press.

Gregg, P. and Machin, S. (1991) 'Changes in union status, increased competition and wage growth in the 1980s', *British Journal of Industrial Relations* 29, 4: 603–611.

Gregg, P. and Yates, A. (1991) 'Changes in wage setting arrangements and trade union presence in the 1980s', *British Journal of Industrial Relations* 29, 3: 361–376.

Guest, D. E. (1989) 'Human resource management: its implications for industrial relations and trade unions', in J. Storey (ed.) *New Perspectives on Human Resource Management*, London: Routledge.

—— (1996) 'Leadership and management', in P. B. Warr (ed.) *Psychology at Work* 4th edn, Harmondsworth: Penguin.

Guest, D. E. and Hoque, K. (1994) 'The good, the bad and the ugly: employment relations in new non-union workplaces', *Human Resource Management Journal* 5, 1: 1–14.

—— (1996) 'Human resource management and the new industrial relations', in I. Beardwell (ed.) *Contemporary Industrial Relations: A Critical Analysis*, Oxford: Oxford University Press.

Guest, D. E. and Rosenthal. P. (1993) 'Industrial relations in greenfield sites', in D. Metcalf and S. Milner (eds) *New Perspectives on Industrial Disputes*, London: Routledge.

Hain, P. (1986) *Political Strikes: State and Trade Unionism in Great Britain*, New York: Viking Penguin.

Haiven, L., Edwards, P. K. and Belanger, J. (1994) 'Conclusion: globalization, national systems, and the future of workplace industrial relations', in J. Belanger, P. K. Edwards and L. Haiven (eds) *Workplace Industrial Relations and the Global Challenge*, Ithaca, NY: ILR Press.

Hall, S. (1992) 'The question of cultural identity', in S. Hall, D. Held and T. McGrew (eds) *Modernity and Its Futures*, Oxford: Polity Press.

Hardin, R. (1982) *Collective Action*, Baltimore, Md: Johns Hopkins University Press.

Harris, L. (1988) 'The UK economy at a crossroads', in J. Allen and D. Massey (eds) *The Economy in Question*, London: Sage.

Hartley, J. F. (1992) 'Joining a trade union', in J. Hartley and G. M. Stephenson (eds) *Employment Relations: the Psychology of Influence and Control At Work*, Oxford: Blackwell.

Harvey, D. (1989) *The Condition of Postmodernity*, Oxford: Blackwell.

Hassard, J. (1993) 'Postmodernism and organizational analysis: an overview', in J. Hassard and M. Parker (eds) *Postmodernism and Organizations*, London: Sage.

Hearn, J. and Parkin, W. (1993) 'Organizations, multiple oppressions and postmodernism', in J. Hassard and M. Parker (eds) *Postmodernism and Organizations*, London: Sage.

Heath, A. (1976) *Rational Choice and Social Exchange: a critique of Exchange Theory*, Cambridge: Cambridge University Press.

Hebdige, D. (1989) 'After the masses', in S. Hall and M. Jacques (eds) *New Times*, London: Lawrence and Wishart.

Heckscher, C. (1996) *The New Unionism* 2nd edn, Ithaca, NY: ILR Press.

Hedges, B. (1994) 'Work in a changing climate', in R. Jowell, J. Curtice, L. Brook and D. Ahrendt (eds) *British Social Attitudes: the 11th Report*, Aldershot: Dartmouth.

Heery, E. (1997) 'Performance-related pay and trade union de-recognition', *Employee Relations* 19, 3: 208–221.

Held, D. (1992) 'Liberalism, Marxism and democracy', in S. Hall, D. Held and T. McGrew (eds) *Modernity and its Futures*, Oxford: Polity Press.

Hendy, J. (1993) *A Law Unto Themselves: the Conservative Employment Laws* 3rd edn, London: Institute of Employment Rights.

Hewstone, M. (1989) *Causal Attribution: From Cognitive Processes to Collective Beliefs*, Oxford: Blackwell.

Hewstone, M. and Brown, R. (1986) 'Contact is not enough: an intergroup perspective on the "contact hypothesis"', in M. Hewstone and R. Brown (eds) *Contact and Conflict in Intergroup Encounters*, Oxford: Blackwell.

Higgs, F. (1994) 'Briefing report on Shell Haven UK', in House of Commons Employment Committee, Third Report, *The Future of Trade Unions, Volume II, Minutes of Evidence*, 154–155, London: HMSO.

Hill, S. (1976) *The Dockers*, London: Heinemann.

Hindess, B. (1988) *Choice, Rationality and Social Theory*, London: Unwin Hyman.

Hinkle, S. and Brown, R. (1990) 'Intergroup comparisons and social identity: some links and lacunae', in D. Abrams and M. A. Hogg (eds) *Social Identity Theory: Constructive and Critical Advances*, Hemel Hempstead: Harvester Wheatsheaf.

Hinton, J. (1983) *Labour and Socialism: a History of the British Labour Movement 1867–1974*, Brighton: Wheatsheaf.

Hinton, J. and Hyman, R. (1975) *Trade Unions and Revolution: the Industrial Politics of the Early British Communist Party*, London: Pluto Press.

Hobby, C. (1994) *The Increase in Grievances Against Management in the Years 1983–1993*, London: London School of Economics MSc thesis.

Hobsbawm, E. (1952) 'Economic fluctuations and some social movements since 1800', in E. Hobsbawm *Labouring Men*, London: Weidenfeld & Nicolson, 1964.

Hofstede, G. (1984) *Culture's Consequences: International Differences in Work-Related Values*, abridged edn, London: Sage.

Hogarth, R. M. and Reder, M. W. (1987) 'Introduction: perspectives from economics and psychology', in R. M. Hogarth and M. W. Reder (eds) *Rational Choice: the Contrast Between Economics and Psychology*, Chicago: University of Chicago Press.

Hogg, M. A. and Abrams, D. (1988) *Social Identifications: a Social Psychology of Intergroup Relations and Group Processes*, London: Routledge.

Hogg, M. A. and McGarty, C. (1990) 'Self-categorization and social identity', in D. Abrams and M. A. Hogg (eds) *Social Identity Theory: Constructive and Critical Advances*, Hemel Hempstead: Harvester Wheatsheaf.

Hollingsworth, M. and Norton-Taylor, R. (1988). *Blacklist: the Inside Story of Political Vetting*, London: Hogarth Press.

Hollingsworth, M. and Tremayne, C. (1989) *The Economic League: the Silent McCarthyism*, London: National Council for Civil Liberties.

Hotz-Hart, B. (1992) 'Switzerland: still as smooth as clockwork?', in A. Ferner and R. Hyman (eds) *Industrial Relations in the New Europe*, Oxford: Blackwell.

Howard, M. C. and King, J. E. (1992) *A History of Marxian Economics: Volume II, 1929–1990*, London: Macmillan.

Hyman, R. (1971) *Marxism and the Sociology of Trade Unionism*, London: Pluto Press.
—— (1972) *Strikes*, London: Fontana.
—— (1974) 'Workers' control and revolutionary theory', *Socialist Register 1974*, 241–278.
—— (1975) *Industrial Relations: a Marxist Introduction*, London: Macmillan.
—— (1978) 'Pluralism, procedural consensus and collective bargaining', *British Journal of Industrial Relations* 16, 1: 16–40.
—— (1986) 'Reflections on the mining strike', *Socialist Register 1985/1986*, 330–354.
—— (1989a) 'Why industrial relations?', in R. Hyman *The Political Economy of Industrial Relations*, London: Macmillan.
—— (1989b) 'Class struggle and the trade union movement', in R. Hyman *The Political Economy of Industrial Relations*, London: Macmillan.
—— (1989c) *The Political Economy of Industrial Relations: Theory and Practice in a Cold Climate*, London: Macmillan.
—— (1991) 'Plus ca change? the theory of production and the production of theory', in A. Pollert (ed.) *Farewell to Flexibility?*, Oxford: Blackwell.
—— (1992) 'Trade unions and the disagggregation of the working class', in M. Regini (ed.) *The Future of Labour Movements*, London: Sage.
—— (1994a) 'Theory and industrial relations', *British Journal of Industrial Relations* 32, 2: 165–180.
—— (1994b) 'Changing trade union identities and strategies', in R. Hyman and A. Ferner (eds) *New Frontiers in European Industrial Relations*, Oxford: Blackwell.
—— (1996) 'Changing union identities in Europe', in P. Leisink, J. van Leemput and J. Vilrokx (eds) *The Challenges to Trade Unions In Europe: Innovation or Adaptation*, Cheltenham: Edward Elgar.
Hyman, R. and Brough, I. (1975) *Social Values and Industrial Relations*, Oxford: Blackwell.
Inglehart, R. (1990) *Culture Shift in Advanced Industrial Society*, Princeton, NJ: Princeton University Press.
ISR (1995) *Employee Satisfaction: Tracking European Trends*, London: International Survey Research Ltd.
Jackson, D. and Sweet, T. (1979) 'The world strike wave', *Omega: The International Journal of Management Science* 7, 1: 43–53.
Jackson, M. P. (1991) *An Introduction to Industrial Relations* 3rd edn, London: Routledge.
Jacobi, O. (1986) 'Trade unions, industrial relations and structural economic "ruptures"', in O. Jacobi, B. Jessop, H. Kastendiek and M. Regini (eds) *Economic Crisis, Trade Unions and the State*, London: Croom Helm.
—— (1988) 'New technological paradigms, long waves and trade unions', in R. Hyman and W. Streeck (eds) *New Technology and Industrial Relations*, Oxford: Blackwell.
Jameson, F. (1989) 'The postmodern debate', *New Left Review* 176: 31–45.
Jasny, N. (1972) *Soviet Economists of the Twenties*, Cambridge: Cambridge University Press.
Jeffery, K. and Hennessy, P. (1983) *States of Emergency: British Governments and Strikebreaking Since 1919*, London: Routledge and Kegan Paul.
Jefferys, S. (1988) 'The changing face of conflict: shopfloor organization at Longbridge, 1939–1980', in M. Terry and P. K. Edwards (eds) *Shopfloor Politics and Job Controls*, Oxford: Blackwell.
Jessop, B. (1982) *The Capitalist State*, Oxford: Martin Robertson.

Johnston, P. (1994) *Success While Others Fail: Social Movement Unionism and the Public Workplace*, Ithaca, NY: ILR Press.

Jones, C. and Novak, T. (1985) 'Welfare against the workers: benefits as a political weapon', in H. Beynon (ed.) *Digging Deeper: Issues in the Miners' Strike*, London: Verso.

Jowell, R. *et al.* (eds) (1984–1996) *British Social Attitudes*, Aldershot: Gower/Dartmouth.

Kagitcibasi, C. (1994) 'A critical appraisal of individualism and collectivism: toward a new formulation', in U. Kim, H. C. Triandis, C. Kagitcibasi, S-C. Choi and G. Yoon (eds) *Individualism and Collectivism: Theory, Method, and Applications*, London: Sage.

Kalecki, M. (1943) 'Political aspects of full employment', *Political Quarterly* 14, 4: 322–331.

Kaufman, B. E. (1993) *The Origins and Evolution of the Field of Industrial Relations in the United States*, Ithaca, NY: ILR Press.

Kaufman, B. E. and Kleiner, M. M. (eds) (1993) *Employee Representation: Alternatives and Future Directions*, Madison, Wisc: Industrial Relations Research Association.

Kavanagh, D. (1990) *British Politics: Continuities and Change* 2nd edn, Oxford: Oxford University Press.

Keenoy, T. (1985) *Invitation To Industrial Relations*, Oxford: Blackwell.

Kelley, M. R. and Harrison, B. (1992) 'Unions, technology and labor–management cooperation', in L. Mishel and P. B. Voos (eds) *Unions and Economic Competitiveness*, New York: M. E. Sharpe.

Kelly, C. and Breinlinger, S. (1996) *The Social Psychology of Collective Action: Identity, Injustice and Gender*, London: Taylor and Francis.

Kelly, J. (1988) *Trade Unions and Socialist Politics*, London: Verso.

—— (1996) 'Union militancy and social partnership', in P. Ackers, C. Smith and P. Smith (eds) *The New Workplace and Trade Unionism*, London: Routledge.

—— (1997) 'The future of trade unionism: injustice, identity and attribution', *Employee Relations* 19, 5: 400–414.

—— (forthcoming) *Industrial Relations, Social Democracy and Anti-Communism: A Political Biography of Allan Flanders*, in preparation.

Kelly, J. and Heery, E. (1989) 'Full-time officers and trade union recruitment', *British Journal of Industrial Relations* 27, 2: 196–213.

—— (1994) *Working For The Union*, Cambridge: Cambridge University Press.

Kelly, J. and Kelly, C. (1991) '"Them and us": social psychology and the "new industrial relations"', *British Journal of Industrial Relations* 29, 1: 25–48.

—— (1992) 'Industrial action', in J. Hartley and G. M. Stephenson (eds) *Employment Relations: the Psychology of Influence and Control at Work*, Oxford: Blackwell.

Kelly, J. and Nicholson, N. (1980) 'Strikes and other forms of industrial action', *Industrial Relations Journal* 11, 5: 20–31.

Kelly, J. and Waddington J. (1995) 'New prospects for British labour', *Organization* 2, 3/4: 415–426.

Kern, H. and Sabel, C. F. (1992) 'Trade unions and decentralized production: a sketch of strategic problems in the German labour movement', in M. Regini (ed.) *The Future of Labour Movements*, London: Sage.

Kerr, C. and Siegel, A. (1954) 'The inter-industry propensity to strike – an international comparison', in A. Kornhauser, R. Dubin and A. Ross (eds) *Industrial Conflict*, New York: McGraw-Hill.

Kessler, I. (1994) 'Performance pay', in K. Sisson (ed.) *Personnel Management: a Comprehensive Guide to Theory and Practice in Britain* 2nd edn, Oxford: Blackwell.

Kessler, S. and Bayliss, F. (1995) *Contemporary British Industrial Relations* 2nd edn, London: Macmillan.

Kirkbride, P. (1985) 'Power in industrial relations research: a review of some recent work', *Industrial Relations Journal* 16, 1: 44–56.

—— (1992) 'Power', in J. Hartley and G. M. Stephenson (eds) *Employment Relations: the Psychology of Influence and Control at Work*, Oxford: Blackwell.

Klandermans, B. (1984a) 'Mobilisation and participation in trade union action: a value expectancy approach', *Journal of Occupational Psychology* 57, 2: 107–120.

—— (1984b) 'Mobilisation and participation: social psychological expansions of resource mobilisation theory', *American Sociological Review* 49, 5: 583–600.

—— (1988) 'The formation and mobilization of consensus', *International Social Movement Research* 1: 173–196.

—— (1989a) 'Introduction: social movement organizations and the study of social movements', *International Social Movement Research* 2: 1–17.

—— (1989b) 'Introduction to Part II', *International Social Movement Research* 2: 117–128.

—— (1992) 'The social construction of protest and multiorganizational fields', in A. D. Morris and C. M. Mueller (eds) *Frontiers in Social Movement Theory*, New Haven, Conn.: Yale University Press.

—— (1997) *The Social Psychology of Protest*, Oxford: Blackwell.

Klandermans, B. and Tarrow, S. (1988) 'Mobilization into social movements: synthesizing European and American approaches', *International Social Movement Research* 1: 1–38.

Kleinknecht, A., Mandel, E. and Wallerstein, I. (eds) (1992) *New Findings in Long-Wave Research*, London: Macmillan.

Kochan, T. A. and Osterman, P. (1994) *The Mutual Gains Enterprise*, Boston: Harvard Business School Press.

Kochan, T. A., Katz, H. C. and McKersie, R. B. (1986) *The Transformation of American Industrial Relations*, New York: Basic Books.

Kondratieff, N. D. (1979) 'The long waves in economic life', *Review* 2, 4: 519–562 (first published 1926).

Kumar, P. (1993) *From Uniformity to Divergence: Industrial Relations in Canada and the United States*, Kingston, Ontario: IRC Press.

Kuwahara, Y. (1993) 'Industrial relations in Japan', in G. J. Bamber and R. D. Lansbury (eds) *International and Comparative Industrial Relations* 2nd edn, London: Routledge.

Lane, T. and Roberts, K. (1971) *Strike at Pilkingtons*, London: Fontana.

Lash, S. and Urry, J. (1987) *The End of Organized Capitalism*, Oxford: Polity Press.

Leadbeater, C. (1989) 'Power to the person', in S. Hall and M. Jacques (eds) *New Times*, London: Lawrence and Wishart.

Legge, K. (1989) 'Human resource management: a critical analysis', in J. Storey (ed.) *New Perspectives On Human Resource Management*, London: Routledge.

—— (1995a) 'Rhetoric, reality and hidden agendas', in J. Storey (ed.) *Human Resource Management: A Critical Text*, London: Routledge.

—— (1995b) *Human Resource Management: Rhetorics and Realities*, London: Macmillan.

Leggett, C. (1993) 'Corporatist trade unionism in Singapore', in S. Frenkel (ed.) *Organized Labor in the Asia-Pacific Region*, Ithaca, NY: ILR Press.

Lembcke, J. (1992) 'Why 50 years? Working class formation and long economic cycles', *Science and Society* 55, 4: 417–445.

Levi, P. (1987) *If This Is A Man/ The Truce*, London: Sphere.

Levinson, H. M. (1969) 'Wage determination under collective bargaining', in A. Flanders (ed.) *Collective Bargaining*, Harmondsworth: Penguin.

Lilja, K. (1992) 'Finland: no longer the Nordic exception', in A. Ferner and R. Hyman (eds) *Industrial Relations in the New Europe*, Oxford: Blackwell.

Littler, C. (1990) 'The labour process debate: a theoretical review', in D. Knights and H. Willmott (eds) *Labour Process Theory*, London: Macmillan.

LRD (1991) 'Sexuality: a trade union issue?', *Labour Research* 80, 6: 10–12.

Lukes, S. (1974) *Power: a Radical View*, London: Macmillan.

Lyddon, D. (1996) 'The car industry, 1945–79: shop stewards and workplace unionism', in C. Wrigley (ed.) *A History of British Industrial Relations, 1939–1979*, Cheltenham: Edward Elgar.

Lyddon, D. and Smith, P. (1996) 'Editorial: Industrial relations and history', *Historical Studies in Industrial Relations* 1: 1–10.

McAdam, D. (1988) 'Micromobilization contexts and recruitment to activism', *International Social Movement Research* 1: 125–154.

McCarthy, W. (1992) 'Time to move on: or reflections on forty years of industrial relations research', *IRRU Research Review* 5: 2–5.

—— (1994) 'Of hats and cattle: or the limits of macro-survey research in industrial relations', *Industrial Relations Journal* 25, 4: 315–322.

McCarthy, W. E. J. and Parker, S. R. (1968) *Shop Stewards And Workshop Relations*, London: Royal Commission On Trade Unions and Employers' Associations, Research Paper 10.

McIlroy, J. (1985) '"The law struck dumb?" – labour law and the miners' strike', in B. Fine and R. Millar (eds) *Policing the Miners' Strike*, London: Lawrence and Wishart.

—— (1997) 'Still under siege: British trade unions at the turn of the century', *Historical Studies in Industrial Relations* 3: 93–122.

McIlroy, J. and Campbell, A. (1997) *The Communist Party and Industrial Politics, 1964–1975*, British Trade Unionism Conference paper, University of Warwick, September.

MacInnes, J. (1987) *Thatcherism at Work*, Milton Keynes : Open University Press.

McLennan, G. (1992) 'The Enlightenment project revisited', in S. Hall, D. Held and T. McGrew (eds) *Modernity and Its Futures*, Oxford: Polity Press.

McLoughlin, I. and Beardwell, I. (1989) *Non-Unionism and the Non-Union Firm in British Industrial Relations*, London: Kingston Business School, Occasional Paper 7.

McLoughlin, I. and Clark, J. (1988) *Technological Change at Work*, Milton Keynes: Open University Press.

McLoughlin, I. and Gourlay, S. (1994) *Enterprise Without Unions: Industrial Relations in the Non-Union Firm*, Buckingham: Open University Press.

Maguire, P. (1996) 'Labour and the law: the politics of British industrial relations, 1945–79', in C. Wrigley (ed.) *A History of British Industrial Relations, 1939–1979*, Cheltenham: Edward Elgar.

Maksymiw, W., Eaton, J. and Gill, C. (1990) *The British Trade Union Directory*, London; Longman.

Mandel, E. (1975) *Late Capitalism*, London: Verso.

—— (1992) 'The international debate on long waves of capitalist development: an intermediary balance sheet', in A. Kleinknecht, E. Mandel and I. Wallerstein (eds) *New Findings in Long Wave Research*, London: Macmillan.

—— (1995) *Long Waves of Capitalist Development: a Marxist Interpretation* 2nd edn, London: Verso.

Marchington, M. and Parker, P. (1990) *Changing Patterns of Employee Relations*, Hemel Hempstead: Harvester Wheatsheaf.

Marchington, M., Goodman, J., Wilkinson, A. and Ackers, P. (1992) *New Developments in Employee Involvement*, Sheffield: Employment Department, Research Series 2.

Marginson, P. (1998) 'The survey tradition in British industrial relations research: an assessment of the contribution of large-scale workplace and enterprise surveys', *British Journal of Industrial Relations* 36, 2:

Marginson, P., Edwards, P. K., Martin, R., Purcell, J. and Sisson, K. (1988) *Beyond the Workplace*, Oxford: Blackwell.

Margolis, H. (1981) 'A new model of rational choice', *Ethos* 9: 265–279, in P. Abell (ed.) *Rational Choice Theory*, Aldershot: Edward Elgar.

Marshall, G., Newby, H., Rose, D. and Vogler, C. (1988) *Social Class in Modern Britain*, London: Hutchinson.

Martin, J. and Roberts, C. (1984) *Women and Employment: a Lifetime Perspective*, London: HMSO.

Martin, R. (1981) 'Power', in A. Thomson and M. Warner (eds) *The Behavioural Sciences and Industrial Relations*, Aldershot: Gower.

—— (1992) *Bargaining Power*, Oxford: Clarendon.

Marwell, G. and Ames, R. E. (1979) 'Experiments on the provision of public goods. I. Resources, interest, group size, and the free-rider problem', *American Journal of Sociology* 84, 6: 1335–1360.

—— (1981) 'Economists free ride, does anyone else?', *Journal of Public Economics* 15, 3: 295–310. Reprinted in P. Abell (ed.) *Rational Choice Theory*, Aldershot: Edward Elgar.

Marwell, G. and Oliver, P. (1993) *The Critical Mass in Collective Action: a Micro-Social Theory*, Cambridge: Cambridge University Press.

Marx, K. (1847) *The Poverty of Philosophy* in K. Marx and F. Engels *Collected Works Volume 6*, London: Lawrence and Wishart.

Mason, B. and Bain, P. (1991) 'Trade union recruitment strategies: facing the 1990s', *Industrial Relations Journal* 22, 1: 36–45.

Meltz, N. M. (1991) 'Dunlop's *Industrial Relations Systems* after three decades', in R. J. Adams (ed.) *Comparative Industrial Relations: Contemporary Research and Theory*, London: HarperCollins.

Melucci, A. (1988) 'Getting involved: identity and mobilization in social movements', *International Social Movement Research* 1: 329–348.

Menshikov, S. (1992) 'The long wave as an endogenous mechanism', in A. Kleinknecht, E. Mandel and I. Wallerstein (eds) *New Findings in Long-Wave Research*, London: Macmillan.

Metz, R. (1992) 'A re-examination of long waves in aggregate production series', in A. Kleinknecht, E. Mandel and I. Wallerstein (eds) *New Findings in Long-Wave Research*, London: Macmillan.

Miliband, R. (1969) *The State in Capitalist Society*, London: Quartet.

Miller, R. W. (1991) 'Social and political theory: class, state, revolution', in T. Carver (ed.) *The Cambridge Companion to Marx*, Cambridge: Cambridge University Press.

Millward, N. (1990) 'The state of the unions', in R. Jowell, S. Witherspoon and L. Brook (eds) *British Social Attitudes: the 7th Report*, Aldershot: Gower.

—— (1994) *The New Industrial Relations?*, London: Policy Studies Institute.

Millward, N. and Hawes, W. R. (1995) 'Hats, cattle and IR research: a comment on McCarthy', *Industrial Relations Journal* 26, 1: 69–73.

Millward, N. and Stevens, M. (1986) *British Workplace Industrial Relations 1980–1984*, Aldershot: Gower.

Millward, N., Stevens, M., Smart, D. and Hawes, W. R. (1992) *Workplace Industrial Relations in Transition*, Aldershot: Dartmouth.

Milne, S. (1994) *The Enemy Within: MI5, Maxwell and the Scargill Affair*, London: Verso.

Milner, S. (1993) 'Overtime bans and strikes: evidence on relative incidence', *Industrial Relations Journal* 24, 3: 201–210.

—— (1995a) 'Where do we go from here?', *British Journal of Industrial Relations* 33, 4: 609–615.

—— (1995b) 'The coverage of collective pay-setting institutions in Britain, 1895–1990', *British Journal of Industrial Relations* 33, 1: 69–91.

Milner, S. and Richards, E. (1991) 'Determinants of union recognition and employee involvement: evidence from London Docklands', *British Journal of Industrial Relations* 29, 3: 377–390.

Minkin, L. (1991) *The Contentious Alliance: Trade Unions and the Labour Party*, Edinburgh: Edinburgh University Press.

Monks, J. (1993) 'A trade union view of WIRS3', *British Journal of Industrial Relations* 31, 2: 227–233.

Morris, A. D. and Mueller, C. M. (eds) (1992) *Frontiers in Social Movement Theory*, New Haven, Conn.: Yale University Press.

Morris, T. and Wood, S. (1991) 'Testing the survey method: continuity and change in British industrial relations', *Work, Employment and Society* 5, 2: 259–282.

Mort, F. (1989) 'The politics of consumption', in S. Hall and M. Jacques (eds) *New Times*, London: Lawrence and Wishart.

Mulgan, G. (1989a) 'Uncertainty, reversibility and variety', in S. Hall and M. Jacques (eds) *New Times*, London: Lawrence and Wishart.

—— (1989b) 'The power of the weak', in S. Hall and M. Jacques (eds) *New Times*, London: Lawrence and Wishart.

Murray, R. (1989) 'Fordism and post-Fordism', in S. Hall and M. Jacques (eds) *New Times*, London: Lawrence and Wishart.

NACAB (1990) *Hard Labour*, London: National Association of Citizens' Advice Bureaux.

—— (1993) *Job Insecurity*, London: National Association of Citizens' Advice Bureaux.

—— (1997) *Flexibility Abused*, London: National Association of Citizens' Advice Bureaux.

Naylor, R. (1989) 'Strikes, free-riders and social customs', *Quarterly Journal of Economics* 104, 4: 771–785.

Newman, G. (1982) *Path to Maturity: NALGO, 1965–1980*, Manchester: Cooperative Press.

Nichols, T. and Armstrong, P. (1976) *Workers Divided*, London: Fontana.

Nichols, T. and Beynon, H. (1977) *Living with Capitalism*, London: Routledge and Kegan Paul.

Nolan, P. and Edwards, P. K. (1984) 'Homogenise, divide and rule: an essay on *Segmented Work, Divided Workers*', *Cambridge Journal of Economics* 8, 2: 197–215.

Nolan, P. and Walsh, J. (1995) 'The structure of the economy and labour market', in P. K. Edwards (ed.) *Industrial Relations: Theory and Practice in Britain*, Oxford: Blackwell.

Noon, M. and Blyton, P. (1997) *The Realities of Work*, London: Macmillan.

Norton, B. (1988) 'Epochs and essences: a review of Marxist long-wave and stagnation theories', *Cambridge Journal of Economics* 12, 2: 203–224.

OECD (1997) *Employment Outlook July 1997*, Paris: Organisation for Economic Co-operation and Development.

Offe, C. (1985) 'New social movements: challenging the boundaries of institutional politics', *Social Research* 52, 4: 817–868.

Offe, C. and Wiesenthal, H. (1985) 'Two logics of collective action', in C. Offe *Disorganized Capitalism*, Oxford: Polity Press.

O'Lincoln, T, (1985) *Into the Mainstream: the Decline of Australian Communism*, Sydney: Stained Wattle Press.

Oliver, P. (1984) '"If you don't do it, nobody else will": active and token contributors to local collective action', *American Sociological Review* 49, 5: 601–610.

Oliver, P. and Marwell, G. (1988) 'The paradox of group size in collective action: a theory of the critical mass II', *American Sociological Review* 53, 1: 1–8.

Olson, M. (1971) *The Logic of Collective Action*, Cambridge, Mass.: Harvard University Press.

—— (1982) *The Rise and Decline of Nations: Economic Growth, Stagflation and Social Rigidities*, New Haven, Conn.: Yale University Press.

—— (1992) 'Foreword', in T. Sandler *Collective Action: Theory and Applications*, Hemel Hempstead: Harvester Wheatsheaf.

Paloheimo, H. (1990) 'Between liberalism and corporatism: the effect of trade unions and governments on economic performance in eighteen OECD countries', in R. Brunetta and C. Dell'Aringa (eds) *Labour Relations and Economic Performance*, London: Macmillan.

Panitch, L. (1981) 'Trade unions and the capitalist state', *New Left Review* 125: 21–44.

Parker, S. R. (1974) *Workplace Industrial Relations 1972*, London: HMSO.

—— (1975) *Workplace Industrial Relations 1973*, London: HMSO.

Peak, S. (1984) *Troops in Strikes*, London: Cobden Trust.

Pimlott, B. and Cook, C. (eds) (1991) *Trade Unions in British Politics* 2nd edn, London: Longman.

Piore, M. J. and Sabel, C. F. (1984) *The Second Industrial Divide*, New York: Basic Books.

Pollert, A. (1981) *Girls, Wives, Factory Lives*, London: Macmillan.

Poole, M. (1984) *Theories of Trade Unionism* 2nd edn, London: Routledge and Kegan Paul.

—— (1986a) *Industrial Relations: Origins and Patterns of National Diversity*, London: Routledge and Kegan Paul.

—— (1986b) *Towards a New Industrial Democracy: Workers' Participation in Industry*, London: Routledge and Kegan Paul.

Poole, M. and Jenkins, G. (1990) *The Impact of Economic Democracy: Profit Sharing and Employee Share-Holding Schemes*, London: Routledge.

Popkin, S. (1988) 'Political entrepreneurs and peasant movements in Vietnam', in M. Taylor (ed.) *Rationality and Revolution*, Cambridge: Cambridge University Press.

Premack, S. L. and Hunter, J. E. (1988) 'Individual unionization decisions', *Psychological Bulletin* 103, 2: 223–234.

Price, R. (1991) 'The comparative analysis of union growth', in R. J. Adams (ed.) *Comparative Industrial Relations: Contemporary Research and Theory*, London: HarperCollins.

Purcell, J. (1979) 'The lessons of the Commission on Industrial Relations' attempt to reform workplace industrial relations', *Industrial Relations Journal* 10, 2: 4–22.

—— (1981) *Good Industrial Relations*, London: Macmillan.

—— (1991) 'The rediscovery of the management prerogative: the management of labour relations in the 1980s', *Oxford Review of Economic Policy* 7, 1: 33–43.

Rainnie, A. F. (1989) *Industrial Relations in Small Firms: Small Isn't Beautiful*, London: Routledge.

Ram, M. (1994) *Managing To Survive: Working Lives in Small Firms*, Oxford: Blackwell.

Ramsay, H. (1977) 'Cycles of control: worker participation in sociological and historical perspective', *Sociology* 11, 3: 481–506.

Rentoul, J. (1989) *Me and Mine: the Triumph of the New Individualism?*, London: Unwin Hyman.

Richardson, R. and Rubin, M. (1993) 'The shorter working week in engineering: surrender without sacrifice?', in D. Metcalf and S. Milner (eds) *New Perspectives on Industrial Disputes*, London: Routledge.

Roberts, B. C. (1962) *Trade Unions in a Free Society*, London: Hutchinson.

Rollinson, D. (1993) *Understanding Employee Relations: a Behavioural Approach*, Wokingham: Addison-Wesley.

Royal Commission on Trade Unions and Employers' Associations, 1965–68 (Donovan Report) (1968) London: HMSO, Cmnd. 3623.

Rubinstein, S., Bennett, M. and Kochan, T. A. (1993) 'The Saturn partnership: co-management and the reinvention of the local union', in B. E. Kaufman and M. M. Kleiner (eds) *Employee Representation: Alternatives and Future Directions*, Madison, Wisc.: Industrial Relations Research Association.

Rule, J. B. (1989) 'Rationality and non-rationality in militant collective action', *Sociological Theory* 7, 2: 145–160.

Runciman, W. G. (1966) *Relative Deprivation and Social Justice*, London: Routledge and Kegan Paul.

Rustin, M. (1989) 'The trouble with New Times', in S. Hall and M. Jacques (eds) *New Times*, London: Lawrence and Wishart.

Salamon, M. (1992) *Industrial Relations: Theory and Behaviour* 2nd edn, London: Prentice Hall.

Sandler, T. (1992) *Collective Action: Theory and Applications*, Hemel Hempstead: Harvester Wheatsheaf.

Sayer, A. (1992) *Method in Social Science* 2nd edn, London: Routledge.

Sayer, A. and Walker, R. (1992) *The New Social Economy: Reworking the Division of Labour*, Oxford: Blackwell.

Scase, R. (1977) *Social Democracy in Capitalist Society*, London: Croom Helm.

Scott, A. (1992) 'Political culture and social movements', in J. Allen, P. Braham and P. Lewis (eds) *Political and Economic Forms of Modernity*, Oxford: Polity Press.

Scott, A. (1994) *Willing Slaves? British Workers Under Human Resource Management*, Cambridge: Cambridge University Press.

Screpanti, E. (1984) 'Long cycles and recurring proletarian insurgencies', *Review* 7, 2: 509–548.

—— (1987) 'Long cycles in strike activity: an empirical investigation', *British Journal of Industrial Relations* 25, 1: 99–124.

—— (1989) 'Some demographic and social processes and the problem of Kondratieff cycle periodicity', in M. di Matteo, R. Goodwin and A. Vercelli (eds) *Technological and Social Factors in Long Term Fluctuations*, Berlin: Springer-Verlag.

Seifert, R. (1984) 'Some aspects of factional opposition: Rank and File and the NUT 1967–1982', *British Journal of Industrial Relations* 22, 3: 372–390.

Sen, A. (1977) 'Rational fools: a critique of the behavioural foundations of economic theory', *Philosophy and Public Affairs* 6, 4: 317–344.

Sexton, P. C. (1991) *The War on Labor and the Left*, Boulder, Col.: Westview Press.

Shaikh, A. (1992) 'The falling rate of profit as the cause of long waves', in A. Kleinknecht, E. Mandel and I. Wallerstein (eds) *New Findings in Long-Wave Research*, London: Macmillan.

Shalev, M. (1992) 'The resurgence of labour quiescence', in M. Regini (ed.) *The Future of Labour Movements*, London: Sage.

Shaw, W. H. (1984) 'Marxism, revolution, and rationality', in T. Ball and J. Farr (eds) *After Marx*, Cambridge: Cambridge University Press.

Shipley, P. (1976) *Revolutionaries in Modern Britain*, London: Bodley Head.

Shorter, E. and Tilly, C. (1974) *Strikes in France, 1830–1968*, Cambridge: Cambridge University Press.

Silver, B. (1992) 'Class struggle and Kondratieff waves, 1870 to the present', in A. Kleinknecht, E. Mandel and I. Wallerstein (eds) *New Findings in Long-Wave Research*, London: Macmillan.

Sisson, K. (1993) 'In search of HRM', *British Journal of Industrial Relations* 31, 2: 201–210.

—— (1994) 'Personnel management: paradigms, practice and prospects', in K. Sisson (ed.) *Personnel Management: a Comprehensive Guide to Theory and Practice in Britain* 2nd edn, Oxford: Blackwell.

Smith, P. and Morton, G. (1993) 'Union exclusion and the decollectivization of industrial relations in Britain', *British Journal of Industrial Relations* 31, 1: 97–114.

—— (1994) 'Union exclusion: next steps', *Industrial Relations Journal* 25, 1: 3–14.

Snow, D. A. and Benford, R. D. (1992) 'Master frames and cycles of protest', in A. D. Morris and C. M. Mueller (eds) *Frontiers in Social Movement Theory*, New Haven, Conn.: Yale University Press.

Snow, D. A., Rochford Jr, E. B., Warden, S. K. and Benford, R. D. (1986) 'Frame alignment processes, micromobilization, and movement participation', *American Sociological Review* 51, 4: 464–481.

Sorge, A. and Streeck, W. (1988) 'Industrial relations and technical change: the case for an extended perspective', in R. Hyman and W. Streeck (eds) *New Technology and Industrial Relations*, Oxford: Blackwell.

163

Spencer, B. (1989) *Remaking the Working Class? An Examination of Shop Stewards' Experiences*, Nottingham: Spokesman.

Spencer, P. (1996) 'Reactions to a flexible labour market', in R. Jowell, J. Curtice, A. Park, L. Brook and K. Thomson (eds) *British Social Attitudes: the 13th Report*, Aldershot: Dartmouth.

Storey, J. (1992) *Developments in the Management of Human Resources*, Oxford: Blackwell.

Storey, J. and Sisson, K. (1993) *Managing Human Resources and Industrial Relations*, Buckingham: Open University Press.

Strinati, D. (1982) *Capitalism, the State and Industrial Relations*, London: Croom Helm.

Stroebe, W. and Frey, B. S. (1982) 'Self-interest and collective action: the economics and psychology of public goods', *British Journal of Social Psychology* 21, 2: 121–137.

Tailby, S. and Whitston, C. (eds) (1989) *Manufacturing Change: Industrial Relations and Restructuring*, Oxford: Blackwell.

Tarrow, S. (1991) *Struggle, Politics, and Reform: Collective Action, Social Movements, and Cycles of Protest*, Ithaca, NY: Cornell University, Center for International Studies, Occasional Paper 21.

—— (1994) *Power In Movement: Social Movements, Collective Action and Politics*, Cambridge: Cambridge University Press.

Taylor, A. J. (1987) *Trade Unions and Politics: a Comparative Introduction*, London: Macmillan.

Taylor, D. M. and Moghaddam, F. M. (1987) *Theories of Intergroup Relations*, New York: Praeger.

Taylor, M. (1988) 'Rationality and revolutionary collective action', in M. Taylor (ed.) *Rationality and Revolution*, Cambridge: Cambridge University Press.

Taylor, R. (1978) *The Fifth Estate: Britain's Unions in the Seventies*, London: Routledge and Kegan Paul.

—— (1993) *The Trade Union Question in British Politics*, Oxford: Blackwell.

—— (1994) *The Future of the Trade Unions*, London: André Deutsch.

Terry, M. (1983) 'Shop steward development and managerial strategies', in G. S. Bain (ed.) *Industrial Relations in Britain*, Oxford: Blackwell.

—— (1985) 'Combine committees: developments of the 1970s', *British Journal of Industrial Relations* 23, 3: 359–378.

—— (1986) 'How do we know if shop stewards are getting weaker?', *British Journal of Industrial Relations* 24, 2: 169–179.

Terry, M. and Edwards, P. K. (eds) (1988) *Shopfloor Politics and Job Controls*, Oxford: Blackwell.

Thompson, K. (1992) 'Social pluralism and post-modernity', in S. Hall, D. Held and T. McGrew (eds) *Modernity and Its Futures*, Oxford: Polity Press.

Thompson, M. (1993) 'Industrial relations in Canada', in G. Bamber and R. Lansbury (eds) *International and Comparative Industrial Relations* 2nd edn, London: Routledge.

Thompson, P. (1989) *The Nature of Work* 2nd edn, London: Macmillan.

—— (1990) 'Crawling from the wreckage: the labour process and the politics of production', in D. Knights and H. Willmott (eds) *Labour Process Theory*, London: Macmillan.

—— (1993) 'Postmodernism: fatal distraction', in J. Hassard and M. Parker (eds) *Postmodernism and Organizations*, London: Sage.

Thompson, P. and Ackroyd, S. (1995) 'All quiet on the workplace front? A critique of recent trends in British industrial sociology', *Sociology* 29, 4: 615–633.

Thompson, P. and Bannon, E. (1985) *Working the System: the Shop Floor and New Technology*, London: Pluto Press.

Thompson, W. (1992) *The Good Old Cause: British Communism 1920–1991*, London: Pluto Press.

Tilly, C. (1978) *From Mobilization to Revolution*, New York: McGraw-Hill.

Tinbergen, J. (1984) 'Kondratiev cycles and so-called long waves. The early research', in C. Freeman (ed.) *Long Waves in the World Economy*, London: Frances Pinter.

Touraine, A., Wieviorka, M. and Dubet, F. (1987) *The Workers' Movement*, Cambridge: Cambridge University Press.

Towers, B. (1992) *A Handbook of Industrial Relations Practice* 3rd edn, London: Kogan Page.

Traxler, F. (1992) 'Austria: still the country of corporatism', in A. Ferner and R. Hyman (eds) *Industrial Relations in the New Europe*, Oxford: Blackwell.

Triandis, H. (1989) 'The self and social behaviour in different cultural contexts', *Psychological Review* 96, 3: 506–520.

Trotsky, L. (1921a) 'Report on the world economic crisis and the new tasks of the Communist International', in L. Trotsky *The First Five Years of the Communist International Volume 1*, London: New Park (1973).

—— (1921b) 'Flood tide – the economic conjuncture and the world labour movement', in L. Trotsky *The First Five Years of the Communist International Volume 2*, London: New Park (1974).

—— (1922) 'The fifth anniversary of the October Revolution and the Fourth World Congress of the Communist International', in L. Trotsky *The First Five Years of the Communist International Volume 2*, London: New Park (1974).

—— (1923) 'The curve of capitalist development' in L. Trotsky *Problems of Everyday Life*, New York: Monad Press (1973).

TUC (1980) *General Council Report*, London: Trades Union Congress.

—— (1994) *Human Resource Management: a Trade Union Response*, London: Trades Union Congress.

—— (1997) *TUC Directory 1997*, London: Trades Union Congress.

Turner, J. C., Hogg, M. A., Oakes, P. J., Reicher, S. D. and Wetherell, M. S. (1987) *Rediscovering the Social Group: a Self-Categorization Theory*, Oxford: Blackwell.

Turner, L. (1991) *Democracy at Work: Changing World Markets and the Future of Labor Unions*, Ithaca, NY: Cornell University Press.

Tylecote, A. (1991) *The Long Wave in the World Economy*, London: Routledge.

Undy, R. (1996) 'Mergers and union restructuring: externally determined waves or internally generated reforms?', *Historical Studies in Industrial Relations* 2: 125–137.

Undy, R., Ellis, V., McCarthy, W. E. J. and Halmos, A. M. (1981) *Change in Trade Unions*, London: Hutchinson.

Undy, R., Fosh, P., Morris, H., Smith, P. and Martin, R. (1996) *Managing the Unions: the Impact of Legislation On Trade Unions' Behaviour*, Oxford: Clarendon Press.

Urry, J. (1989) 'The end of organised capitalism', in S. Hall and M. Jacques (eds) *New Times*, London: Lawrence and Wishart.

Valkenburg, B. and Zoll, R. (1995) 'Modernization, individualization and solidarity: two perspectives on European trade unions today', *European Journal of Industrial Relations* 1, 1: 119–144.

van Duijn, J. J. (1984) 'Fluctuations in innovations over time', in C. Freeman (ed.) *Long Waves in the World Economy*, London: Frances Pinter.

van Vuuren, T., Klandermans, B., Jacobson, D. and Hartley, J. (1991) 'Employees' reactions to job insecurity', in J. Hartley, D. Jacobson, B. Klandermans and T. van Vuuren (eds) *Job Insecurity*, London: Sage.

Verma, A. and Cutcher-Gershenfeld, J. (1993) 'Joint governance in the workplace: beyond union–management cooperation and worker participation', in B. E. Kaufman and M. M. Kleiner (eds) *Employee Representation: Alternatives and Future Directions*, Madison, Wisc.: Industrial Relations Research Association.

Visser, J. (1989) *European Trade Unions in Figures*, Deventer, Netherlands: Kluwer Publishers.

—— (1992a) 'The strength of union movements in advanced capitalist democracies: social and organizational variations', in M. Regini (ed.) *The Future of Labour Movements*, London: Sage.

—— (1992b) 'The Netherlands: the end of an era and the end of a system', in A. Ferner and R. Hyman (eds) *Industrial Relations in the New Europe*, Oxford: Blackwell.

Visser, J. and Waddington, J. (1996) 'Industrialization and politics: a century of union structural development in three European countries', *European Journal of Industrial Relations* 2, 1: 21–53.

Vittorini, P., Field, N. and Methol, C. (1986) 'Lesbians against pit closures', in V. Seddon (ed.) *The Cutting Edge: Women and the Pit Strike*, London: Lawrence and Wishart.

von Prondzynski, F. (1992) 'Ireland: between centralism and the market', in A. Ferner and R. Hyman (eds) *Industrial Relations in the New Europe*, Oxford: Blackwell.

Waddington, D. (1987) *Trouble Brewing: a Social Psychological Analysis of the Ansells' Brewery Dispute*, Aldershot: Avebury.

Waddington, J. (1992) 'Trade union membership in Britain, 1980–1987: unemployment and restructuring', *British Journal of Industrial Relations* 30, 2: 287–324.

—— (1995) *The Politics of Bargaining: the Merger Process and British Trade Union Structural Development, 1892–1987*, London: Mansell.

—— (1997) 'External and internal influences on union mergers: a response to Roger Undy', *Historical Studies in Industrial Relations* 3: 81–92.

Waddington, J. and Whitston, C. (1996) 'Collectivism in a changing context: union joining and bargaining preferences among white-collar staff', in P. Leisink, J. van Leemput and J. Vilrokx (eds) *The Challenges to Trade Unions in Europe: Innovation or Adaptation*, Cheltenham: Edward Elgar.

Walton, R. E. and McKersie, R. M. (1965) *A Behavioral Theory of Labor Negotiations* (new edn 1991), New York: McGraw-Hill.

Webb, S. and Webb, B. (1920) *The History of Trade Unionism, 1666–1920* 2nd edn, London: Longmans.

Westwood, S. (1984) *All Day, Every Day: Factory and Family in the Making of Women's Lives*, London: Pluto Press.

Williams, K., Cutler, T., Williams, J. and Haslam, C. (1987) 'The end of mass production?', *Economy and Society* 16, 3: 405–439.

Winchester, D. (1983) 'Industrial relations research in Britain', *British Journal of Industrial Relations* 21, 1: 100–114.

Womack, J. P., Jones, D. T. and Roos, D. (1990) *The Machine That Changed the World*, New York: Rawson Associates.

Wood, S. J. (1991) 'Japanization and/or Toyotaism?', *Work, Employment and Society* 5, 4: 567–600.

Woolfson, C. and Foster, J. (1988) *Track Record: the Story of the Caterpillar Occupation*, London: Verso.

Wright, M. (1996) 'The collapse of compulsory unionism? Collective organization in highly unionized British companies, 1979–1991', *British Journal of Industrial Relations* 34, 4: 497–513.

Yates, C. (1992) 'North American autoworkers' response to restructuring', in M. Golden and J. Pontusson (eds) *Bargaining for Change: Union Politics in North America and Europe*, Ithaca, NY: Cornell University Press.

Zeckhauser, R. (1987) 'Comments: behavioural versus rational economics: what you see is what you conquer', in R. M. Hogarth and M. W. Reder (eds) *Rational Choice: the Contrast Between Economics and Psychology*, Chicago: University of Chicago Press.

NAME INDEX

SUBJECT INDEX